# COUNTERFACTUALS

**ALSO AVAILABLE FROM BLOOMSBURY**

*Slow Philosophy*, Michelle Boulous Walker
*Technic and Magic*, Federico Campagna
*The Many Futures of a Decision*, Jay Lampert
*Everyday Examples*, David Cunning
*Dying for Ideas*, Costica Bradatan

# COUNTERFACTUALS

Paths of the Might have Been

**Christopher Prendergast**

BLOOMSBURY ACADEMIC
LONDON • NEW YORK • OXFORD • NEW DELHI • SYDNEY

Bloomsbury Academic
Bloomsbury Publishing Plc
50 Bedford Square, London, WC1B 3DP, UK
1385 Broadway, New York, NY 10018, USA

BLOOMSBURY, BLOOMSBURY ACADEMIC and the Diana logo are
trademarks of Bloomsbury Publishing Plc

First published in Great Britain 2019

Copyright © Christopher Prendergast, 2019

Christopher Prendergast has asserted his right under the Copyright, Designs and
Patents Act, 1988, to be identified as Author of this work.

For legal purposes the Acknowledgements on p. viii constitute an extension of
this copyright page.

Cover image: a detail of an Alexander Calder mobile
© Tim Brown / Alamy Stock Photo
Cover design by Catherine Wood

All rights reserved. No part of this publication may be reproduced or transmitted
in any form or by any means, electronic or mechanical, including photocopying,
recording, or any information storage or retrieval system, without prior
permission in writing from the publishers.

Bloomsbury Publishing Plc does not have any control over, or responsibility for,
any third-party websites referred to or in this book. All internet addresses given
in this book were correct at the time of going to press. The author and publisher
regret any inconvenience caused if addresses have changed or sites have ceased
to exist, but can accept no responsibility for any such changes.

A catalogue record for this book is available from the British Library.

A catalog record for this book is available from the Library of Congress.

ISBN: HB: 978-1-3500-9008-8
PB: 978-1-3500-9009-5
ePDF: 978-1-3500-9007-1
eBook: 978-1-3500-9010-1
XML: 978-1-3500-9011-8

Typeset by RefineCatch Limited, Bungay, Suffolk

To find out more about our authors and books visit www.bloomsbury.com
and sign up for our newsletters.

Look at what's in front of you,
but think about what is missing.
**Benedict Anderson**

# CONTENTS

Acknowledgements viii

Introduction: The Conjectural Breeze of Time 1
1 A Naile, a Nose and a Traitor 27
2 Just the Facts, Ma'am: Fact and Counterfact 49
3 Flying Blind: *Angelus Novus* and *Allegory of Prudence* 67
4 Crossroads: Three Tales, Three Gamblers 87
5 Looking Back: From Metanoia to Buyer's Regret 119
6 Not, Never or Forever Being Me 151
7 On the Run with Fernando Pessoa 177

Notes 193
Index 235

# ACKNOWLEDGEMENTS

The roaming brief of this book has required the support of many intellectual and scholarly companions for it to have been able to wander at all. My thanks are due to a large number of colleagues and friends in King's College, Cambridge (as well as more generally to an institution in which conversation and consultation can move between the disciplines more or less at the drop of a hat): Anna Alexandrova, John Barrell, Franco Basso, Michael Bate, Nathanael Berestycki, Peter de Bolla, Bill Burgwinkle, Tim Clark, Aytek Erdil, Ingo Gildenhard, Simon Goldhill, Tim Griffin, Ross Harrison, John Henderson, Carrie Humphrey, Martin Hyland, James Laidlaw, Geoffrey Lloyd, Jean-Michel Massing, Robin Osborne, Martin Rees, Hamid Sabourian, Michael Sonenscher and Godela Weiss-Sussex. And, in a special place of his own, there is Bernard Williams, alas deceased, but whose scintillating intelligence remains a living force. It has touched various extended moments in this book, most notably in its later chapters.

My thanks are also due to Dorothy Edgington, Imre Galambos, Raymond Geuss, Miranda Gill, Emma Gilby, Peter Hainsworth, Timothy Hampton, Jane Haynes, Andrew Huddleston, Katherine Ibbett, Dominique Jullien, Hugh Mellor, Michael Moriarty, Alexander Nehamas, Timothy Reiss, Thomas Romer, Simon Schaffer, Richard Scholar and Michael Wood. Extended thanks go to Stanley Corngold, Catherine Gallagher and Eric Méchoulan for their helpful comments and suggestions in respect of more or less the entire manuscript.

My thanks also to the team at Bloomsbury, my unfailingly patient editor, Liza Thompson and all the others involved in the production of the book.

Finally, there is Bridget, where thanks seem pointless because they are endless. This book is lovingly dedicated to her for the simultaneously enlivening and unnerving cornucopia of counterfactuals she brought to me with Julia's Story, along with that other counterfactual: without her, the book might not have existed.

# INTRODUCTION THE CONJECTURAL BREEZE OF TIME

*That blind chancy darkness which we call the future.*

**WILLIAM FAULKNER**

## I

'We pass forks in the road and forget them, concentrating in memory only on the single road we took.' This is Michael Wood (in his superb *The Road to Delphi*) on 'story' and how we typically read narrative, ruthlessly culling what might obstruct our unilinear through-movement to what happens both next and finally. This relentless drive can, however, be checked and complicated (it is what a writer like Proust, for example, does all the time with Time, crucially including the time of reading). But there is also something else, and in several ways it furnishes the guiding rationale of this book. Wood recounts an unexpected experience while reading a work by the French anthropologist, Claude Lévi-Strauss that gave him electrically charged pause for thought: 'I remember being shocked, even outraged, when I read in Lévi-Strauss's book on totemism that what actually happens in any given situation is just one of the logical possibilities on offer.' Shock (and even outrage) give way, however, to the acceptance of an invitation: 'he was inviting us to see the fork in the road', the place where the 'actual' and the 'possible' meet in a relation of productive tension, the relation between what 'actually happens' and what might have happened in its place. Finally, there is also something recovered: 'a form of freedom in imagining even lost possibilities, especially lost possibilities, if we can avoid the forlorn nostalgia that goes with such exercises ... We could be reminding ourselves that our choices are choices, and that not even an oracle can take this freedom from us.'[1]

Some of this is, of course, debatable. It is doubtful, for example, that Oedipus – whom Wood goes on immediately to discuss, and who will also appear in this book (at a fork in the road he doesn't take) – would be completely at home with the thought that his 'choices' really were *his* (or at least only his), given what he eventually learns to his tragic cost: that the script had been entirely pre-written, and an abbreviated (and enigmatic) version of it entrusted to the oracle at Delphi. Historical variation and cultural difference will thus call for much discrimination in connection with the reach of the 'we', 'us' and 'our' in Wood's account. Nevertheless, the general thrust of his three-stage journey from initial shock through acceptance to recovery remains exemplary for this inquiry – into some of the ways in which the actual, the possible, and the fork in the road furnish the basic coordinates of the counterfactual as it is analysed, narrated and lived.

The counterfactual is a category of thought and language, but its instantiations are plural, not merely because there are lots of them about, but because their types and functions vary greatly. It is one of the aims of this book to show something of that variety, while acknowledging that there is much debate and disagreement about what counterfactuals are plausibly for and how they properly work. They certainly cast a long shadow, from, say, metaphysics to movies. They can take in Heidegger's question 'why is there something rather than nothing?' and reformulate it as what would a possible world look like if it had nothing in it (an intriguing thought-experiment that philosophy does indeed occasionally run[2]). On the more local and less ontologically dizzying plane of two human lives contingently intersecting, there is the film, *Brief Encounter*, in which actual encounter yields the poignant counterfactual encounter over which falls the twilight silhouette of the might-have-been. Its enduring power derives from its understated quality, like a scent that lingers tantalizingly as the perfume of the possible, quite unlike the cheap fragrance splashed all over the might-have-been that irrupts into the cinematic banality appropriately titled *La La Land*.

The latter can stand also as the name of a vast country in the world of counterfactuals, with a correspondingly vast population. There is inevitably a province reserved for wonderings about the careers of movie stars themselves: would Al Pacino have become a star if Robert Redford had accepted the part of Don Corleone, that sort of thing.[3] We will soon encounter a very special example of this category, in far-fetched but intriguing connection with Baroness Shirley Williams. More broadly, very many inhabitants of La La Land are there courtesy of being close friends of the Queen of neighbouring Wonderland ('why, sometimes I've believed as many as six impossible things before breakfast'). There will be occasion to visit both countries, most notably in connection with the difficult issue (the topic of Chapter 1) of how to distinguish the silly and the serious. There are some sceptics, principally in the discipline of history, who take the view that in fact pretty well all counterfactuals live here, as a collection of fantastical beings disconnected from what happens on planet earth. One member of the historians' tribe has confessed to suffering 'allergic' reactions when in their company, though this is very hard to separate from polemical fever in the waging of a turf war and the policing of disciplinary boundaries, as if counterfactuals were ill-educated usurpers intent on putting 'normal' history out of business.[4] That is an error, the best antidote for which is perhaps a version of Wood's shock therapy. Polemic, however, is also the name of a further large country in the geography of the counterfactual, and, teeth-gritted, we will also have to go there from time to time. It is part of the price one has to pay for entrance into the places that matter.[5]

These, I have already stressed, are manifold. If huge numbers of unemployable counterfactuals lounge about in La La Land, very many do productive work in an impressive range of disciplines that include philosophy, history, social sciences, economics, art history, linguistics, jurisprudence, cosmology, biology, and cognitive and behavioural psychology. In this book, I roam freely both in and across several of these intellectual territories and disciplinary frameworks (expertise disclaimers registered here), I do so because, unless expressly restricted by deliberate choice, the kind of interests the topic of the counterfactual arouses and sustains almost inevitably entails a form of roaming. The emphasis on range here is not, of course, meant to entail the aim of 'coverage' (an insane ambition, and in any case this is not a 'survey'). It is more a function of what I want to call 'resonance'. By this I mean tuning into how the counterfactual resonates in some of the numerous places where the counterfactual is thought and felt by human beings struggling to understand the world they inhabit from the point of view of what Faulkner majestically terms 'that blind chancy darkness which we call the future', and the retrospective assessments we run when that future in turn becomes a past. For want of better terms, I have bundled these 'listening' exercises under the general heading of an 'anthropology' of the counterfactual. I use the term primarily, and loosely, in its original sense of the 'study' of the 'human', but also as intersected by the modern, specialized sense of the discipline of social anthropology and the issues associated with notions of cultural difference or even incommensurability. Do all cultures operate counterfactuals, and, if so, to what ends? For example, the allusion to the complicating case of the Oedipus story suggests a larger story of variation, as an instance of a world in which, as Bernard Williams put it, 'counterfactual thought runs into the ground even more readily than it does ordinarily'.[6] We shall see that proposition being put to the test later (in Chapter 4).

But take another example. The grammar and syntax of Chinese do not permit counterfactual constructions after the manner of European languages. What, however, are we to infer from that? It would be odd, even as devotees of the Sapir-Whorf school, to infer solely from this linguistic fact that Chinese people do not think counterfactually or experience feelings of a type involving counterfactual considerations.[7] The only way (for non-Chinese) to find out is, of course, to ask or, in the formally procedural terms of the anthropologist, to carry out some 'field work' with 'informants'. Studies along these lines have produced confusing results. When presented with counterfactual expressions in the form of 'if $x$ had been the case, then $y$ would/might have ensued', reactions included 'unnatural', 'un-Chinese' and even, in one case, 'evil'. Making sense of them required conversion to statements in the conceptually precautionary form of: '$x$ is not the case, but if $x$, then $y$.' On the other hand, Mao, who spoke no European languages, was much taken with counterfactual arguments (expressed in the converted form), with the truly paradoxical consequence that, according to one body of reader-response research, Western readers of his writings found them (in translation) more congenial than many native Chinese readers (in the original). The confused picture points to real conceptual differences, but of an operational rather than substantive nature, to do with the circumstances, terms and conditions under which counterfactual reasoning is put to work. The Chinese example speaks not of conceptual incommensurability, but of a different cultural and cognitive relationship to the counterfactual realm. It suggests less an unfamiliarity with the counterfactual as such rather than an unease around pure hypotheticals known by definition to be false (whence the prefatory addition: '$x$ is not the case, but if $x$, then ...'). Without the introductory caveat, the counterfactual is seen as either potentially misleading or simply meaningless, a waste of valuable cognitive time.[8]

The question of cultural difference in respect of counterfactuals belongs in the wider anthropological enterprise of the social 'mapping' of Time.[9] When, in Chapter 3, I examine a sixteenth-century painting by Titian, I do so in part from the point of view of a compositional arrangement of faces and gazes that mirrors the modern Western spatial conceptualizations of time: the past lies 'behind', the future 'ahead'. This schema is in turn mapped as a left/right relation; from the spectator's point of view, the past is placed on the left side of the picture and the future on the right. The left/right distribution of time is echoed in the practice of left to right reading and – a point cognitive science makes much of – in the sequencing of ordinals. Some cognitive scientists maintain that this is a universal of mankind's mental ordering of time. Anthropologists are likely to demur, pointing to, for example, the linguistic placing of past and future in Mandarin ('below' and 'above' respectively); or the reversal operated by Aymara, spoken in the Andes region of South America, where the future is 'behind' and the past 'in front'; or the aboriginal Pormpuraawan community in Australia, which spatializes time on a cardinal basis, from east to west, the points of the temporal 'compass' shifting according to how and where the body is positioned.

Do these various conceptual systems and spatial metaphors all enable or even welcome counterfactuals? And if so, do they manifest themselves in the same ways? Is counterfactual thinking more likely to occur in 'modern' societies with life worlds characterized by higher levels of 'choice' and histories with fast acceleration rates that generate 'crisis' moments and decisive turning points more often than in other societies?[10] Are we to think the relation between social time and counterfactuals, if not exclusively then principally, in terms of Reinhart Koselleck's account of the temporalities of 'modernity', as an endless rush towards imagined futures saturated with retrospective might-have-beens, and a correspondingly distinctive relation between memory and forgetting?[11] Is the venerable distinction 'culture' and 'civilization' pertinent here? Régis Debray reminds us of what is at stake in the etymology of the two words: 'culture' goes with 'agriculture' and the relatively settled because repeated rhythms of the rural, while 'civilization' hails from 'civis' and the more agitated life of cities.[12] Might it be that counterfactuals are more prominently a feature of the urban? In short, do counterfactuals matter to 'us' in ways that don't necessarily apply to 'others', such that our thinking counterfactually about their histories does not coincide with how they think counterfactually about themselves, assuming they do so at all? Is there, in fact, such a thing as the 'time of the other', or is that construction, as Johannes Fabian has argued, merely an ethnocentric prejudice?[13] I touch on aspects of some of these questions in various guises as the book unfolds, but for the most part its frame of reference is limited to the histories with which I am familiar. This necessarily places a question mark over what it means to invoke the earlier sense of 'anthropology', in the belief that what we do with counterfactuals and what they do to us are integral to the task of 'making sense of humanity'. One blunt response to the question mark might be to say: show me a human being who has never, in some form or other, entertained a counterfactual thought, and I'll show you a dead one. This may, of course, be a mistake.

Against that background, the book falls broadly into two halves. The opening three chapters lay some ground work. The first chapter grapples with the criterion of 'scale' in various dimensions to consider how far the remit of the counterfactual can extend before becoming unmanageable, implausible or downright silly, while nevertheless maintaining that the stretch is far greater than many accounts allow for. To that end, I resurrect, along with some other examples, the canonically discredited because allegedly laughable example of Cleopatra's Nose to suggest that it is in fact no laughing matter. The second chapter investigates the complex relation of the counterfactual and the factual by raising some questions in connection with what we understand 'facts' to be and the conditions under which we access them. Special thanks are here due to Kellyanne Conway for the helpfully clarifying addition of the category of the 'alternative fact', with which the counterfactual should never be confused. The latter is at once a derivative and a dependent of fact, not its adversary. It can however also be deployed as a sceptical instrument with which to work critically on the factual order, by opening up what is ideologically 'cemented' into it. This chapter describes some of the ways in which that can be done, as part of what we can call a 'politics' of the counterfactual.[14] The third chapter takes up temporary abode with the angels in the house of art history, in particular revisiting Klee's *Angelus Novus* and the place of the counterfactual in Walter Benjamin's celebrated interpretation of Klee's image (renamed as the 'Angel of History'), while also pausing over Titian's more secular way with time in painting (his late work, the *Allegory of Prudence*). The Klee-Benjamin sources are windows onto thinking about the counterfactual energies buried in ruined pasts, and, specifically in connection with Benjamin, the utopian dimension of counterfactual thought experiments. Titian's painting takes us on a journey through life's 'seasons' and turning points, with a first intimation of the story of 'Hercules' Choice' and the related core emblem of the crossroads.

Chapter 4 – on the 'Crossroads' theme – is in some respects the pivotal chapter. A junction point for many of the book's principal concerns, it is also where the figurative 'paths' of my title acquire literal form. The crossroads is the place of the 'fork(s) in the road' and the moment of dilemma and decision, haunted not only by the mythological goddess, Hecate, but also by counterfactual scenarios of the ways in which things might have gone. I illustrate something of the cultural history of crossroads symbolism with three journey-tales taken respectively from antiquity (Oedipus), the late middle ages (Petrarch) and the early modern period (Ignatius of Loyola). They track a development from a story of over-weening confidence to tales exemplifying the modern confrontation with doubt.

Chapters 5 and 6 explore aspects of the human, all-too-human, act of looking back to forks both taken and not taken. The first is on the theme of 'regret' in relation to the long history of the Greek concept of *metanoia*, ending with the cultural attitudes and legal practices associated with the phenomenon of 'buyer's regret'. The second deals with questions of personal 'identity', especially what can go awry when certain kinds of counterfactual thinking threaten to undermine the sense of a self by bringing us to imagine ourselves as either 'someone else' or 'no-one' at all (most radically in the wish never to have been born). The final chapter, however, reopens the question of the respects in which counterfactuals support the construction of divided and multiple identities, by looking at what it is that enables a writer such as Fernando Pessoa to say of himself 'I am what I am and am not'.

## II

'A form of freedom in imagining', governed by certain constraints, is a useful formula for counterfactually driven inquiry. I emphasize 'constraint' here, for the general reason already mentioned (staying clear of La La Land), but there are other more particular reasons. One has to do with the association of 'imagination' with imaginative literature and more specifically the genres of literary fiction. This is not one of the concerns of this book. It begins, of course, epigraphically with a novelist, and the latter (William Faulkner) will reappear at various junctures, along with many other passing literary references and a more extended look at Sophocles' *Oedipus Tyrannus*. The book also ends by handing the baton to literature (with Fernando Pessoa as the runner). However, I largely bypass questions to do with counterfactual fictions or counterfactuals in fiction, partly because there is already a substantial body of work in this area, some of which is outstanding (most notably by Catherine Gallagher). Gallagher has raised interesting and important issues of meaning and reference in connection with 'the peculiar language game of certain kinds of fiction', and her answers can scarcely be bettered. One of her examples is Napoleon Bonaparte in three different discursive settings: a personal letter (the one in which Hegel describes Napoleon as 'world history on horseback'), a novel (Tolstoy's *War and Peace*) and a counterfactual history (Louis-Napoléon Geoffroy-Château's *Napoléon et la conquête du monde*). Gallagher resurrects the question as to whether in these generically different contexts the proper name can be taken to refer to the 'same' person. How can a Napoleon actually seen by Hegel in Jena, who appears on the same battlefield as the fictional character Pierre Bezukhov, or who in Geoffroy-Château's alternative history does something that never happened (march on St Petersburg), be the 'same' person? Gallagher's own answer, in the face of certain theoretical objections, is a robustly argued 'yes, he is'.[15] On the other hand, there is something about this question that can potentially threaten one's sanity, akin perhaps to what happens in the grimly hilarious counterfactual plot of the novel, *L'Homme qui se prenait pour Napoléon* by Laure Murat. Napoleon escapes from St Helena and returns clandestinely to Paris. When finally he reveals his true identity, he is declared a mad imposter and taken to the Charenton asylum, where he discovers that all the inmates are lunatics suffering from the same delusion (of being none other than who he actually is, Napoleon Bonaparte).

There is, however, another reason for leaving the case of fiction to one side: the epistemological chaos caused by raiding parties launched from the territory of Polemic, whose basic aim (in so far as one can peer through the fog) is to discredit non-fictional counterfactuals by corralling and forcing them into the ill-fitting uniform of the fictional (that is to say, in order to place them on parade as 'mere' fictions). Branding non-fictional counterfactuals as 'fictions' is a common way of dismissing them, but it is rare to encounter the commonplace elevated to the status of a 'fundamental' question about 'borders'. Here is the historian, Richard

Evans: 'the idea of counterfactual history seemed to raise in a new way the fundamental questions about the borders between fact and fiction.'[16] The fact/fiction distinction, of course, runs back to Aristotle's *Poetics*, and, whatever the refinements that have been subsequently added, this isn't one of them. Historical counterfactuals are not aids to understanding the boundaries that separate the domains of the factual and the fictional; what they assist is our understanding of the boundaries between the factual and the counterfactual. Evans superimposes one binary on the other and in the process blurs both, the inevitable consequence of a persistent reduction of counterfactual history to being effectively a branch of the 'entertainment' industry, at whose outer limit counterfactual constructions are but 'baroque products of the imagination'.[17] Here and there an effort is made to distinguish the reputably 'useful' and the frivolously 'entertaining', but the distinction keeps buckling beneath the sheer weight of animus to the category as such. The proposition that summarizes the basic claim remains the dismissive one: 'counterfactual history essentially belongs in the same world as these other more obviously fictional works of the imagination.' It doesn't. There are no 'essences' here, and, if there were, they would be quite distinct, if occasionally entering into neighbourly contact.

Despite valiant efforts elsewhere (those of Thomas Pavel, for example[18]) to develop a general account of fiction as a branch of 'possible worlds' theory, backed by a view of counterfactuals as fiction's 'natural habitat', the logic of fiction in general starts from a different place, not in the assumption of a 'what-if', but in the operation of an 'as-if' (the philosopher Vaihinger's *als ob*, adopted by Frank Kermode for the account of the nature of fictional narrative in *The Sense of an Ending*). Counterfactual fictions are a subgenre of the class of fiction in which the 'as-if' is married to a 'what-if', but the two are not the same. Consider the intriguing triple counterfactual, one nested inside another, staged by the opening sentences of Philip Roth's novel, *The Plot Against America* (whose counterfactual premise has Charles Lindbergh beating Franklin Roosevelt in the 1940 presidential election): 'I wonder *if* I would have been a less frightened boy *if* Lindbergh hadn't been president or *if* I hadn't been the offspring of Jews' (my emphasis). This takes some unpacking. What, for instance, of the counterfactual imagining by the narrator in respect of his birth: 'if I hadn't been the offspring of Jews'. This is fundamental to the novel's strenuous probing of an historical America imagined as radically antisemitic. But it also throws the reader off balance: if our first person narrator hadn't been born the way he was, then whoever else he would have been, he wouldn't have been him. There is here perhaps a slight nod in the direction of a joke concerning the peculiar things that certain kinds of fiction can do. And then reconsider the counterfactual lobbed into the novel as its first words ('if Lindbergh *hadn't* been president', my emphasis). This works to counter the counterfactual on which the entire novel is based (Lindbergh as president). Suppose we take the narrator's musing seriously and ask what indeed if Lindbergh hadn't won? For the fictional narrator it makes perfect sense to speculate along these lines. For the reader it sends the whole fictional game into a vertiginous spin.[19] There is, for the real-world reader, a possible world that more or less comfortably locks onto the statement 'if Lindbergh had been President' (though not a candidate in the actual election, he was an influential player who could have been the Republican Party's candidate). However, when detached from the voice of a fictional narrator (or rather *this* fictional narrator), it is not so obviously straightforward to posit a world that intelligibly yields a Lindberghian counterpart in respect of the statement 'If Lindbergh *hadn't* been President . . .'[20] It is truly uncanny to encounter a rock-solid historical fact functioning as the counterfactual of a character inside a fiction. But whatever questions this raises, they are distinctively questions for fiction; they cannot be transported elsewhere, and, since they can't, they don't invite us to worry much about 'borders', and still less to fret about illegal crossings.[21]

## III

There is also something else this book is not that calls for (lengthier) clarification. While many of the descriptions and arguments in it involve theoretical considerations, in some cases extensively, it does not attempt *a* theory of the counterfactual, nor even a developed contribution to an existing one. While I dissent from some of the grounds on which Geoffrey Hawthorn bases his claim, I fully assent to the claim itself (in *Plausible Worlds*): 'there can be no theoretical answer to the question of precisely which counterfactuals to admit.'[22] These are wise words, often ignored by theoretical legislators and gatekeepers. There is, however, a basic frame, the shape of which I try to describe here. The philosopher who invented the expression 'counterfactual conditionals' (Nelson Goodman) wrote in the opening sentence of the ground-breaking paper in which he introduced the expression: 'The analysis of counterfactual conditionals is no fussy little grammatical exercise.'²³ It certainly isn't (either fussy or little). It is big, but also most definitely grammatical (Goodman's emphasis is presumably to be taken as rhetorical rather than substantive, a way of stressing the philosophical importance of his topic). The theoretical scaffolding of counterfactuals is undergirded by a sentence type that combines a subordinate 'if' clause and a consequential main clause ('if *x*, then *y*, where *x* is the antecedent "if" clause and *y* is the responsive clause delivering the entailed or asserted consequent').

The form permits of syntactical and grammatical variation. The syntax can invert ('John might have perceived other options, if he had thought counterfactually'). While in most cases inversion makes no significant difference, classical scholars have claimed that it does affect meaning and emphasis in, for example, Homer and Thucydides. Grammatical variation is essentially a matter of tense and mood, subject to the precise temporal relation in question. Here I am mostly concerned with the 'if' clause in the pluperfect subjunctive ('if John had thought . . .') and the main clause in the perfect conditional ('he might have perceived . . .'). The example of Greek also figures here in providing two terms for these two clauses (which survive only in specialist usages, for the most part in linguistics): *Protasis* and *Apodosis*. To the modern lay ear, these two splendid terms may seem like the names of gods or mythological creatures presiding over the world of conditionality and the empire of the possible. In fact, their morphology suggests more a loving couple than gods, heroes or beasts. The verbal noun *tasis* attached to the preposition *pro* ('before') signifies a 'stretching' – towards, of course, the waiting *apodosis*, which is itself a compound of the preposition *apo* ('back') and the verbal noun *dosis* as a 'giving'. Whence the implication of a bond of reciprocity, the 'before' of the *protasis* reaching for the *apodosis* which turns 'back' to it.

In this model of linguistic mutuality, we find the schematic form of all counterfactual statements and propositions. But like most complex relationships, it is not always easy; it can become notably strained by virtue of controversial views as to what can plausibly go into each clause and what a 'proper' relation between the two might be. In ancient Greece the *protasis–apodosis* structure was deployed in fields as varied as logic, oratory and divination.²⁴ In the more specialized fields of the modern 'disciplines', everything depends on the nature of the particular counterfactual thought-experiment being conducted and the often fiercely partisan views of what is 'admissible' as either logically or empirically viable ('warranted assertability' is the technical buzzword).

All sentence forms of the relevant type juggle a double temporal perspective: back to a point in time where a hypothetical 'if'-governed change is introduced to the fabric of reality, and then forward to the putative consequences of the switched or modified antecedent. In tracing this double movement, one key issue, especially for the discipline of history, is where the starting point is to be, either looking back to a past from a position of known outcomes, or projecting forwards from the assumed point of view of historical actors facing an as yet unknown future. The two perspectives, of course, interconnect and interact, and can be separated only for analytical purposes. Some, however, have sought to drive a wedge between them, with a view to privileging one over the other.

One school of thought prefers the backwards look; indeed in some quarters it is the very ground of an evaluative distinction between 'good' and 'bad' counterfactual history ('restrained' and 'exuberant' the terms often used).[25] It is certainly the case that with known outcomes as the point of departure, one has a 'restraining' control mechanism for testing hypotheses, usually of a causal sort: by highlighting how something that happened might not have, we arrive at a better explanation of what, as a matter of historical fact, did occur. This is safer and, it is implied, more intellectually respectable than attempts to 'explain' what did not occur as if it (conditionally) had. On the other hand, and especially when proffered as the basis of a prescriptive methodological blueprint, laudable restraint can harden into exclusionary restrictive practices. It is not only nature that abhors a vacuum. If we imagine something that happened as not having happened (the French Revolution, say), the speculative chain does not conveniently halt at a posited historical absence (no French Revolution); a hypothetical something else has to occur in its place. It seems perfectly reasonable to try and develop some tools for thinking about what that might have been: a continuation of the *Ancien Régime* in different historical dress; or, as some have counterfactually proposed, an agreeably modern liberal order whose midwives were agreeably enlightened eighteenth-century aristocrats. Hindsight is a wonderful thing, but the view from the stern of the known can end by closing off avenues of inquiry into realms of 'possibility' which it is the job of the counterfactual imagination to explore. Its ideological *reductio*, the all-mastering endpoint that can be reached as one of the potential consequences of the selected starting point, is the infamous End of History, the latter's winners securely on the throne. The backwards look is powerful, but sometimes in the wrong sense of the term.

The alternative starting point faces forwards rather than backwards, immanent to the past in which historical actors individually or collectively contemplate an unknown future as a horizon of the possible, typically in conditions of stress, urgency and perplexity. These are at their most acute when an individual, a group, or an entire society reaches forks in the road, each of which represents, in varying degrees of scale, a different 'option'. The methodological suggestion is to start here, by trying, as best one can, to enter a thought-world at a crossroads moment or on the approach to that moment.[26] More specifically, the principal objects of investigation are the consciously pondered and explicitly recorded thoughts around which gather the might-bes of a future that will become might-have-beens once that future faced has become a future past.[27] This helps us capture something of the weird temporal cartwheel performed by counterfactuals. There is, however, a question as to *where* exactly on the landscapes of the past it can be performed. One objection is that it is at home only in connection with certain kinds of historical interest and inquiry (notably, high politics, diplomacy and warfare), and is accordingly attractive to fans of the 'great men' version of history ('the actions of a few princes and rich men', in Braudel's words).[28] It looks less appealing, or even workable, in respect of the slower-moving rhythms of *longue durée* history, in large measure not only slow or 'cold', but where the anonymity of mass social formations means there is often little if anything by way of recorded 'thoughts' for us to access (what, again, Braudel describes as 'anonymous history, working in the depths, and most often in silence').[29]

For the 'forwards' perspective to be able to capture more, the frame of reference needs to broaden, from the consciously 'thought' to the structurally or systemically 'thinkable' and the terms in which the parameters of the latter are set (collective 'mentalities', historical 'epistemes' and so forth). These circumscribed orders of the thinkable are usually seen as limiting, fixing the boundaries to what can be thought in a given place at a given historical moment and hence setting limits to what can count as an 'option' for historical actors. If in the ancient world you shared Aristotle's view that being a slave was a 'natural' condition, counterfactual musings of an abolitionist kind were not just unlikely to have any place in the thought-world; they were unlikely to have any place there even if one didn't share Aristotle's view. The concern with the limits of the thinkable is thus also a concern with the *unthinkable*, primarily to avoid anachronism and unrealistic expectations. But, along with embargoing illicit imports from one culture or period to another, there is, within a given formation, also the question of the thinkable and the unthinkable *for whom*. That question involves the social distribution of knowledge, the political control of information, the authority of custom, the availability and understanding of technological resource, and the areas of ignorance remediable by educational means. Mapping that is simply vast, and it is little surprise that historians interested in trying to operate counterfactuals in the context of larger collective movements tend to focus on leaders, advisers and experts in the making and implementing of public policy (what Hawthorn refers to as 'public bodies'). This is not just another version of Great Men history, but, from a Braudelian point of view, there is much it simply cannot encompass.

On the other hand, even where tightly constraining, these systems need to be examined not only for what they exclude but also for what they permit, above all at the outer limits of the historically given universe of the thinkable. When Lucien Febvre took Abel Franc to task for having suggested that Rabelais was a closet atheist, he did not do so on the grounds that the evidence pointed strongly to Rabelais being a believer (it does), but on the larger claim that, in the sixteenth century, atheism was not an option because it was 'unthinkable'.[30] In terms of sixteenth-century intellectual resource, however, there was a strong but no absolute bar to thinking the allegedly 'unthinkable'. The question is not whether an atheist position could be thought, but whether it could be openly stated or published, that is to say, a question of power and authority. When under new pressures that authority weakens, possibilities emerge that can also include an enriched understanding of the might-have-beens or 'lost possibilities' of a past repressed, concealed or dormant in a world poised between the thinkable, the thought and the declared.[31] We can perhaps characterize such examples as existing at the 'edge' of what the culture permits or prohibits, as instances of what (though his purposes here are somewhat different) Hawthorn calls the 'imaginative extensions' of a given thought-world to what 'might have been considered'.[32]

Another way of describing the issue underlying Febvre's claim would be to say that it is less what Rabelais could or might have thought than what he could have *done* with those thoughts. However much our understanding of the 'thinkable' is enlarged by the principle of 'imaginative extension', it has to be steadied by a corresponding sense of the 'doable'. Flying to the moon was not an 'option' for the seventeenth century in the counterfactual form of a missed opportunity merely because one was able to go there in a utopian fiction by Cyrano de Bergerac. The Incas were conversant with the principle of rotary motion, but did not adopt the wheel for the practical organization of everyday transportation; given the mountainous terrain, it was not a workable option. It is a truism that a counterfactual claim to the effect that such and such could (and might) have been done is meaningful only if it is a fact that it could have been done ('could have' is the modal specifically for the category of the doable). There is, however, space for considerable debate over what that 'fact' about counterfactual possibility truly looks like. As we shall see in Chapter 2, versions of the 'facts' can have an imprisoning rather than an anchoring effect, as the mask that 'realism' wears when acting as the servant of power. It is always important to remember that counterfactuals fold two statements into one: about something that might have been the case, they are also about something that wasn't. The latter can serve in turn as a crisp reminder that in some scenarios there simply were no alternatives. On the other hand, there is the converse, the role of the former as a reminder that the 'no alternative' claim can also be guilty of wishful thinking inducing a (usually self-interested) form of blindness to real possibilities. Historically circumscribed forms of 'how it is' sometimes give you the answer as to why notions of how it might have been are 'fantastic' in the sense of delusional, but sometimes also provide no answer at all other than in the terms of a question-begging ideological diktat. The doable and the non-doable are often, but not always, simply 'given', as realists often seem to imply. If they are given, it is in many cases because they are 'given' by someone, constructed by those who tell others what can and cannot be done, and counterfactually what could and could not have been done. Those constructions are neither immutable nor exempt from critical challenge. That can indeed be one of the tasks of the counterfactual, pressing against the construction in the name of the possibilities it excludes (we will see more of this in Chapters 2 and 3). For now, Emily Dickinson's wonderfully ambiguous poem comes to mind:

> *What I can do – I will –*
> *Though it be little as a Daffodil –*
> *That I cannot – must be*
> *Unknown to possibility –*

To which one response can be: unknown not because not there, but because unseen. The temporal cartwheel of the counterfactual, flipping between the 'before' and the 'after', mixes elements of forecast and retrospect in a manner that disconcerts but that can also illuminate. Echoing the 'hindcast' of meteorology,³³ we can call this the disorientating perspective of the 'retrocast', a form of predicting the past by means of a closer look at the trampled seedbeds in which the little Daffodil stands. There may indeed be no real alternatives, paths strictly unknown to possibility (in which case the counterfactual has no purchase and is generally but a receptacle for idle dreams or disappointed hopes). Or there may be, but as ones scarcely perceptible and, if perceived, not easily taken then and there, outlier options with low chances.³⁴ But not being front and centre of an individual's or a society's range of options does not mean that they cannot be found elsewhere, at another point along the 'edge', where possibilities gather in the shadowy halfway house between the present and the absent. The classic cases are moments of convulsive transition.³⁵

Positing the alternative and then imagining it as adopted belong in the *protasis*, the place where the 'if'-governed substitution occurs. The function of the *apodosis* is to state a view of what consequentially follows. This is, can be only, a probability construction. That, however, excludes retro-prediction of what is sometimes oddly called a hundred per cent probability. If the doable is part of what counterfactuals descriptively refer to (realms of possibility), it is also a constitutive part of counterfactuals themselves, what they themselves can do. Some things they cannot do, at least with any degree of conviction or guarantee of success. Further strain in the *protasis–apodosis* relation can arise from attributing to counterfactuals a capacity for delivering what they are not equipped to deliver. This can stem from either inflated expectations (someone's pipe dream) or wilful misattribution (setting them up to fail where they could never pass). It bears repeating more than once that the tasks that counterfactuals can perform are multiple. But one thing their special combination of conditional and subjunctive elements cannot supply, other than in some highly specialized scientific settings, is a 'proof'. Niall Ferguson highlights a class of historical counterfactuals that, in his eyes at least, glitter diamond-like, but are nevertheless to be found wanting; they are 'brilliantly formulated counterfactual *questions*, not answers' (one of his examples is Hugh Trevor-Roper's reflections on how the seventeenth-century Stuart monarchy could have been preserved).³⁶ Literally, this is, of course, untrue; the makers of the glittering specimens are all too eager to garland them with answers. What Ferguson means is that they are not *good* answers; they fail to convince. But what counts as a good answer? That depends on what the test is. While – assuming criteria that reasonable people can agree on – some historical counterfactuals are clearly more plausible than others, none at all can ever qualify as 'proofs'; in that sense they are *always* questions without answers. Experimentally posed and pursued, they do not supply answers other than provisionally; they play with possibility to show that, whatever the historical world is made of, it isn't reinforced concrete. The fact that a question lacks an answer isn't necessarily a reason for not asking it; asking it can be a way of exploring the limits of answerability (useful for everyone including historians). 'The answer must in the end be open' concludes Hawthorn in connection with one of his case studies.[37] That is true of all historical counterfactuals because it is intrinsic to them.

We can take this set of questions further by way of a particular grammatical property of the *apodosis*, specifically the choice of the modal auxiliary, and the various hostages to fortune when the preference is for 'would have' claims. The confidence with which one can enter a 'would-have' counterfactual claim is justified in very few domains of inquiry. The deductive logic of truth-conditional semantics is one such, as is the philosophy of science concerned with theories of causation in terms of what is held to be the law-bound behaviour of physical phenomena. But in any other context, and especially those that involve empirical and epistemic questions of verifiability, that 'would' is extremely precarious, even though we often come across it on parade like some intellectual peacock.[38] The discipline of history is littered with them, not only strutting boldly, but careering like wild horses towards a brick wall of an apodotic outcome.[39] The key issue is that of causation. This is difficult enough in respect of 'normal' history (Hawthorn recommends that we just forget about it). One need only gaze upon the panoply of types and models of causal explanation placed before us by Stephen Mumford and Rani Lill Anjum (physicalist, primitivist, pluralist, dispositionalist and so on);[40] or bury oneself in the marvel of what has to be one of the most beautiful creations of analytical philosophy, the Mackie formula for 'inus-conditions' (insufficient but necessary features of a condition that itself is unnecessary but sufficient);[41] and then, wrapped around all this, the neo-Humean reminder in connection with inferences drawn from the observation of past regularities: correlation is not causation.

How, other than in fiction, one might readily carry that weighty package into the counterfactual realm is anyone's guess, but guessing is all it can be. Counterfactuals, as I intimated earlier, are often used heuristically to test causal explanations of what actually happened; indeed causal explanations can themselves be construed as supplicants at the court of the counterfactual, implicitly calling on counterfactuals to act as their assessors. In history and the social sciences, this is where we encounter the legacy of Weber and the notion of so-called 'causal imputation'. A textbook example is Fogel's 'cliometric' delving into the evidence bank of nineteenth-century American economic history. Fogel asked what the effect on economic growth rates would have been had there been no railways. His answer was very little. But the point of the statistics-based exercise is purely heuristic; it was not to suggest that there was a counterfactual option for the United States whereby no railways would have been built; this crossed no-one's mind.[42] That, however, is very different from devising an alternate timeline with specified causal characteristics. It is far from clear how one establishes a persuasive causal sequence to 'explain' something in the realm of *irrealis* that never actually happened, above all how the hypothesis can cope with the chain of postulated knock-on effects, feedback loops and game-theoretical adjustments that, in any sequence involving human decision, would intervene in the speculative journey from the *protasis* to the *apodosis*.

One might perhaps feel justified in using a 'would have' construction in the vaguer form of 'if x had not been the case, then things would have turned out differently', where 'differently' is given no determinate content. But even in that indeterminate guise, there is an obvious weakness: apart from being of little interest, it is eminently possible that the supposed consequent of the antecedent switch comes out as (more or less) identical to that which actually occurred. Same-outcome counterfactuals are an intriguingly special sub-class, generally used for the inspection of causal explanations, but they also appear in connection with ideas of 'fate' (we will see something of this in Chapter 4 in relation to the Oedipus story). Then there are the *ex eventu* circular forms in which the 'would have' is run: in the knowledge that the coin came up heads, I can say 'if I had called heads, I would have won'. The 'would have' claim is both (uninterestingly) true and (importantly) false. It is false since, at the time point that matters (calling the outcome *before* the toss), I cannot know what will turn out to have been the case.[43] It is also a spoof example, associated in particular with the legendary Sydney Morgenbesser, renowned for the poker-faced wryness with which he set philosophical traps for hapless interlocutors. I like to think, though probably wrongly, that he might have enjoyed the company of Aslan when responding to Lucy in *Prince Caspian*: 'to know what would have happened, child? . . . No. Nobody is ever told that.'

The author of the great counterfactual fiction of our time, Philip Roth, in *Sabbath's Theater* seems, with his central character, to turn against 'what ifs' in no uncertain terms: 'Shoulda, woulda, coulda. The three blind mice.' He doesn't however include 'mighta' on the list of the futile modals, though whether that is because it covers too many possibilities to be even worth bothering with, or because it has a reasonable claim to exemption from scorn, is not broached. 'Might haves' are definitely a different animal, if in some instantiations wide-eyed (anything goes), at least not blind. The grammar of might-have is where most of us abide in our counterfactual navigations, and its more tentative nature needs to be respected. Probabilistic all the way through, it directs us away from a fixation on 'proof', from a pipe dream in search of an unattainable certainty. In some Lewisian quarters we can find more than a hint of disdain for might-haves, as if they were the modal vehicle of counterfactuals for wimps. This is rightly felt elsewhere to be a serious limitation. Keith DeRose has offered a robust defence of 'might-have' counterfactuals, explicitly advertised as a rejoinder to Lewis's semantics (which he identifies as LT (Lewis's Thesis)). In DeRose's argument, there is a vast class of 'context-sensitive' counterfactuals, meaning sensitive to contingent states of knowledge on the part of the speaker or 'case-constructor' at the time the counterfactual speculation is made. Thus, if it is known that John has no money in his pocket, one can assert that 'if John had put his hand in his pocket, he would have found no money in it'. But what if John (or Lewis) doesn't know or can't be sure (a perfectly normal state of affairs in any money-using world recognizable to us)? All that can be said by either is that, if John had put his hand in his pocket, he might have found some money. The closed world of Lewisian deduction in its pure form seems to be marked by indifference to these epistemic contingencies, the consequence of which is briskly stated: ignoring them is exactly the point at which LT finds itself 'in *deep* trouble' (De Rose's pointed emphasis).[44] That sounds like a wake-up call that needs to be heeded.

In probabilistic constructions informed by epistemic considerations, would-haves, if they are not to appear wantonly assertive or emptily tautological, survive only in terms of degrees and weightings of probability; that is, retention of 'would have' is acceptable only when adverbially modified by 'probably' or 'possibly', or 'perhaps' or 'maybe'. These are, of course, crudely imprecise measures for weighting probabilities, but they are at least intellectually courteous. Even more courteous is the delightfully modest use of 'perhaps' by Charles Renouvier, in his *Uchronie*, one of the major nineteenth-century sources for the development of thinking history counterfactually. Renouvier envisaged a history of Europe 'not as it has been, but as it might have been'. However extravagant some of Renouvier's imaginings, fans of the thrusting 'would-have' may have a lot to learn from the display of intellectual modesty in his use of the cautious 'might have'. It certainly stands as a quiet corrective to this from Walter Rathenau: 'History does not conjugate in conditionals, it speaks of what is and what was, not what would have been.' I cite this because Richard Evans does, as, in the concluding words of his book, a flourish in pole position to conclude the entire irritating business; what more, runs the implication, needs to be said on the matter? Several things, as it happens. Missing from Rathenau's *obiter dictum* are, crucially, the 'only' that needs to be inserted after 'speaks' if the passage is to mean what it ostensibly says, plus the 'might have been' that belongs alongside 'would have been'. However, once that has been tacked on, the question of how history 'conjugates' becomes very much an open one.[45]

Furthermore, probabilistic judgements of both forecasts and retrocasts are not only analytical. We don't carry computerized Bayesian Nets around in our heads. Our judgements are also bound up with the intuitions and beliefs we draw upon in the application of practical reason to the conduct of our daily lives. In those contexts, the relevant sense of 'probability' goes all the way back to ancient sources and understandings of the 'probable' as based in *doxa* (common opinion and socially ratified assumptions) that predate the emergence of the early modern 'mathematized' conceptions explored by Ian Hacking.[46] 'If he had been smart, he would have made a lot of money' scarcely qualifies as 'scientific', but is characteristic of a belief-system within a particular kind of society (call it, in shorthand, the 'Trump' kind). It is true that in stylized mathematical models one can get that curiously oxymoronic thing, a hundred per cent probability, and inside the model it makes perfect sense. But that is a stylized representation of a real world. In the latter, a hundred per cent probability makes no coherent sense. A human world in which there are hundred per cent chances is a world in which there is no place for chance.

# IV

All counterfactuals are thought experiments of a particular kind, and the *protasis–apodosis* sentence type can be conceived as housing the figurative laboratory in which the experiments are carried out. We can also think of them as 'games', on a spectrum from the sophisticatedly game-theoretical to the notionally, though deceptively, frivolous sort evoked by the historian, Daniel Milo, in the name of the shake-it-up project he calls 'experimental history'. In a gesture both designed and guaranteed to exasperate, Milo flamboyantly enlists Marx (the Groucho one) to his cause, citing the episode in *A Night in Casablanca* where, as the new manager, Groucho orders a redistribution of the hotel room numbers; when his assistant objects 'think of the confusion', back comes the reply 'But think of the fun'. 'Experimental history', according to Milo, is 'carnavalesque' and 'disrespectful', it proposes rearranging some of the furniture just to 'see' ('pour voir'), and the counterfactual has an important part to play in the rearranging. Above all, it is crucial to the experiment that it be allowed to 'fail'.[47] We will revisit this remarkable laboratory in Chapter 2. More soberly, though rivetingly, the philosopher, Dorothy Edgington, also describes counterfactuals as a 'game', in relation to which she asks two questions, a 'how' question and a 'why' question. 'The problem of counterfactuals', she writes, 'has always been: what are the rules of the game.'[48] That's the 'how' question, how to play the game according to a coherent and shared set of rules. This, of course, is the necessary constraint on potential intellectual anarchy (imagine Groucho playing chess with his assistant and announcing there are no longer any rules). On the other hand, and as I have already intimated, a consolidated, fixed set of operational rules (a rule *book*) cannot encompass all the games that legitimately support and enact counterfactuals without thinning their field of reference or in some cases inflicting major distortions.

For there is also, Edgington writes, the 'why' question ('why play this game?'). What's the point of it? For philosophers on the whole the point consists primarily in using analytical means to get it right in the sense of the 'objectively correct'. But for people in their daily lives, Edgington observes, counterfactuals 'play other roles'. In this context, the question might be: what, for counterfactual thinking, is the benefit of 'The Benefit of Hindsight' (the subtitle of Edgington's paper)? Is there any? Some (for example, the band of Yoloists we shall meet in Chapter 5) maintain there is none at all. Edgington herself provides a general reason why there is, rooted in psychology: 'It's hard to believe that many of our desires, beyond the most basic hard-wired ones, would survive if we were always indifferent to what has happened.'[49] 'Desire' however is a treacherous thing, and its relation to counterfactuals is, to put it mildly, complicated.

In relation to our desiring being and how we use the might-have-beens of a past as we move into a future, do counterfactuals sap our energies or recharge them? Are they, in E. H. Carr's withering description, merely the 'favourite consolation of the defeated', or a spur to transformation (as illustrated, for instance, by the history of the concept of *metanoia* I look at in Chapter 5)? More modestly, are they 'nudges' in the balancing acts of reason and intuition sponsored by the new 'behavioural' sciences? Are they a source of creative thinking or of mere wishful thinking (in the coin-tossing story, if I'd called heads as if *only* I'd called it). Or are they, in desperate circumstances, what Faulkner's *Absalom, Abasalom* describes as the 'might-have-been which is the single rock we cling to above the maelstrom of unbearable reality'?

There is something else we might want to add (I certainly do). One of the considerable virtues of counterfactual exploration is as a stimulant of unadulterated curiosity and the desire to wander far and wide (at your own risk of course). I have already spoken of the roaming properties of this book in terms of its eclectic set of intellectual and disciplinary interests (the risks taken on that front are entirely my own responsibility). One of the forms of wandering spurred by counterfactual curiosity is along the arc of time towards what, in the following chapter, I call the class of counterfactual 'Ultimates'. Two such concern beginnings and endings. The Book of Genesis offers a version of the First Humans, and (at least) two counterfactual questions hang over it, one about God's attitude to what he has made and the other the feelings of Adam and Eve about what they have done. The disaster that befalls Eden is a story of how things were not meant to be, and thus accompanied by the counterfactual suggestion that – on assumptions regarding divine powers and plans – they might have been otherwise. This is not just a question for a story, a narrative question. It is also a richly theological one, especially of Pauline inspiration (the theme explored in *Corinthians* and *Romans* of Christ as the Second Adam who comes to put right what originally went wrong in the Garden). Does this mean that God 'regretted' his original creation; and, if so, that he wished he had dealt the cards differently. But if this *was* the 'plan', how could things have been otherwise?[50]

Then fast forward projectively to the prospect of the 'post human' in the age of robotics. The question that has dogged successive and evolving iterations of the Turing Machine is whether computational simulations of the human mind mean that the 'thinking' machine becomes progressively indistinguishable from the human mind; or, perhaps more profoundly, whether there is a paradox at the heart of the whole enterprise (the 'black holes' of mathematics that are not so much a problem for, as central to, what mathematics is) whereby the closer the simulation gets to human mental processes, the less it actually is what it seems to be. The question arises with some urgency in connection with AI algorithms that can, we are told, 'learn from mistakes'. Is this the same as 'after thoughts' and 'changing one's mind' in the senses associated with *metanoia*? Can it involve counterfactuals? If so, can it do so in relation to ethical deliberations and affective attitudes? Can it experience 'regret' over bad decisions? Don't be silly, expostulates one hard-headed expert in the field of algorithmically driven high-speed trading: 'Algorithms are designed to act without emotion.' Is the thought that they might 'feel' not just a fantasy in the Blade Runner 2049 mode? Yet here's Boer Deng in *Nature* on 'ethical robots', rehearsing the ways in which a programme can be designed to cope with the counterfactual scenarios involved in well-known ethical thought experiments (he cites the famous example of the runaway railway trolley dilemma that is a favourite of the moral philosophers).[51] And, if generally speaking the jury is still out, here is neuroscientist Ryota Kanai casting his vote, under the eye-popping title 'How Introspection and Imagination Make Robots Better' (presumably including the sense of the expression 'better human beings'):

> Our AIs already have sophisticated training models, but they rely on our giving them data to learn from. With counterfactual information generation, AIs would be able to generate their own data – to imagine possible futures they come up with on their own ... If we consider introspection and imagination as two of the ingredients of consciousness, perhaps even the main ones, it is inevitable that we eventually conjure up a conscious AI, because those functions are so clearly useful to any machine.[52]

Gathering counterfactuals, it will be seen, is indeed a quirky business, and it will surprise no-one if it occasionally resembles woolgathering (the lovely activity of purposeless daydreaming[53]). That is in large measure because they are themselves quirks, strange folds in what the Chilean writer, Roberto Bolaño, calls the 'conjectural breeze of time'. The word 'quirk' in fact crops up routinely in actual discussion of counterfactuals (not least the splendid fact that one of the major linguist-logicians interested in them was called Quirk). Thus we have the 'cognitive quirks of counterfactuals'; 'some logical quirk about counterfactuals'; the 'mind-bending quirks' of 'the counterfactual quantum'; and – a special pleasure – 'a quirk of New Zealand law' (which consists in 'considering multiple counterfactuals'). This sort of thing is the collector's delight, and thus the moment arrives for a confession. One of the truly quirky yet addictive pastimes an interest in counterfactuals can spawn is that of the Collector. Whether this is a virtue or a vice is up for debate, but in my case it has proven to be irresistible. I dream of a vast catalogue, a *Dictionnaire des contrefactuels*, to offer as a belated homage to Gustave Flaubert. It could also eventually yield a taxonomy: there would be the commonplace specimens and the rare breeds, the wan and the brightly coloured, the memorable and the forgettable, and, of course, the personal favourites. So here is a very short list of five of my own favourites plucked from what is now a very large personal archive. Some were mined while working in the trenches, while others turned up as unexpectedly serendipitous acquisitions. They are chosen not solely for their straightforward analytical yield. There is more than a touch of Groucho about some of them, and are essentially invitations to play (in the strong sense of the play of the mind). Together, they reflect some of the many things counterfactuals can happily (and sometimes unhappily) do for, and to, us (making us think, wonder, laugh, admire, and squirm come to mind here).

The first is unsurprisingly opaque given that it is from Kafka and his bottomless chest of 'baffling questions'; here is his contribution at once to ancient history and to the course of world history (one to pair perhaps with Pascal's example of the famous queenly nose).[54] It is vintage Kafka, utterly arresting because of its distinctive mix of the transparent and the inscrutable, simultaneously indifferent to interpretive commentary while seeming to beseech it:

> It is conceivable that Alexander the Great, in spite of the martial successes of his early days, in spite of the excellent army that he had trained, in spite of the power he felt within him to change the world, might have remained standing on the bank of the Hellespont and never have crossed it, and not out of fear, not from infirmity of will, but because of the mere weight of his own body.

The second came my way – to deliver another kind of 'shock' – by a chance attendance at a philosophy seminar (of the Serious Metaphysics Group in Cambridge) devoted in part to counterfactual conditionals. It is perhaps only in such contexts that one could encounter the following gracefully demented specimen (served up for exemplary illustrative purposes, it teaches you a lot once you have recovered from the shock). Take two factually true statements, convert and link them as the *protasis* and *apodosis* of a counterfactual conditional, and, Groucho-style, you have:

If Canberra were the capital of Australia, the moon would have craters.

The third is an offering of Doris Lessing's and comes perfumed with a hint of the *louche*. I include it after the fashion of the connoisseur (in this instance arising from having been a life-long devotee of Stendhal; he also makes a brief appearance in the concluding chapter). Stendhal famously loved women, but suffered from a dysfunction that in his private journals he discreetly termed the 'fiasco'. Lessing puts an interestingly joyous counterfactual gloss on this:

He acquired a reputation for impotence, but, as we know from literature and from life, this could – had he used it – have lured women to his bed, because of their instinct to repair the situation.

The fourth (technically the least qualified, but morally compelling) is from a parliamentary speech by Charles James Fox in 1806, on the bill to abolish slavery:

So fully am I impressed with the vast importance and necessity of attaining what will be the object of my motion this night, that, if, during the almost forty years that I have had the honour of a seat in Parliament, I had been so fortunate as to accomplish that, and that only, I should think I had done enough.

This is not a pure counterfactual conditional. It hovers between an indicative and a subjunctive, which are then lobbed into an imagined future past governed by the concluding pluperfect ('I should think I had done enough'). However, the bill did not pass that night, and eventually did so only after Fox's death. Chronologies, political and personal, thus confer the sense of a 'what if' on his sentence, and thus steer it to honorary as well as honourable membership of the counterfactualist catalogue. For its nobility of sentiment and its syntactic majesty, this is as good as it gets, and the one all collectors should have.

The fifth has a special significance for me, dispiriting at first sight, but also an essential tonic that I have kept about my person. As already noted, the book's central emblem is the Crossroads. A sustained concern with crossroads scenes reflexively conjures up the book's own counterfactuals (the forks in the road it might have taken but didn't). If there were a temptation to forget this, my friend and colleague, Geoffrey Lloyd, has been there to remind me of it with his own bracing counterfactual:

> If I had written a book about counterfactuals, I wouldn't have done it this way.

# 1 A NAILE, A NOSE AND A TRAITOR

*Little Needles, Big Differences.*
                    **TATTOO PARLOUR, SAN FRANCISCO**

*I wonder if there's other worlds like this, he said. Or if this is the only one.*
                                        **CORMAC McCARTHY**

# I

'For want of a naile the shoe is lost, for want of a shoe the horse is lost, for want of a horse the rider is lost', so runs a truncated ancient proverb in George Herbert's *Outlandish Proverbs*, published in 1640. Its earliest known reference is to the fate of Richard at the Battle of Bosworth, and the allusion to the fall of a monarch and the loss of a kingdom is made explicit in the fuller version recorded in 1758 by Benjamin Franklin in *Poor Richard's Almanack*:

> For want of a nail the shoe was lost.
> For want of a shoe the horse was lost.
> For want of a horse the rider was lost.
> For want of a rider the message was lost.
> For want of a message the battle was lost.
> For want of a battle the kingdom was lost.
> And all for the want of a horseshoe nail.

The ruling idea here can be retroactively construed as a folk wisdom version of a modern scientific theory, and, in a sort of dialectical tourniquet, popular (as distinct from scientific) accounts of the theory itself can be loosely and figuratively construed as a modern form of folk wisdom: namely 'chaos theory' (the quiver of a butterfly wing on one side of the world is connected to the eruption of a storm on the other). The theory itself uniquely combines rigorous determinism and radical unpredictability, expressed as the tendency of dynamical systems to generate uncertainty in proportion to increased timespan. Lyapunov translated it mathematically as an exponential formula whereby a doubling of the time scale – the time elapsing between original event and final one – entails a quadrupling of the unpredictable. Scale is thus fundamental, and is mirrored in both the form and the content of the proverb. Within the framework of formal repetition (line-initial 'for want of' and line-terminal 'was lost'), there is a textual scaling up, matched by a thematic expansion of the historical terrain itself, the latter represented as a process of causal 'stretch' running from a tiny contingency to a hugely consequential outcome. The expansion is what matters (foregrounded in the summarizing seventh line). In the run from nail loss to shoe loss to horse loss in the first two lines, the stretch looks manageable. But the run from nail loss all the way to kingdom loss ends by looking a bit of a stretch in the more idiomatic sense, especially where the conclusion in its turn opens onto longer-term consequences for the political future of an entire nation.[1] The implicit counterfactual is, of course, that, if the nail had not been lost, that future might, indeed would, have turned out very differently. Many historical counterfactuals are like this (a famous example I discuss later in this chapter, in the company of Cleopatra). Indeed the proverbial nail is the source for the title of a collection of essays on such cases, probably the best known of which is the Catholic Wind fable.[2] As starting points or hypothetical 'antecedents', nail and wind hover between an appearance of pure contingency ('chance' or 'luck' the common names) and an affirmation of causal linkage in virtue of which things very different in magnitude as well as distant from each other in both time and space are seen as connected, if unpredictably, after the fashion of chaos theory.[3]

This proverbial gathering of counterfactuals furnishes a window onto a more general set of questions. Might any one particular in everything that has happened not have happened? But if so, what follows logically: does it mean that, in what follows temporally, nothing would have been the same? This view of radical connectedness, all the way down, back and through, is truly dizzying (chaos theory and its cousin, fractal geometry, look modest by comparison). Something like this is to be found in Leibniz's metaphysics (though what exactly Leibniz meant by 'connection' in space–time is much debated). The metaphysical argument is grounded in a theistic conception whereby God as 'clockmaker' or 'designer' created the world in a certain way, and that is the way it ineluctably remains. This does not mean, according to Leibniz, that it could not have been otherwise. There is an indefinite number of possible worlds in the mind of God, constrained only by the law of non-contradiction such that God could not create a world in which there are simultaneously more trees than mountains and more mountains than trees. Any one of these possible worlds could have been switched for this one; in that sense the existence and form of this world are counterfactually contingent. But God is not like the deity imagined by Nietzsche in a later addition to *The Birth of Tragedy*, the 'totally unthinking and amoral artist' playing imperiously and nonchalantly with worlds as if they were plastic works of art. Once created, this world unfolds according to laws prescribed for it, as a harmoniously ordered ensemble and the 'best possible'. God, in short, doesn't play dice. Counterfactuals may slosh around inside the divine mind, but they cannot in principle be questions for us.

That did not, however, prevent them continuing to preoccupy Leibniz along with those his metaphysics either inspired or annoyed.[4] In the very act of theoretically closing down the topic of counterfactuals as God's business alone, he opened a Pandora's box. What in this connection has been called 'possible-worlds providentialism' generated all manner of counterfactual speculations, most of them in the dystopian form, famously satirized by Voltaire in *Candide*, of how things could have been worse (so-called 'downward' counterfactuals).[5] Some of the issues reappeared in a sphere dominated by Leibniz's contemporary, Isaac Newton (with whom, at the initiative of Caroline, the Princess of Wales, Leibniz indirectly corresponded through the intermediary of an exchange with Samuel Clarke). Their differences (over the nature of 'space', for example) need not detain us. What might, if only briefly, is the discipline of which Newton is one of the founding fathers. Cosmology is a theory of the origins, nature and history of the universe (or multiverse) that is haunted by counterfactuals in the context of the greatest beginning-story of all time (precisely because all time is its subject). For Leibniz, in the beginning was God the clockmaker. For the modern cosmologist, in the beginning was the Bang. The physics of the first 'instant' is unknown, its singularity a mystery (was there just one Bang or many, for example?).

But if the observational methods and mathematical equations do not permit of inferential access to the moment of the Bang itself, its immediate aftermath (possibly a mere nanosecond) is generally posited as a scene of countless initial conditions that include all manner of possibilities, a cosmic host of unrealized might-have-beens. What we call 'our' world is a matter of a few crucial numbers (the former Astronomer Royal, Martin Rees, lists six), which represent the 'fine-tuned' parameters that make our world possible, including our being here to think these things (the principle of so-called 'anthropic selection'). 'Untuned', and there are no stars and no life. Eminently possible small variations in the numbers mean the Bang could have given birth to a stillborn cosmos (of which there may in fact be many 'elsewhere', perhaps as the product of other Bangs). If the expansion rate of the universe had been slower, it would have re-collapsed to a 'crunch'; or if nuclear forces were just slightly different, there would have been no chemicals other than hydrogen (a counterfactually grounded warning to beware of 'carbon chauvinism' in thinking of life as the inevitable outcome of natural 'constants').

Unless there is a fine-tuning clockmaker at work in this, there is no reason to believe that things had to be the way they have turned out. What we call the 'laws of nature' may be, in Rees's words, mere 'local bylaws governing our cosmic patch', and even these may have changed with the ageing of the patch (as the universe cooled).[6] The Bang didn't fix the law-like behaviour of the universe at one go; it has a history marked by turning points, at which it could have gone in different directions. No scientist is, of course, obliged to think about these might-have-beens (they may reasonably say they already have enough on their hands trying to understand what is). And in any case, for those so inclined, counterfactual dalliances at the cosmic crossroads are only for tiny bands of specialists in physics and mathematics. Their more general interest, however, is as examples of what in the Introduction I baptized 'Ultimate' counterfactuals, partly because of their physical immensity, but also because they lead back to ultimately remote starting points and then unfurl forwards along various axes of the great chain of planetary being.

Though far less remote from the cosmological point of view. Evolutionary biology is another example, at least if we entertain Stephen Jay Gould's thought experiment which asks about an alternative biological trajectory if, hypothetically, we were to wind the evolutionary tape back to the beginning and start it again. According to Gould, many outcomes are likely to have been different, and the chances in particular of 'anything remotely like a human being' emerging are 'effectively nil'.⁷ There are many other questions arising from what have been called 'Darwinian counterfactuals'.⁸ There is also a caricatural version of this type of back-to-the beginning counterfactual, arising from readings of Genesis touched upon in the previous chapter. What if Eve had not partaken of the apple at the serpent's urging? As with stillborn cosmoses, we wouldn't, of course, be here as their descendants to ask. But since we are, one question could be: might what we know as serpents have had legs? Since God's punishment for the urging is to condemn all serpents henceforth to the slithering mode of legless locomotion, speculation about alternative modes becomes a legitimate question in an alternative world where the serpent doesn't tempt Eve. It is also a nice question as to how the original tempting serpent itself moved, but not unreasonable to classify it as a question only for biblical literalists. The main problem with 'Ultimates' is that they are likely to end by putting counterfactuals out of business for the purely practical reason that there are few, if any, shoulders broad enough to carry their intellectual burden. But these are not to be confused with those that never open for business in the first place, not by virtue of their unmanageable weight, but because of their flagrant pointlessness (are we really going to wonder about how serpents got around in Paradise and might have continued to do so if Adam and Eve had not disobeyed?).

## II

How then – the principal question for this chapter – to distinguish between the vacuous and the non-vacuous? What, for example, of a counterfactual in a teacup? If for breakfast on a given morning, a farmer in Shropshire had drunk a third cup of tea instead of his customary two, what might that have meant for him, or indeed for everything? The thoroughly vacuous observation that everything that has occurred, is occurring and will occur, has in the present moment the feature of preceding, succeeding or coinciding with the event of that third cup, will be of no interest to anyone including even the most pathologically narcissistic Shropshire farmer. As for causal linkage, to, for example, an aggravated monsoon in India, board that train of thought and the likely intellectual destination for chaos theory is chaos itself. But scale up once more (this time to a very large number) and head off instead to nineteenth-century China with historian, Ian Morris, in search of the secrets of the historical 'success' of the British Empire and more generally the West: 'Victoria's countrymen broke Daognang and shattered his empire for that most British of vices – a cup of tea (or, to be more precise, several billion of cups of tea).'[9] It's an interesting causal thesis that the vicar's wife having a nice cup of tea in the rectory garden was part of the story of British steamboats making their determined way up the Yangtze. There is even better to come: if the collective addiction to tea had not been so all-embracing, what might have been the consequences for the Chinese empire and its emperor, and – even more exotically – for Albert, Victoria and Looty?

We are given an answer in the form of an extraordinary narrative reversal, a counterfactual fable in which an armed flotilla bears the Daognang down the Thames to a waiting Victoria and Albert, who swear allegiance before the Consort is carted off to China, where, never to return, he goes native, grows a Manchu pigtail, learns to speak fluent Mandarin, and becomes increasingly versed in the Chinese classics. The counterfactual has, of course, to be a mere 'device', a fantastical tale told solely to throw into sharper relief a fact-based (though controversial) historical argument centred on the triumph of the West. But then we get something else. First a nugget: after Albert's death, a group of British officers back from China express their condolences by presenting Queen Victoria with a Pekingese dog stolen from the Imperial Summer Palace. She baptized him 'Looty' (hopefully, reports that a joke was intended are accurate). This, believe it or not, is fact-based history, and it is not for nothing that Morris cites the old chestnut 'History is often stranger than fiction'. And so indeed it proves in the following guise. Around the charming tale of canine loot, a further question is asked, its form such as to blur completely the dividing line between history and fiction: 'Why', writes Morris, 'did history follow the path that took Looty to Balmoral Castle, there to grow old with Victoria, rather than the one that took Albert to study Confucianism in Beijing?'

We need to take a deep breath here and continue holding onto the belief that Morris clearly does not 'mean' his Albert story to stand as an actual historical option. Yet the formulation (Looty brought to Balmoral 'rather than' Albert disappearing to Beijing) positions it as exactly that; it evokes, if only for heightening purposes, the counterfactual not as an invented tale, but as a genuine alternative 'path', a fork in the historical road to which another was preferred. We are thus situated in two parallel worlds, in both of which we encounter a grieving Queen of England. In the counterfactual world Victoria grieves for the loss and then death of a spouse in Beijing; in the 'real' world she also grieves over the death of a spouse but is fortunate in being able to console herself by stroking a hound pilfered from Beijing. It would not be unreasonable to see the parallels as putting great strain on the conceptual antimony of *realis* and *irrealis*. Indeed the would-be counterfactualist might well at this point experience stirrings of another loss (of the will to live). They are likely to grow much stronger on reading the accolade conferred by one of the doyens of counterfactual history: Niall Ferguson blurbs that this book is 'the nearest thing to a unified field theory of history we are ever likely to get'. This would make it an honorary member of the 'Ultimates' category, as history's cousin to cosmology; a unified field theory of history could stand proudly alongside the 'theory of everything' in physics.

But if certain thoughts about the history of the cosmos (including its might-have-been forks in the road) are, in Rees's words, 'speculative physics', they are also, as he goes on to add, 'physics, not metaphysics', and their counterfactual components, though by definition unobservable, nevertheless count as part of science. A Confucian consort of Queen Victoria cannot be said to sit other than entertainingly alongside counterfactually posited variations in gravitational forces. If there is a parallel of sorts with the cosmological, it does not come as a recommendation. What the imagined fate of Albert in Beijing tells us is that, like the model of an ever-expanding universe, counterfactuals are limitless; apart from death, one can 'what-if' anything, on virtually any imaginable 'scale'. This is the opposite of a selling point, the limitless not as a call to the wide plains of intellectual adventure, but as a recipe for another sort of big bang, in which the counterfactual enterprise simply shatters. Many preliminary clarifications of a methodological nature are necessary if counterfactual inquiry is to prosper, as distinct from languishing in the front room as a collection of mere 'parlour games'. I have touched on some of these in the Introduction. They must include the unmanageability of the prospect of counterfactuals without end along with the related task of distinguishing between the serious and the non-serious.

As noted in the Introduction, silly counterfactuals are legion, from the comically batty to the outright scary, with a generously proportioned space reserved for cases whose analytical yield is somewhere south of zero. There is, of course, nothing in this that is unique to counterfactuals;

more or less any sentence type can be used to produce nonsense, and it would itself be silly to single out the *protasis–apodosis* structure as specifically and especially vulnerable to abuse and misuse. It is nevertheless important to discriminate, partly as a check to an increasingly pervasive exploitation of the trivial counterfactual in the everyday life world, and partly because of the ways in which these uses can be seized upon by critics to discredit the counterfactualist enterprise as such. Since mercy is here synonymous with parsimony, three especially egregious instances from and for our times will suffice for illustrative purposes. All three wrap a justificatory counterfactual around violence, two of them addressing the nexus of politics and war (the place in which historical counterfactuals, from Herodotus to the present, so often dwell, whether as dispassionate analysis or partisan rationalization). The first, threaded into a political biography, is a coolly appraisive offering from our champion of historical counterfactuals:

> Arguments that focus on loss of life in strategically marginal countries – and there is no other way of describing Argentina, Bangladesh, Cambodia, Chile, Cyprus, and East Timor – must be tested against this question: how, in each case would an alternative decision have affected US relations with strategically important countries like the Soviet Union, China, and the major western European powers?[10]

Counterfactuals are usually despised by political 'realists' (the world is as it is, and there is little point in thinking how it might have been otherwise). This chilling exercise in utilitarian calculus is an exception, actively embraced by a form of political realism in the service of great power interests and the vindicatory legitimation of one of its outstandingly repulsive modern representatives. Swift's 'Modest Proposal' comes to mind, though entirely bereft of both his irony and intellectual rigour. In its haste to rationalize Kissinger's policy in the terms of *realpolitk*, the counterfactual overlooks how its premise implies its pointlessness: if the listed countries were not 'strategically important', what does it matter whether or not, for example, Cambodia is carpet-bombed? In the meantime, we can console ourselves with the thought that somewhere between the napalm descending and the flesh burning, the victims consoled themselves with the thought that their lives were of minor strategic importance.

The second example is, in its own ghastly fashion, a collector's item – Donald Trump on the Orlando shootings in 2017:

If some of those wonderful people had guns strapped right here, right to their waist or right to their ankle, and this son of a bitch comes out and starts shooting and one of the people in that room happened to have it and goes boom, boom. You know what, that would've been a beautiful, beautiful sight, folks.[11]

This deranged utterance admits of no rational engagement, other than a musing on what movie might have been passing through Trump's mind (*The Gunfight at the OK Corral*?). It contains, of course, a coded message of support for the Base, the National Rifle Association and assorted 'Second Amendment people'. But if actually parsed as a counterfactual, it is certifiable: the envisaged 'consequent' is not that guns fired in self-defence would have saved lives, but that the spectacle 'would've been a beautiful, beautiful sight', thus impressively extending the meaning of the 'beautiful' to include the hideous. 'Silly' is not quite the appropriate adjective for a counterfactual aesthetics of bullets and corpses, though, if we think its madness places it in a league of its own, there are in fact rivals for the top spot. On an analytical view, one such (from Tony Blair's former Director of Operations, John McTernan) makes Trump look vaguely sane: 'If Jeremy Corbyn had stopped Tony Blair invading Iraq, dictators and jihadists would rule the world today.'[12] In terms of both its assumed 'antecedent' and its inferred 'consequent', this is counterfactual reasoning seemingly bent on staging the shipwreck of Reason.

These are, of course, easy targets, caricatures of the silly genre, rightly attracting not just the politely suburban description of 'parlour games' (E. H. Carr's analogy), but the more insulting term used by E. P. Thompson (the original German best retained for its properties of aggressive sibilance): *Geschichtscheissenschlopf*. Thompson's implicit call for buckets, mops and cleaning materials is, however, directed indiscriminately to historical counterfactuals as such, as one of a set of moves and counter-moves in a polemical Punch and Judy show, with each side of the debate taking it in turn to play an unintended parody of Punch. Thus, while Thompson turns on the hoses, the conservative historian, Andrew Roberts, responds to Thompson and his perceived intellectual allies with an unusually tawdry defence of counterfactual history: if the opposition are against it, we're for it ('anything condemned by Carr, Thompson and Hobsbawm is clearly to be recommended').[13] These are the qualifications for high office in the country called Polemic.

Inanity, it will be seen, is contagious, in respect not just of suggested counterfactuals but also of their justification or denunciation. Appearances can, however, also prove deceptive. What if – to reprise occupancy of that small corner of La La Land devoted to counterfactual movie castings – the makers of the film *National Velvet* had cast Shirley Williams for the part of the horse-crazy Velvet Brown? The informed reader of that sentence might already be reeling. Both first and last names being fairly common, surely they refer to a 'Shirley Williams' other than the erstwhile Labour minister, founder of the Social Democrats, former wife of philosopher Bernard Williams (who figures prominently in this book)? Or does the name in fact refer to the distinguished politician, as one of those outlandish counterfactual speculations that give the whole business a very bad name, altogether less plausible than, say, what if Donald Trump had auditioned for the main part of *The Terminator* or Manuel Barroso for the part of Jordan Belfort in *The Wolf of Wall Street*? In many ways, the example is on a par with the tale of Fidel Castro's abortive destiny as the pitcher with a curveball so good that the New York Giants wooed him with the offer of a contract. Castro declined and the rest, as they say is history. But there remains the counterfactual: what if Fidel had accepted? Baseball scouts might have reoriented the course of world history. Allowing for qualitative difference at the level of the 'consequent' (leadership of the Cuban revolution presumably weightier than a ministerial career in British politics), the two counterfactuals are prima facie similarly bizarre. But there is one very real difference. The option of an alternative career in baseball for Castro is an urban myth, widely disseminated and believed to be true by many (including Senator Eugene McCarthy, challenger in the 1968 presidential primaries). The fact remains that Castro was never offered a contract, nor even considered for one. The tale now serves primarily as an example of a joke counterfactual.[14]

The case of Shirley Williams is not like this. I said earlier that a basic problem with counterfactuals is their limitlessness, the unlicensed freedom, for those so inclined, to 'what-if' anything. Why on earth (and notwithstanding Ronald Reagan's inverse story) speculate about an alternative career path in the movies for this British politician? The answer, of course, is because she auditioned for the part.[15] Auditioning for it is not the same thing as actually being offered it, and Baroness Williams was after all only 12 years old at the time. It is a weak counterfactual, and of little interest outside the personal memoir or the gossip columns of the media. On the other hand, it also tells us that, on the matter of silliness, the protocol should be: not so fast. We need to bear in mind that there are kinds and degrees of silliness and that distinguishing them is a first step on the (long) road to constraining unregulated what-iffery. But we can productively go about this task by also reminding ourselves again that the purposes of counterfactual thinking are just that, plural; all depends, as I suggested in the Introduction, on the type of question being asked. To see why and how, let us examine two very remarkable counterfactuals, both of which seem absurd, and one of which genuinely but instructively is. Both involve considerations of 'scale', in the first case circus leaps across logical space, and in the second gigantic leaps across historical space. Together, they raise or disclose important lines of inquiry concerning what we can and cannot do with counterfactuals.

## III

The first example – which casts the founding director of the FBI in a role for which one can imagine no-one auditioning – is purely formal, situated within the airtight world of analytical philosophy, and more specifically the logical semantics of possible-worlds theory. The type of question this counterfactual addresses has something in common with the ancient inventors of the *modus ponens* and *modus tollens* models of inferential reasoning, but, in this particular case, in a manner that doubles back on itself in self-exploding ways. That is its intended point. It is expressly meant by its inventor to come out as a botched job, less an instance of faulty reasoning than a conscious demonstration of it; it is a kind of philosopher's pastiche in the sense of furnishing an exemplary lesson in how *not* to do things with counterfactuals. In one possible world (the fictional one of Philip Roth's *The Plot Against America*), J. Edgar Hoover counterfactually serves a fascist Lindbergh president, an imagining in some ways consistent with fact, given Hoover's later recruitment of Nazi war criminals in the post-war fight against Communism. Imagine then the shock of finding Hoover in another possible world (philosophical rather than fictional) where he becomes his own and his country's worst enemy, that dread beast, a Communist, and thus a traitor, whose likely fate is to be eventually hauled before and exposed by the House Committee on Un-American Activities. Its judgement would be incontrovertible, not, however, on grounds of evidence (there is none), but by deduction from within a closed but crazy world of inference. This

Hoover features in the major and minor premises of a 'hypothetical' syllogism invented by the philosopher, Robert Stalnaker, and glossed by David Lewis, as an example of what the latter calls 'counterfactual fallacies'.[16] The rigged deck of cards in question goes by the fetching name of 'the fallacy of transitivity', and is based on the process known as 'strengthening the antecedent' in the inferential movement from major to minor premise ('if $x$ is this, then it is also that; and if that, then...'). Under certain conditions, both premises are deemed to be true, but also incompatible, such that, albeit true, they lead to a false conclusion, an impossible possible world. Here is the syllogism, in all its wondrous wackiness:

> If J. Edgar Hoover had been born a Russian, he would have been a communist.
> If J. Edgar Hoover had been a communist, he would have been a traitor.
> Therefore, if J. Edgar Hoover had been born a Russian, he would have been a traitor.

Wondrous indeed this is, a daring adventure of the Predicate, gliding from proposition to proposition across syllogistic space, while stopping off to refuel at various possible worlds situated at varying degrees of remoteness from the actual world. Three initial questions arise from the voyage: how does the vessel travel; why does it sink on arrival at its final destination; and why bother finding out? Answers to the first two questions provide terms for answering the third, and in doing so lay a groundwork for sketching, if not a counterfactuals handbook, at least some elementary guidelines. The use-value, both negative and positive, of the dotty syllogism lies here. The journey (from Russian to communist to traitor) functions under two constraints. The first consists of fixed background assumptions centred on known facts of the actual world (here two-fold: the historical J. Edgar Hoover was the American director of the FBI; a high-ranking servant of the Soviet state would typically have been a member of the Communist Party). The second concerns the limiting pressure of the 'minimal rewrite' requirement for counterfactuals. This works in two interrelated dimensions, one quantitative, the other qualitative (both forms of what Lewis calls 'parsimony').

In the quantitative dimension, the counterfactual is constrained by the application of the *ceteris paribus* (or all-else-being-equal) clause, which, for the construction of any possible world, allows for only one changed variable at the level of the antecedent, or, if more flexibly applied, for a strictly controlled substitution. The limitation here is one of number. It is often used in economics to isolate a variable which, if conditionally removed or altered, helps understand certain outcomes (classically in connection with the 'law' of supply and demand). But it is also deployed in other disciplines, from medical science to philosophy of causation. In the qualitative dimension, the counterfactual is constrained by the principle of 'closeness' or 'similarity' whereby a given possible world must not stray far from the texture of the actual world, the criteria for which include both remaining subject to the same 'laws of nature' (pigs can't be allowed to fly), and sensitive to the pertinence of local context and immediate environment (counterfactual reflections on the lives of Hoover's mediaeval ancestors are of no helpful relevance to the 'alternative' Hoover we are here being invited to consider). Nor would they be helpfully relevant to a Hoover in a society without an advanced police bureaucracy (a Hoover, shall we say, as a Trobriand Islander). In short, the resemblance between actual and possible worlds has to be strong. Another way of putting this would be to say that the Hoover of the possible world, though different in certain respects, has to be recognizably the same as the Hoover in the actual world. It is an 'identity' constraint (some of the complications of which I consider in Chapter 6).

If then, armed with these constraining principles, we return to the analysis of the syllogism, we can state the following. The world closest to the one at which Hoover is a Russian is a world in which he is also a communist. This is because, under the *ceteris paribus* condition, the possible world in question remains in all other respects the same as the actual world in which Hoover historically existed. This must include Hoover's known commitments as a loyal patriot. A Russian Hoover therefore will have the same intensity of commitment, but in the terms standardly available to a Russian patriot of the Soviet period, that is, as a fervent (anti-American) communist. Hoover switches sides because the premise places him on the other side (of the Iron Curtain). The second premise, however, has Hoover voluntarily switching ideological sides. Again by virtue of the *ceteris paribus* clause, if we find Hoover at a possible world in which he is a communist, then everything else remains the same as before, which includes Hoover being an American and the director of the FBI; and thus a willing traitor. Propositions which successively advance both a Russian communist Hoover and an American communist Hoover are clearly irreconcilable, and lead inexorably to a self-contradictory conclusion in which the sequitur comes folded into a non sequitur. The prior incarnations of Hoover appear, so to speak, turned inside out, as possible worlds collide and bits of one are incorporated into the other. In one possible world, he is a communist and a loyal Soviet citizen; in another he is also a communist, but an American one and so a 'traitor'; but he can be a traitorous American only if he is also Russian, since the latter is the condition of his being a communist in the first place. If this is the point to invite the understandably somnolent to wake up and smell the coffee, it is to be assumed that it is not in respect of the product in the famous pastiche syllogism which the logic of the Hoover exercise resembles:

A cold coffee is better than nothing.
Nothing is better than a warm coffee.
Therefore a cold coffee is better than a warm coffee.

The explanation for the vessel's foundering just as it enters the notionally safe harbour of a deductive conclusion stems from the presence of two gaping holes in its design, out of which the ballast of 'closeness' profusely leaks. One of the holes is at the syllogism's pivot or midpoint, a junction from which two channels head off in opposite directions, one to the east and one to the west, like two Cold War adversaries. The middle term is 'communist' (the equivalent of the ambiguous 'nothing' in the coffee syllogism), where one channel comes from Russia (and loyalty) and the other leads to America (and treason). The second hole opens up at the starting point, where in order for the possible world in question to be entertained, the conditional premise has to give up a key background fact (the fact that Hoover was American). This is to give up too much. It may be that, as Lewis observes, a communist Hoover 'is nowhere to be found at worlds near ours'. On the other hand, one cannot wholly discount the contingent possibility of an ideological road to Damascus moment (especially given Hoover's attested tastes in cross-dressing).[17] A Russian Hoover, on the other hand, is just about as remote as it gets, far out in both senses of the expression. Whoever this Hoover is, he can't be the one called 'Hoover' in the actual world. The collision of possible worlds and the collapsing logical edifice that ensues derive primarily from that initial override of plausibility for the conditional antecedent.[18] If I can imagine a Russian Hoover, then pretty well anything is imaginable by way of counterfactual speculation. For instance, what if Stalin had been an American spy ... We are back foursquare in the realm of the limitless and the limitlessly silly, where counterfactuals come out to play and do exactly as they please. Hoover a Russian communist? How about a nineteenth-century Emperor of China seated victorious, so to speak, in Buckingham Palace?

As a how-to lesson in how *not* to, this taxing (and mildly hilarious) imbroglio of imploding predication serves its local purposes well. But what can we take from it back to our framing question: the criteria on which, in the counterfactual universe, we can begin to distinguish between the vacuous and the non-vacuous, or the exuberant and the restrained? Aligned with some of our other examples – from nail to nose via the cosmos and the unhappy experience *inter alia* of Donald Trump orbiting in a counterfactual ecstasy all of his own – this might be the point in our excursus to the outer reaches at which one's thoughts turn after all towards prospects for compiling a counterfactualist primer, with a view to calling the unruly to order. This would nevertheless probably be energy misspent. Several of the examples cited in this chapter illustrate vividly the reasons underlying talk of the need for a sort of highway code for counterfactuals (one codifier has listed nine basic rules or 'criteria' as a bare minimum).[19] On the other hand, as my introductory comments on the *protasis–apodosis* structure suggested, there is something about the very idea of 'rules' that sits uneasily with a speculative field of inquiry defined as a 'world of possibles'. While codified rules of engagement perhaps become increasingly important the more the counterfactual thought experiment is refined, at the more rudimentary level with which we are here concerned, it is better to think of control mechanisms that come with an in-built adaptability that permits of flexible application.

Take, for instance, in relation to the recurring, and vexed, question of 'scale', the two controls identified via the intellectual fiasco of the Hoover syllogism: closeness and *ceteris paribus*. As we have seen, scale is both a structural property of counterfactuals and, largely by virtue of its elasticity, an issue for their viability. It is formed primarily from variations of 'small' and 'big' in respect of the antecedent, the consequent and the relation connecting the two: an example is scale as timescale, the extent of the temporal distance separating antecedent and consequent, brought dramatically into focus by the immense temporal perspectives of the cosmologist. But along with the internal dimension of timeline (degrees of temporal distance between antecedent and consequent), there is also an external dimension, centred on the relation of a possible world to an actual world. Here 'scale' becomes 'distance' understood as degrees of 'similarity' between the two worlds. The two controls – closeness and *ceteris paribus* – are supposed to be a means of reducing the heterogeneous, thus acting as a sort of restraining order on the excessively fanciful (one can posit a counterfactual world so distant – i.e. different – from this world that there is simply no point in going there, assuming means of intellectual transport in the first place). To that end, the controls are also implicated in, indeed methodologically committed to, an ideal of relative 'smallness', whereby the form of a viable counterfactual rests on the making of small-scale adjustments to the actual world, whether of kind, degree or number, and whose basic (though not sole) purpose is to ensure non-violation of laws of nature.

It is nevertheless a question as to when the necessarily restricting becomes the undesirably restrictive or, more bluntly, simply throttles the counterfactual enterprise. Scale variation is not easily tameable. Beyond mere whimsy, the variations are largely a function of the type of question being asked – logical, historical, scientific, metaphysical. They are, to repeat, context-sensitive, and demand flexibility in how they are to be assessed. The *ceteris paribus* clause, for example, is a useful, even indispensable, tool in connection with certain kinds of counterfactual. The theoretical stress-testing of causal explanations by means of elimination is a case in point (hypothetically remove variable *a* from the equation and see what happens). Similarly, it can be the only sensible way with historical examples marked by a short timespan between antecedent and consequent. But where the temporal space between the two is substantially extended, we are unlikely to be able to hold *ceteris paribus* constraints steadily in place for long (it is why some schools of thought maintain that *only* short timespan experiments are manageable). Its enforcement can become indistinguishable from a temporary suspension point or an outright ban on complexity, arbitrarily bracketing what otherwise threatens to overrun the script and defy our more contained notions of the world's regularities. As Allan Meghill puts it, paraphrasing Max Weber, 'contingency is not a train you can get on or off at will'.[20] And where, as in Pascal's *Pensées*, the question being asked isn't really about history at all other than in a metaphysical sense, control by *ceteris paribus* does not even apply. Pascal, as we shall shortly see, has no interest in what a consequential map for 'the entire world' might look like if affected by a speculative variation in the size of Cleopatra's nose. For his distinctive purposes, the greater the apparent difference of scale between antecedent and consequent, the better.

As for the principle of 'closeness', that too has problems of its own, broadly in terms of the point of view from which a question exists *as* a question for *someone*, not the point of view of the Universe (in Sidgwick's, memorable phrase), but specifically located in a here and now and bound up with the – often parochial – needs, hopes, interests and habits of particular human beings. When Adam Smith said something to the effect that, if around bedtime one had had news of an earthquake in China with immeasurable casualties, a 'man of humanity in Europe' would have uttered commiserating noises, only to retire to bed to 'snore with the most profound security over the ruin of a hundred millions of his brethren', he had in mind a particular image of 'closeness' that was not just geographical.[21] In possible-worlds theory, closeness is invoked to ensure analytical rigour, but it can also signify an attachment to the safer shores of the familiar. Familiarity rather than similarity evokes a very different perspective for 'closeness', in which the worlds we hold to be close are the ones that, by accident of birth, custom or prejudice, we hold close; comfort zones in which expectations self-reproduce and go unchallenged; where the 'small' (or the 'parsimonious') is infected by the small-minded.[22]

One way to think about that is by replacing Lewis's 'background assumptions' (as anchor in the 'real' world) with another of his expressions: 'commonplace assumptions'. Commonplaces are generally the register of 'common sense', and the latter is rarely far from the realm of what goes without saying, what goes unquestioned as 'natural'. One of the fans of the idea of a rule-book for counterfactuals, Philip Tetlock, has claimed that they should 'not unduly disturb' the known world.[23] That echoes Lewis's requirement, and, of course, must command assent in so far as one cannot rewrite the laws of nature. But – to anticipate one of the themes of the next chapter – the parochial conception of the 'natural' is not the same as nature (though wants to be confused with it). Tetlock's 'unduly' can also be a rationale for conformity, for closeness as a closing off of our capacity for imagining the 'possible'. The historical life of humans is messy and unstable, and the proposed stabilizers for counterfactual history have also to reckon with that. *Ceteris paribus* struggles to impose order on variables in the interests of securing a steady grip on the consequent (workable ways of assessing its degrees of 'probability'). Closeness bears mainly on the selection of antecedents, in the attempt to keep that 'near' what we call 'our' world, on this side of entry into La La Land. But together, the two basic principles constitute a threshold rather than a system for managing the relation of *protasis* and *apodosis*.

# IV

Blaise Pascal's reflections on the significance of a protuberance – perhaps the most famous nose *in* history because it is alleged to have influenced the course *of* history – is a veritable anthology piece in the counterfactual canon: 'Le nez de Cléopâtre, s'il eût été plus court, toute la face de la terre aurait changé' ['If Cleopatra's nose had been shorter the whole face of the earth would have changed'].[24] Widely quoted, generally derided and commonly misunderstood, its form resembles that of the 'nail' example (with which indeed it is sometimes grouped) in the scaled-up movement from minor antecedent to major consequent; the nose is to Pascal's conception of history loosely what the butterfly is to chaos theory.[25] For detractors, the claim typically provokes a routine snigger at its outlandish implausibility: how on earth could the future of *the* 'earth' (of its 'face' no less) turn on a contingent facial variation of a single individual?[26] Since it takes some nerve to accuse Pascal of silliness (the first to bite back, with an intellectual ferocity likely to cut one off at the knees, being, of course, Pascal himself), some have preferred to construe it as 'satire', an intentional joke at the expense of counterfactual reasoning. However, that is also to misconstrue it. There is almost certainly a parodic element in play, but its target lies elsewhere, and is cold comfort to historians seeking to enlist Pascal for the anti-counterfactualist cause. When he writes that a shorter nose for Cleopatra would have changed the course of history (and not just Roman history), he means it. But what he means *by* it derives from a set of interests and beliefs – specifically seventeenth-century and intrinsically Pascalian – centred on a radical and embracing absence of meaning, the irredeemable meaninglessness of human history as such, whether factual or counterfactual.

Pascal's preoccupations, in other words, are philosophical rather than historical;[27] or, to the extent that they involve statements and claims of a historical character, they operate within the framework of a philosophy of history shaped by a theology. This also holds *a fortiori* for counterfactual history, which, apart from anything else, Pascal's fideist theological commitments would proscribe as hubristic usurpation of the powers and authority of the divine. Pascal has no interest in the routine work of the excavating historian, and makes no effort to substantiate his specific claim in respect of either antecedent or consequent. At the level of the antecedent, he does not investigate the question of Cleopatra's 'beauty' and its alleged power (a controversial topic; Plutarch, for one, thought there wasn't much to write home about on this front[28]), nor, unsurprisingly, does he delve into the murky sphere of Anthony's desiring unconscious. Equally, at the level of the consequent, he conspicuously avoids tracing a detailed counterfactual map of likely outcomes: 'toute la face de la terre' (supported synonymously in the same fragment by 'le monde entier') evokes gigantic consequentialist scenarios, but remains uselessly vague and imprecise. There is, for instance, no mention of anything specifically to do with the Roman Empire, the consequential historical matter most immediately to hand; are we to presume that a shorter nose for Cleopatra signifies no civil war? If so, Pascal doesn't tell us.

This lack of instantiating detail should not, however, constitute a test or bar. 'Failing' Pascal as if before a historians' board of examiners would be to obscure Pascal's purpose, and thus what for him is here the function of a counterfactual speculation. There is unquestionably a conception of history at work, broadly a contingency theory of its determinants, based on accidents and quirks of the most 'trivial' kind. In that respect, the Cleopatra counterfactual is offered seriously. 'Smallness' is key, though we might already discern a hint of irony in the envisaged small-scale historical contingency turning on the small matter of a smaller nose. Another expression used by Pascal – also in the same fragment – for this is: *je ne sais quoi*. In its seventeenth-century context, the expression can refer to several things.[29] One is social and political, for instance the imperceptible inflections of courtier behaviour in the closed claustrophobic world of court culture that can make such a difference to advancement or failure. In Pascal's text, however, the *je ne sais quoi* is explicitly associated with the unanalysable vagaries of the sexual (what in the same fragment he calls 'the causes and effects of love', the latter further described as 'frightful'). In modern parlance the *je ne sais quoi* here belongs crucially in the psychic economy of fetishistic desire.

The nose in particular is a fetish object par excellence; scholars have made the interesting point that Pascal's highlighting of it stands outside the 'classical' ideal of beauty, where the focus would be rather on a 'nobility' of look reflected in the eyes. While instant anachronistic translation of Pascal's words into Freud's analytical terms (let alone those of Jacques Lacan's cryptic dance with the 'speaking nose'[30]) is probably not a self-selecting option, as Freud reminds us, the nose and the olfactory are associated with the 'base' zones of the erogenous. For Pascal, concupiscence is where 'small' as a term of scale joins with small in the moral sense of 'petty' (French 'petitesse' carries both senses) and thus the idea of petty passions, random attractions and contingent objects of desire as the drivers of history. Human history is the product of human actions, and human actions are determined by what men and women want, the paradigmatic form of which is lust, its unfathomable irrationality matched only by its indestructible ferocity. The *je ne sais quoi* of the sexual is also where the small and the petty are conflated with the 'base' (what in a neighbouring fragment Pascal terms 'la bassesse et l'injustice des passions').

Critics who dismiss Pascal's counterfactual as a bagatelle, sometimes do so on the grounds that it falls into the trap of 'reductive inference', by which is meant a simplifying mono-causal explanation of a given or imagined historical outcome, especially where there is a substantial difference of scale as between antecedent and consequent. This, however, mistakenly presupposes that Pascal's primary concern is with the empirical demonstration of a particular causal process. For Pascal, the issue of 'scale', of the disjunctive gap between trivial antecedent and grand consequent, is in fact, and decisively, a non-issue. Although his famous sentence formally proposes just such a disjunction, substantively the disjunction is collapsed into a relation of implied equality. From the *je ne sais quoi* of Anthony's desire to the defeat of 'princes and armies' on the world-historical stage, it all comes to the same, the insignificance of the one matched by the insignificance of the other. There is indeed a 'reductive' move at work in Pascal's utterance, but it has less to do with causation than with equalization. The reduction describes a reverse trajectory, whereby reading from left to right (from antecedent all the way out to consequent) then returns from right to left (from consequent back to antecedent), both components of the counterfactual construct meeting one another in the shared value of zero: the fate of the Roman Empire or indeed of the 'entire world' is ultimately of no more importance than the size of a queen's nose or a man's desire for its possessor.

In the Pascalian lexicon there are two buttressing terms for this sort of reductive equation: *vanité* and *néant* (often aided by a third, *misère*). Together they combine a moralist and an existential vocabulary which describes a view of the human condition, including man as historical being. 'Vanité' provides the title for the section (or 'sheaf') of *pensées* along with which the fragment about Cleopatra's nose appears. The term carries two meanings. There is the sense of 'vain' as the narcissistic cult of appearances, wound into the endlessly repeated pursuit of the empty objects of desire, as mockery of the illusion of disinterested motive and aspiration in human conduct. Second, there is the sense of *in* vain, the futility of human action, especially when animated by projects that flatter the human ego and engender *folie de grandeur*, the risible notion of the 'grandeur de l'homme' that is the title of fragment 30. This can be taken, among other things, as a debunking of the 'Great Men' model of history, the deciders and the doers, statesmen and warriors (or the 'princes' and their 'armies' of fragment 32), vainly (in both senses) assuming the *beau rôle* on the stage of history. This is where the equalizing of 'small' and 'big' is most keenly felt, the 'historical' as merely the noise of the 'passions', all sound and fury signifying nothing, swallowed up by the abyssal nothingness, the Pascalian *néant* at the heart of the human.

Naturally, alternative histories also unfold according to the same dolorous logic. As an act of thought, their construction flirts, as already noted, with the blasphemous, the error-soaked belief in the mind's ability to cast history as an object of rational understanding. And in any case, even if the dice were rolled differently, the differences would make no difference. The imagined alternatives may be alternative, but only as ripples on the surface of the world. The fate of the latter may indeed turn on the size of a nose, but the historical actions triggered by the ruinous 'passions' will ensure catastrophe anyway, if in some other guise. In that sense, the counterfactual is a false counterfactual. Pascal's aim is not to imagine an alternative history, better or worse than, or even fundamentally different from, an actual history. It is rather to place *all* history, actual and possible, under the common aegis of senselessness.[31]

On the other hand, Pascal's counterfactual, while itself implicated in this all-encompassing vision of futile human endeavour, also secures a temporary exemption from it. It permits a moment of 'suspension' in which to look into the abyss. In serving this heuristic function, it comes across more as a philosophical conceit, a form of allegory, or, as his colleague Pierre Nicole suggested, an 'image', remarkable moreover for its 'strangeness', precisely its estranging power in enabling us to step back momentarily from the mad flux of distraction to confront 'the vanity of all human affairs'.[32] This is very different from the folk wisdom of the proverbial nail on the field of the Battle of Bosworth. In Pascal's scheme of things, it matters not who wins or loses that battle, any battle. If there is an echo of the proverbial in his thinking, it is rather that of the old Jewish proverb: 'man plans, God laughs'. It might, however, also take us proleptically to Walter Benjamin (himself very interested in Jewish sayings and with more than a passing interest in Pascal), notably in relation to Benjamin's eschatological account of the Baroque in terms of the broken link of sacred and profane. We might also see something of Benjamin's debris-facing angel, though with no space whatsoever for any meliorist or 'messianic' narrative of secular 'redemption'.[33] In Pascal's view, only a world-renouncing devotion to an other-worldly Christ can provide a chance of that.

Those who, for polemical reasons of their own, see Pascal's preoccupation with 'small' things as itself a small preoccupation make a grave interpretive mistake by ignoring the context to which Pascal's speculation belongs. It is a thought-experiment in a collection of 'thoughts' by a major early modern thinker who is also writing – or more exactly preparing to write – a Christian apologetic, the 'thoughts' a sketch for the full-fledged Apology that Pascal did not live to complete. The 'Cleopatra' counterfactual that, in our times, has on the whole been treated as little more than an amusing party piece acquires a very different value when seen in its original context and in relation to a set of questions that belong to that context. Pascal's counterfactual may no longer speak to a modern lay audience, but, whether or not we choose to listen, there is no doubt that it means much more than it has typically been allowed to say. Branding it silly is likely to rebound on the branders, dispatched after the manner in which Pascal deals with a certain class of Jesuits in his satirical masterpiece, *The Provincial Letters*. It is not only our questions that count, let alone our answers. Pascal's example tells us that there is more than one way to skin the counterfactual cat.

# 2 JUST THE FACTS, MA'AM: FACT AND COUNTERFACT

*The truths of reasoning are necessary and their opposite is impossible; the truths of fact are contingent and their opposites are possible.*

**LEIBNIZ**

*Once again, the facts of life have turned out to be Tory.*

**MARGARET THATCHER**

## I

The 'countering' stance implied by the morphology of the term 'counterfactual' suggests a relation of opposition to the factual order, as at once antonymic and adversarial. I shall return later in this chapter to what we might understand by the adversarial relation, in terms of the questioning and contestatory uses to which the counterfactual can be put. Its antonymic definition is a very different and more complicated matter. There is, of course, an obvious sense in which the counterfact can be seen as fact's opposite, by virtue of referring to something that was never the case (where, as the philosophers say, there is no 'fact of the matter'). This, however, can also be misleading. The true antonym of 'fact' is what now goes under the baptismal name of the 'alternative fact' (a non-fact masquerading as if it were one). The counterfactual, on the other hand, is a supplement not a mask, a substitutive term in an 'instead-of' thought experiment, the aim of which is to represent what factually might have been, whereas the alternative fact is a simple oxymoron (or, more bluntly, a deception). The former is not so much an anti-fact as a hypothetical fact, conceptually rooted in the ancient notion of a 'potential' that bears within it a power to become the actual (except that here the power is aborted and consigned to the realm of the might-have-been).[1] The relation of fact and counterfact is thus better thought of as a mix of the different and the complementary. As the fuller linguistic description of the term makes clear, the counterfactual is not a free-standing lexical category at all; its existence is entirely derivative, held in a relation of parasitic dependency on the term from which it not only stems but in turn morphologically incorporates: the factual.

The latter, while it has its own etymological history (current usage dates from as late as the sixteenth century), seems irreducible, foundational for scientific and historical inquiry, as well as for our commonsense understandings of everyday life.[2] The factual is a crucial component of, in Hume's expression, the 'cement of the universe', alongside which the counterfactual can appear to be but a disposable decoration. Facts are especially central to any set of arguments involving law-bound processes and behaviours, from cosmology to criminology. The etymology indeed has an instructive connection to the latter. As a derivative of Latin *factum* (a participial form of the verb *facere*, 'to do' or 'to act'), the term was interestingly associated in earlier usage with 'criminal' acts (the meaning survives in the juridical expression 'before – or after – the fact'). No surprise then if facts are meat and drink to the scrupulous law officer.

Which brings us without further delay to detective Joe Friday and the injunction indelibly associated with him. 'Just the facts, ma'am' one takes to mean no conjectures, no hypotheses, and above all nothing contrary to fact: no misinformation, and, least helpful for the law officer's purposes, no counterfactuals. Imagine the following exchange: 'Officer, if he had taken the car instead of setting out on foot, my husband might still be alive.' 'Thank you for that, ma'am, but just the facts, please.' However, although it is a fact that the words 'just the facts, ma'am' are widely believed to belong to Joe Friday in the series *Dragnet*, it is not a fact that they were uttered by him; they are the invention of a parodist, in a skit of the series. Ironically, the principle that allegedly matters most to the fictional cop is confounded by the factually inaccurate report of how he is alleged to have articulated it (the report, we might want to say, is of an alternative fact). What Joe actually says is 'all we want are the facts, ma'am', and occasionally 'all we know are the facts, ma'am', a decidedly less peremptory mix of wanting and knowing in relation to the factual order.

The detective's insistence on the primacy of fact is by no means an assertion of its exclusively sovereign authority. 'All we know are the facts', suggests that 'all' is not everything (it's all and only what we know so far), that something else is required, and not just the acquisition of further facts (Joe Friday is not a convert to Mr Gradgrind's cause). Our detective is, of course, but a hair's breadth away from the movement of 'fact' into 'interpretation', the two indeed indissociable from the word go. It's not that Joe seeks to keep them apart. His objective is rather to keep the witness he is questioning at as great a distance as possible from interpretive gloss and judgement, but he does not apply the same rule to himself. What he wants is not to banish interpretation, but to exercise a monopoly of it from within a specializing system of the division of intellectual labour (the expert versus the lay person). If there is a sovereign authority in play, it is the detective's power over the realm of the factual. This is not that far removed from some constructions of the role of the historian. Both the detective and the historian are supposed to know how the facts of the past fit together, as the outcome of an exercise in mustering, ordering and decoding a set of 'clues', some of which turn out not to be clues at all and on (rare) occasion prompting a rueful counterfactual from within their own inquiries ('if I had proceeded differently...').

Fact, interpretation, and power ... there is a long and contentious philosophical story bound up with that particular trio, sometimes punctuated by intellectually disastrous chapters centred on outright denial of the factuality of fact. To play fast and loose with the facts is one thing, a common enough practice since time immemorial, and brought to a new pitch by the contemporary arts of a public discourse propelling us ever deeper into the so-called 'post-factual age' of the mediatized advertising and political campaign (who was the newspaper editor who once said facts are 'sacred'?) The expression 'playing fast and loose' originates, appropriately, in a form of scam artistry (the trick known as the Strap). Its correlate in the domain of modern political spin is of a type so flagrant as to make us long for the return of Mr Gradgrind.[3] But if playing fast and loose with particular facts is par for the course, doing so with the category of Fact itself is another thing altogether. Dissolving the latter in the corrosive acid of a full-blown epistemological scepticism is asking for serious trouble. Notwithstanding certain alluring formulae for successful 'living' which require us to ignore or deny facts inconvenient to us and our interests, the assumption of a world in which there are no facts is not a condition in which one is likely to survive, let alone prosper, for very long. Ms Kellayanne Conway, the purveyor *extraordinaire* of the alt-fact, may well turn out to be the contra-factualist we die for (literally).

The task for the questioning mind is not to deny either facts or factuality. It is to examine them, with a view both to rooting out imposters and, more generally, to understanding their complex – and often unstable – conceptual shape. For, alongside cynical or reckless fact-denial, there are also the habits of thought bound up with fact-complacency. As we shall see later, one of the uses of the counterfactual lies with its potential for awakening us from the deep slumbers induced by complacency. Most of us believe, for the most part happily, that we have a grip on facts and what they 'are'. But the more we navigate the underlying conceptual architecture, the likelier it is that we will find ourselves not only wandering as if through a labyrinth, but also treading on increasingly slippery floors (foundations). It may well be, as the philosopher David Lewis maintains in connection with 'possible-worlds' theory, that counterfactual reasoning crucially depends on 'commonplace assumptions about relevant matters of fact'; in other words, counterfactuals, if they are to be taken seriously, must not stray far from our understandings of what the factual world is like. On the other hand, unless also well-managed, 'commonplace assumptions', as noted in the previous chapter, often function less as a disciplining constraint on the counterfactual imagining of alternatives than as the framework for what we lazily take for granted.

Navigation is not for the faint-hearted. Ask a philosopher what 'facts' are, and the first thing s/he is likely to say is that 'commonplace assumptions' will take you only so far, and the second will be to ask how long have you got. For most of us probably not that much, and, when faced with some of the answers, none at all. Instant exit from the conversation is virtually guaranteed in the event of early encounter with the lumbering beast called 'factualist truthbearer maximalism'. This makes facts sound like labourers, with Philosophy as the employment agency charged with placing them in important and presumably well-paid ('maximal') portering work as the load-bearers of Truth, no less. Yet up from their day job in the trenches of ordinary usage, and arranged in what William Faulkner called 'the shapes and shades of facts', they do make for a colourful conceptual parade. Consider them first as an international gathering, clothed in the uniforms of different languages. French 'fait' is consistent more or less with English 'fact', but what of the '*fait accompli*' (which English has absorbed *faute de mieux*)? If some facts are 'accomplished', are there perforce 'unaccomplished' ones, in the sense of either incomplete or sub-standard? Is there such a thing as half a fact or a poor quality one? And then what of German *Tatsache*, restoring the original meaning of 'deed' or 'act' (fact as literally a compound of 'deed' and 'thing'), alongside the later and more technical *Faktum*. Immanuel Kant, who was primarily interested in the meaning of 'fact' from the conceptual point of view ('the concept of a fact'), drove a wedge between *Tatsache* and *Faktum* in order to strengthen his distinction between two generic kinds of 'fact' – the observable datum, on the one hand, and, on the other, fact as an abstract object of pure reason. This involved the unusual philosophical feat of redesigning *Faktum* to mean something that appeared to have little or no visible link to the empirical, that is, to what was generally taken to be the very ground not only of the existence but also of the intelligibility of 'fact'. Many Kantians and non-Kantians alike have found this baffling.[4]

By contrast, in its handling of the question, English appears at first sight commonsensically business-like – more matter of fact, as it were. Hume's use of the expression 'matter of fact' itself embeds the factual in material reality and the empirical method of verification.[5] But if we think that with English and the Humean tradition we have found a philosophical safe harbour, it is but a matter of time before we are adrift again on the waves of language and the vagaries of idiom. Consider the bizarre echo chamber of the following expressions when listed and juxtaposed: fact matters (the title perhaps of a learned paper on the complex issues thereof); facts matter (they most certainly do if existential car crashes are to be avoided or we are to keep public discourse more or less honest). How do the terms 'a matter of fact' and its syntactical inversion 'the fact of the matter' relate to one another? Then add 'as' to the former: the idiomatic 'as a matter of fact' carries more often than not the sense of 'as it happens', or 'it so falls out', thus edging towards the contingent nature of what happens to be the case and the related thought that 'it' could easily have been otherwise. It is then but a step to fashioning a sentence located somewhere between Lewis Carroll and Samuel Beckett, that begins with 'as a matter of fact, the fact of the matter is ...', a syntactic partnering in what is more a Mad Hatter's waltz than a reasoned exposition of the place of 'fact' in the mortar of the world.

The pliability of the concept is moreover not only linguistic, but also taxonomic. Ask the philosopher again, this time about the different types of fact, and we will find ourselves in for another lengthy parade. It will include a set of pairs, each requiring elaborate clarification: simple/complex; particular/universal; contingent/necessary; formal/substantive; conjunctive/disjunctive; objective/subjective.[6] All the pairs have a bearing on historical facts. Take the last instance: 'objective' designates a fact deemed to refer to something that is incontestably the case and in principle accessible to all (a date, for example, though that in turn is relative to the cultural creation of calendars and chronologies). Subjective (or 'mental') facts are relative to a point of view; they are sometimes called, with empiricist resonances, 'facts of experience' and are particular to ways of being not necessarily accessible to those who do not share them. But there is in addition a further pairing which calls for special note: tenseless/tensed. It also takes us back to Hume. He maintained that there were two kinds of fact, present and absent. Present facts can be observed and thus verified. Absent facts by definition cannot be observed and are thus not verifiable by an observer. They are rather objects of reasoned or reasonable belief, what we can assume to be the case on the basis of what the world normally looks like. The class of absent facts can, however, be further sub-divided on the axis of now/then: one that is synchronous with the present moment but invisible to the subject and hence to be taken on faith by virtue of some authority or other justifying a belief in its existence; one that is non-synchronous, absent by virtue of belonging to a past of which we ourselves were not a part. This kind of fact we might want to call 'tensed'.

A tenseless fact ($2 + 2 = 4$) is everywhere and eternally the case (except in certain recognized fictional contexts, Orwell's *1984*, for example, where it was forced to make 5). Tensed is less clear (some philosophers dispute the very existence of a tensed fact[7]). The concept nevertheless has a long pedigree going back at least to Aristotle's ideas on time and truth, in connection with the famous future-tense statement 'there will be a sea battle tomorrow'. This is not a prediction; Aristotle is not claiming advance knowledge of what tomorrow will bring. The form of the argument is more general: there will be something tomorrow rather than nothing, and whatever it is that will be will be. If it is to be a battle, that will be known only with hindsight, the 'proof' that it was to be consisting in the fact that it happened. In other words, the concern is of a purely logical order: if it is the case that a sea battle will happen tomorrow, it is a fact that it will happen. But there is also the association of the notion of a tensed fact with contingency and transience, whether in the present or the past tense. In this context, the statement 'it is a fact that James is happy today' refers to what is a fact of the matter today, with no presumption that his state precedes or succeeds the 'now' of the present. One can, of course, also say 'James was happy yesterday', as a fact of yesterday. Both examples – present and past – are 'tensed' in so far as they are indexed to a temporality. The one in the past tense corresponds to what we also call a historical fact.

This, however, brings us to a peculiarity in the grammar of history-writing. Consider the following statement: 'It is a fact that in 1940 Germany invaded Belgium.' It is a straightforward, incontrovertible factual claim; one would have to be in a very odd place cognitively speaking to maintain that the claim was but a 'matter of interpretation'.[8] Nevertheless there is something peculiar about its grammatical form. The present tense of the main clause constitutes a sort of puzzle arising from the present narration of a tensed fact that belongs in the past. Should not 'it is a fact' be 'it was a fact'? The distinction is, of course, unlikely to detain anyone for very long. It will sound like a meaningless quibble and, for most practical purposes, that is exactly what it is. If I have here insisted on an otherwise useless distinction, it is to bring something more clearly into view about the nature of what we call 'historical facts': namely, that the present-tense preface 'it is a fact that' to the report of a past event (Germany's invasion of Belgium) marks the status of the fact as 'archival', not the past event as such but its representation as a present object of historical knowledge. And the Archive as a cultural institution, even when populated with the undisputed and the indisputable (Germany invaded Belgium), is also a can of worms.

## II

The primary objective of historical inquiry is to acquire and curate a body of knowledge about the past. There are various material and institutional settings for this pursuit (library, museum, university), along with a range of practical resources from the physical relic and the written document through to the digital database.[9] These are all branches of the over-arching institution, the Archive, the grand depot that houses, in Panofsky's words, 'the records left by man' and deposited in 'the stream of time' on which they travel to successive generations. As both storehouse of the past and transmission for posterity, the Archive inhabits a Janus-faced temporality of its own. Located in a present (of consultation), it is simultaneously turned to a past (recorded) and a future (addressee) that frame and define an archival existence forever unfinished, not only because of the prospect of always being able to add to it, but also because, however copiously stocked, it registers never more than a fraction of the history of mankind. Panofsky's magnificent edifice ensures that certain pasts are preserved for the future, but there are also many rooms in it left empty or never built, while many others are but ruins, the residual traces of a past effaced. In short, as itself a man-made artifact, there is always an issue in respect of what exactly goes into – is allowed to enter – the Archive, and then in turn what happens to it once inside.

Archive stems from ancient Greek *arkheon*, the home of the *archon* ('magistrate' or 'governor').[10] The magistrate's home is where official documents were kept. These origins already tell us something important about the construction and maintenance of the archive, run either directly or by means of appointed delegates with quasi-monopoly power over written sources, and evolving through to the modern age as a mix of accredited professionals (scribes, curators, historians, administrators and officials). No surprise then that archives can be – often have been – subject to 'editing' manipulations of one kind or another when the interests of the powerful are at stake. The editing operations vary: exclusion of information deemed embarrassing or compromising (to, for example, the image of a monarch or a regime); falsification of records (including forgery and related ways of re-writing history); outright destruction (the burning of libraries or the shredding of papers). It can also function as a keeper of secrets (by way of the distinction between 'public' and 'classified').[11] But in addition to conscious human interference in making and remaking, there is the far larger class of information that is lost from neglect (accidents of storage, human forgetfulness), or what the mind, individual and collective, represses from memory, either from indifference or from self-censorship. There are also the unintended consequences of technological progress, systems intended to preserve that actually destroy.[12] Finally, and overwhelmingly, there is what gets lost or forgotten because it lies beyond the resources of literate registration, the uninvestigable deep strata of 'history from below'. This is the immeasurable black hole that is *historia abscondita*, occupied by the unknown 'names of history', the anonymous silent majority that never gets into the archive because it never had any chance of doing so. E. H. Carr, notoriously hostile to counterfactuals, nevertheless said of historical facts that they are 'like fish in the Ocean'. We catch only what lies near the surface; what lies in the unfathomable depths the fisherman-historian cannot reach. Thus, if the Archive is a huge remembering machine, its hinterland is an unexplorable sump of oblivion on a planetary scale.

This is not to say that the Archive is so flawed or untrustworthy as to wreck the discipline of history as a viable enterprise, and it has its own procedures for correcting a falsified record when uncovered or for plugging gaps in an incomplete one (where future pasts are concerned, the great desert hinterland will doubtless be increasingly colonized by the technologies of Big Data; everyone will enter the archive and all 'names' registered). On the other hand, its limits and imperfections are a humility-inducing reminder of two things: that what we know is small compared to what we don't know; and that what we know is more precisely, and non-vacuously, described as what we think we know. This can make for a warranted degree of caution in respect of the historian's main articles of faith. We think of the archivally lodged fact as the building block of historical knowledge, used to construct the bridge that takes us to the historian's holy grail: the past as it 'really' was, or – in a striking modification of Ranke's famous formula – as it 'essentially' was (as if an essentialist account of the past were somehow more modest in its aspirations than a realist one).[13] Secure in the real or the essential (not to mention the 'actual'[14]), the claim to the knowable and the known is often the ground for lofty dismissal of the counterfactual. In a jolly little exchange with a leading British politician (a former student of classics as he tirelessly reminds us), a well-known ancient historian stated that she wasn't 'interested in what might have happened, counterfactuals, all I'm interested in speaking about is what we know to have happened'. There is something to be envied in that hearty, straight from the hip epistemological confidence. But it might go down better if 'we think' were inserted between 'what' and 'we know' (and possibly a more guarded way with the first person plural).

The epistemic question that haunts all historical counterfactuals concerns the nature of the evidence the historian can access when dealing with something that never happened (more exactly, something that might have happened but didn't). But there are also major epistemological issues for the historian in the domain of the factual when the latter is proposed as the support of 'what we know to have happened'. The fault-lines running through the archival edifice directly implicate what it means to 'know' the past. There are broadly four sceptical takes on the knowability of the past. The most general and least interesting draws on the arguments of radical scepticism as to the knowability of *anything* (it need not concern us given the intrinsically self-defeating logic of the statement 'I know ... nothing'). The second is the offspring of relativism, an extreme version of which insists on the conceptual and cultural incommensurability of the societies being investigated with that of the investigator. A third turns on fundamental reservations as to the knowability of human agency as such; making sense of humanity is doomed if its aim is the transparency of the human to the investigating gaze. The fourth and the most compelling is also the simplest: I can't know because I wasn't there.[15] There is an engagingly tonic response to that, by way of an adapted version of comedian Tony Hancock's reminder that 'you don't have to fall off a cliff to know that it hurts'. On the other hand, what this form of the sceptical take importantly tells us is that the past is not 'another country' in the sense of the metaphor favoured by members of the Incommensurabilist Party, according to which the alleged 'otherness' of past societies is such that we have no legitimate conceptual passport that permits us to cross their borders or at least to speak their language. It is not that borders are closed to us by virtue of the non-validity of travel documents, but rather that the country we might wish to visit no longer exists. If there is an incurable skin irritation the historian has to live with but can never cease to scratch, this is it. We can, as space scientists, visit the moon to inspect it, or, as anthropologists, visit the Trobriand Islands to converse with 'informants'. But, other than by means of fictional time travel, we cannot visit the eighteenth century. What we visit is an etiolated surrogate, the Archive.

There is a refreshingly tonic reminder of this in a letter from Charles Carrington to the military historian, Michael Howard: 'When I meet some clever young scholar from Queen's or Keble who has written on World War 1, I say to him as politely as I can, "My dear chap, I was there at the time and it wasn't at all as you describe".[16] In its jaunty English way, this last sentence should be posted for inquirers into the past at the entrance of the Archive, just as the words 'Know thyself' were teasingly posted at the *pronaos* (or forecourt) of the temple at Delphi for consultants of the oracle wishing to inquire about the future. Since we weren't there at the time and have no means of going there, strictly speaking, we do not, cannot, know what happened; all we can do is to take a more or less educated view of what *may have* happened, an assessment based on inferences from information at our disposal and judgements as to its credibility and quality.[17] In very many cases, there will be no reasonable grounds for doubting that what is believed by reasonable people to have happened in fact did, but the knowledge-judgements involved should not be confused. The aim of historical investigation is to understand the past, but understanding is not the same as knowing; what we know, because we can consult it, is what we know to be in the archive.[18]

The switch of verb tense to 'may have' is not merely precautionary. It reflects a decisive re-positioning in relation to the 'facts' of the past as we can claim to know them. It also induces a more self-conscious understanding of what is reductively compacted in the baldly generalized pronoun 'what' of 'what happened'; 'what' covers when, why, how, to whom, for whom, and so on. The point especially matters in relation to historical instances of so-called 'subjective facts' or 'facts of experience'. What Mr Gradgrind deplores in his soul-draining celebration of the reign of fact – 'imagination', or 'empathy' – is precisely what the historian most needs when it comes to trying to access the interiority of historical actors (s/he also needs imagination when it comes to the filling of lacunae in the factual record). To be sure, their interiority is not that of aliens (in the sense of other-planetary), and imagining what it felt like to be a fourth-century Goth is doubtless empathetically easier for humans than imagining what – in Thomas Nagel's fearlessly chosen example – it's like to be a bat. Nevertheless, the attempt to see – 'know' – the past from the point of view of the past is a guessing game. Anyone setting up their stall on the terrain of showing us how for past actors 'it really was' is unlikely to conclude many sales, or, if they do, the goods will come without warranty.

## III

None of these caveats is likely to dissuade practising historians from going about their daily business, and nor should that be their aim, unless we want to reduce historical inquiry to something resembling Steven Runciman's cavorting way with the factual in history, his willingness 'to frolic in the evidential void with abandon', as his biographer, Minoo Dinshaw, puts it.[19] They do, however, open a hiatus or pause in the relevant thought-spaces, from which several things can emerge. One is an emphasis on the value of the counterfactual. In connection with the limits and instabilities of the archive as a depot for facts, two very substantial kinds of counterfactual come immediately into view: counterfactuals *of* the archive and counterfactuals *in* it. The first group concerns the record of the factual and the epistemological status of the archive as such, in the form of speculations on how the past might have come to us if, whether by accident or design, the annals had not been deficient (if, in the terms of Carr's metaphor, the 'catch' had been bigger and more varied). The prospects for these counterfactuals bearing empirical fruit depend, of course, on a mix of luck and diligence, and, even under the best conditions, the harvest is likely to be poor; most of 'absconded' history has gone for good, and drooling over a dream of recovering the irrecoverable little more than wish-fulfilment with virtually no chance of gratification. But that is no justification for simply averting one's gaze from the frailties of the archive, and mulling the counterfactual is an intellectual device for keeping the gaze focused on them. The second group (counterfactuals *in* the archive) includes the counterfactual thoughts, projects and hopes of actors in respect of their perceived possible futures, along with more impersonal evidence of possible forks in the historical road which, if taken, might have produced different outcomes. Typically, the record here will be fragmentary, given that the recording process favours what was decided and done rather than what might have been done but was not. But to the extent that they are lodged in the archive, they are themselves 'facts', instances of a hypothetical entertained by historical actors. As the notionally paradoxical class of factual counterfactuals, they belong in the domain that Quentin Deluermoz and Pierre Singaravélou call the 'extension of the factual'.[20]

Bringing the counterfactual into the family of facts will, of course, look prima facie perverse. A basic distinction seems to blur and a conceptual architecture to wobble. But the conditions under which we can meaningfully see the counterfactual as itself a form of fact implies rather a specific set of affinities, a convergence in various cooperative tasks (crucially the collaborative work the two can do with the testing of causal explanations). But there is another more turbulent convergence and a more fractious kinship system, within which fact and counterfact are held more in a relation of symbiotic tension, each exerting pressure on the other. Fact can usefully, even indispensably, serve to de-limit the scope of 'what if' speculation, most notably in the application of the so-called 'minimal rewrite' principle, where a condition of counterfactual minimalism is factual maximalism, a situating of the counterfactual 'alternative' in a thick setting of fact. The counterfactual, on the other hand, can assume the role of the aggressive troublemaker bent on disturbing the peace of the given which the more placid reign of fact will prefer ('just the facts, ma'am').

In this latter context, the family relation shifts from one of cooperation to one of provocation, and to what, in the Introduction, I described as a contestatory 'politics' of the counterfactual. It is where we can return to the project of 'experimental history' espoused by Daniel Milo. 'Provocation' is the term used by Milo to describe one of its purposes. By 'experiment' Milo intends an explicit analogy with the scientific experiment. At the same time, he is careful to circumscribe the analogy; the archive is not the laboratory (though meddlers, marauders and forgers can treat it as if it were effectively such). The differences are, of course, manifold and obvious. Human facts are not reducible to physical properties. In the laboratory the experiment can be repeated, whereas, despite theories of recurring patterns from Polybius to Hegel, the discipline of history, as Paul Valéry put it, is 'the science of what never happens twice'. Above all, except when at the receiving end of malpractice, the archive does not permit what is always possible in the laboratory – intervention that, for experimental purposes, modifies the object. The historical past cannot be 'altered' in the way the chemist in the lab can alter physical reality by varying compound combinations. It is a grievous misrepresentation of historical thought-experiments, including the counterfactual kind, that what they offer are 'altered pasts'. They do not alter anything; they evoke and explore possibilities and in doing so can *imagine* it as other – not at all the same thing. If they alter anything, it is not the past but our understandings of it.

It is in this properly hedged form that Milo pursues his analogy, in particular listing six experimental 'techniques' that together sustain the irreverent shake-up he intends.

1  *Injection*: adding to element $y$ an element $x$ that is foreign to $y$.
2  *Amputation*: removing from $y$ an element $x$ that is normally a feature of $y$.
3  *Estrangement*: displacing $x$ from the environment where one is used to seeing it.
4  *Variation of scale*: moving $x$ through different levels of observation.
5  *Decategorization*: detaching $x$ from its customary conceptual settings.
6  *Juxtaposition*: placing $x$ alongside $y$ where $x$ and $y$ are normally kept apart.[21]

The counterfactual has an active part to play in this venture. Its full provocative potential would lie in an amalgam of elements drawn from all six of these techniques. But in terms of the conflictual version of the fact/counterfact relation, the most important is without doubt the third, the tactic of wilful 'estrangement' (or 'defamiliarization'), with its echo of avant-garde aesthetics and the project of making it strange. In this connection, the counterfactual as agent provocateur appropriates and adapts the tactic for the purpose of disturbing the deep sleep that can overcome the factual order when enveloped in taken-for-grantedness and systematically naturalized (what John Stuart Mill called the 'deep slumber of decided opinion'). Just as counterfactuals can unsettle received causal explanations, they can also seriously disturb factual descriptions, how we habitually describe our world to ourselves and to others when beset by fact-complacency. It is defamiliarization as an exercise in de-naturalization.

Alongside 'matters of fact' (and, in Hume's terms, subsuming them) are ineluctable 'facts of nature'. The latter are part of the stitching of reality. Quine highlights this by inverting Hume's 'matters of fact' to 'facts of the matter', a move designed, for the purposes of the philosophy of science, to emphasize brute physicality, natural fact as ontologically foundational ('factuality ... is internal to our theory of nature').[22] Any attempted de-naturing of facts of nature in this sense is either foolish or perilous. De-naturalization, however, is another process altogether, directed at man-made social and historical constructions that are presented *as* facts of nature and experienced as belonging to the natural order of things. The contexts in which naturalization operates are both formal and informal. The area of the formal is largely that of the disciplines. Milo highlights the uses to which in the nineteenth century natural history (geology and biology) were put in the naturalization of social history. Durkheim's use of the concept of 'fact' to represent the social (*faits sociaux*) in the development of a positivist sociology and its further elaboration as a 'thing' (*chose*) might also belong here, though that is subject to fierce debate. Durkheim assigned to both 'fact' and 'thing' specialized meanings designed to ensure that social phenomena were understood as supra-individual, functioning independently of the intentions of individual actors. But the idiom does also exert an intrinsic semantic pull towards reification and the construal of 'social facts' as if they were facts of nature.[23]

The methodological self-consciousness of the humanistic disciplines nevertheless affords some sort of a check, if not always successful, to fact-naturalization. The latter is to be found most extensively (and insidiously) at work in the informal circuits of everyday life and its reproduction by means of repetition, habit, custom and the assumptions of 'tacit knowledge'. Since the main purpose of naturalization is to preserve the given as if natural, it is principally a characteristic of conservative descriptions of the world. The essence of Conservatism according to a Conservative politician is 'to accept the world as it is'. That is clearly preferable to engaging with it in a delusional state; sometimes the facts are indeed Tory and acknowledging that is consistent with the ancient virtues of prudence and practical reason (as one of the junctures at which the 'thinkable' and the 'doable' meet). On the other hand, flaunting the world 'as it is' under a particular description of it is all too often tailored to particular ideological requirements (here those of Conservative Man, where the main purpose is to conserve).[24] Appeals to 'fact' as the 'facts of life' (notoriously in the Thatcher slogan) is one move in that project. 'Sorry, kids, wealthy pensioners are a fact of life' opines a leader writer in the conservative newspaper, the *Daily Telegraph*. Get over it is the lesson the young are supposed to draw, this is what it means to live in the world not only 'as it is' but as it is naturally meant to be. It is then, of course, but a step to the creation of the notorious class of facts called 'facts on the ground'.

Matters of fact, facts of life, facts of nature, facts on the ground – these are the expressions that together can acquire something akin to the force of gravity. If there is a reason why the semantics of 'fact' is important, it is here, in the sphere of pure naturalization, where the outcomes of the exercise of power are subsequently rationalized as if made to the specifications of eternity. It is the place where meanings and etymologies converge: *factum* as 'act' and 'deed', and *datum* as that which is 'given' (in the sense of the taken for granted) come together in the fact on the ground that is the creature of acts on the ground. To take a notorious example, the West Bank settlements presented by apologists as, precisely, a settled matter, a matter of fact, with the added ideological feature of ring-fencing the installed facts with the claim – the most dangerous of all the ways of playing fast and loose with the facts – that 'there is no alternative'.[25] This is just a flagrant case of the widespread practice of concealing historically contingent (and often violent) origins behind a mask of natural 'thereness'. It corresponds to Althussser's account of the function of fact as 'expression' ('factual expression') and of the role of 'fact' in a 'philosophy of the result' (which posits cause–effect processes in which fact acts as an 'expression' of an allegedly ineluctable outcome). The expression is also a suppression, enabling something born of the 'aleatory' to be packaged as something immovably 'accomplished', precisely the *fait accompli*, whose purpose is to exclude the thought that things might and could have been different, not only as the practically 'doable' but also as the conceptually 'thinkable'.[26] It embodies what Bourdieu implacably described as 'the most implacable' of the forms of 'hidden persuasion', its power deriving from being 'exercised quite simply by *the order of things*'.[27]

Opening up the naturalized to inspection is, of course, a long-standing practice of radical criticism. But if this is to dust down an old hat, it is for the particular purpose of bringing into the foreground the oppositional value of the counterfactual, its 'estranging' energies set to work in 'imagining history otherwise'.[28] And for those who, on this point, find Althusser uncongenial, there is also the example of that great nineteenth-century 'realist' of politics and diplomacy, Metternich, reminding his critics that what seems impossible often reflects merely the fact that 'the obvious is always the least understood'. We might then want to re-baptize de-naturalization as counter-naturalization, the 'countering' action as simultaneously critical analysis of the 'given' and imaginative reaching for the forms of the possible. This is how that great anti-Gradgrindian, Alfred Whitehead, put it:

> Imagination is not to be divorced from the facts: it is a way of illuminating the facts. It works by eliciting the general principles which apply to the facts, as they exist, and then by an intellectual survey of alternative possibilities which are consistent with those principles. It enables men to construct an intellectual vision of a new world.[29]

This is arguably the best formula around for the marriage, at once cooperative and agonistic, of the factual and the counterfactual and their turbulent co-habitation in that other turbulence, the river of time (among other things, Coleridge's image for the active imagination). Heraclitus wisely says you cannot step in the same river twice. It sweeps forward and does not repeat. It does not, however, follow a straight line. Panofsky's image for the archive (of which more in the next chapter) was the 'stream of time' in which the archivally documented past is posted more or less directly to posterity. But the river of time also has its tributaries, bends and forks, represented grammatically by its conditionals and its modals.

Certainly, swimming in the flux of time with the counterfactual as both companion and rival can make the realm of the factual look very different, no longer a collection of static snapshots placed in the archive as if in a photo album. Two famous paintings – the subject of the next chapter – may go some way to telling us why.

# 3 FLYING BLIND: *ANGELUS NOVUS* AND ALLEGORY OF PRUDENCE

*The past is never dead. It's not even past.*
**WILLIAM FAULKNER**

*The living can assist the imagination of the dead.*
**W. B. YEATS**

## I

The Paris street artist, Ender, is known for his angel paintings. One of them has a young man wearing jeans and hoodie, leaning forward, face buried in hands, and sporting a gigantic pair of white wings. The painting's title is 'Même les anges pleurent'. Why 'even' ('même') is unclear, in so far as it oddly implies that weeping is an unusual angelic pastime. It is in fact a recurring feature of the iconography of angels, albeit just one in a tale of visual riches that in its own way yields a correspondingly rich story of religious and moral belief. In Christendom from the fourth century onwards, the predominant images (other than for the fallen ones, on their grimacing and snarling way to all manner of beastly things in Hell) are of serene and joyful countenances participating in God's work. Augustine conceived of angels as citizens of the holy city of God, a view echoed in the sixth century by Pseudo-Dionysus's *Celestial Hierarchy*. The Byzantine conception of the hierarchical divine order is often illustrated by choirlike gatherings of angels as harmonious assembly in the presence and service of God or Jesus (the early modern European painter closest to the Byzantine tradition, El Greco, reproduces this idea of celestial harmony in his *Concert of the Angels*). On the other hand, the art of Renaissance humanism, above all in Italy, did much to bring angels down from heaven to earth and to an existence at once bodily and dynamic ('heavenly manifestations ... conceived in human terms' was how Aby Warburg put it): Raphael's pudgy cherubim; Michelangelo's muscular youth with eagle wings on the ceiling of the Sistine Chapel; Leonardo's ambiguously androgynous angel in the second version of *The Virgin of the Rocks*, and the 'aeronautical' angel of *Annunciation*. The latter's explicit subject matter is, of course, biblical (the angel Gabriel coming to Mary), but there is also both an echo of the Daedalus myth and more than a trace of Leonardo's life-long obsession with the idea of a human flying machine.

Embedding a dream of science in a mythical reference is one of the faces of humanist 'modernity', a token of its immersion in a progress-narrative of futurity and the relation of the latter to a past either discarded or transformed. We cannot, however, forget that the Daedalian story ends badly, with a dead son, Icarus, and an inconsolable, grieving father. Grief, manifested as weeping, is also one of the emotions attributed to angels, in both painting (for example, Giotto's magnificent fresco, *Lamentation on the Death of Christ*) and sculpture (from the angels that adorn early Christian sarcophagi – the most famous the Sarcophagus of Junius Bassus – to Victorian cemetery art, with the distraught angel draped across a tombstone as the most common motif). Ender's paintings carry this tradition into the world of contemporary urban desolation. In the tradition, however, running all the way back to biblical sources, the angels typically watch as well as weep, as impotent observers of mankind's inexhaustible capacity for self-inflicted suffering, a theme memorably echoed in Wim Wender's film, *Wings of Desire* (their sense of hopelessness in stark contrast to Frank Capra's in *It's a Wonderful Life*).[1] And here a first question arises: as the angels watch and weep, what, and how, do they *think*? Crucially, do they, can they, think counterfactually? As they contemplate actual or impending catastrophe, do they, in addition to tears flowing at the pity of it all, also entertain thoughts of how things could have been otherwise? Are the tears, indeed, in part the reflection of a rueful might-have-been?

From very far off in intellectual space, a possible prompt – albeit as little more than a clunky convenience – for addressing this question is the title of a work of journalistic history by Eric G. Swedin, *When Angels*

*Wept: A What-if History of the Cuban Missile Crisis.* Swedin's weeping angels, of course (and thank goodness[2]), make no appearance in his book; they are but the dead letter of a trope feeding a what-if narrative whose analytical yield is somewhat exiguous (the what-if refers to a might-have-been disaster only just averted by the exemplary wisdom of JFK, with a grudging nod to Krushchev, who, for a mad dog of a Soviet Communist, surprised everyone as a leader who 'finally made some rational choices'). The inert metaphor conjoined across a colon with an exercise, however weak, in counterfactual political history may nevertheless propel us back into the highways and byways of angelology (one of the ten major branches of theology). In mediaeval Christian thought, angels are immaterial entities yet also thinking beings (in Islamic theology they are made of light, and in Judaism they come briefly into existence before disappearing back into ontological nothingness). Their assumed immateriality, of course, proved no impediment to painters and sculptors bodying them forth. The assumption did, however, raise difficulties in connection with biblical stories of origin and procreation. What, for example, is the explanation of Cain's progeny? There are no women mentioned in his story, and had there been, given the Ur-genitors, Adam and Eve, they would have to have been sisters. The way round the incest problem was to provide Cain with a partner for reproductive purposes by endowing an angel with female reproductive organs. This creates as many problems as it solves. In the Hebrew Bible angels are male (more accurately, they come disguised as men), as they typically are in paleo-Christian and mediaeval art. But, even when gendered female, there remained the more general problem of angels copulating in the fallen world of the sinful; this is hard to reconcile with the idea of angels as immaculate beings or with Jesus on the virtue of celibacy as rendering humans 'equal to the angels'.

This is perhaps one theological byway we do well to bypass, and instead return to the more rarefied thought-world of the angels. Two great mediaeval philosophers, Ockham and Aquinas (aka the 'Angelic Doctor'), debated the issue (the details are abstruse). Both maintained that angels were disembodied thinking beings; they did not physically speak (since they had no corporeal organs with which to do so), but could think.[3] Ockham and Aquinas took radically different views as to the nature of the cognitive processes involved. But both operated a notion of inter-angelic communication, thoughts intelligibly transmitted as if by a form of 'angelic telephone'. In Aquinas's argument, thought-communication involved an act of will on the part of the sender; the angel has, as it were, to decide to dial up the receiving angel (and, being free to decide not to, can withhold thoughts). For Ockham, on the other hand, the model of thinking was construed as a kind of 'mental speech' that involved a more spontaneous transmission of thoughts as a form of telepathy based on mutual transparency, such that angels can have no secrets from each other.

It is not, however, clear whether, for either philosopher, the shared pool of angelic thoughts included counterfactual musings.[4] The late seventeenth-century Huguenot theologian, Pierre Poiret Naudé, argued strenuously in *L'Economie divine* that angels were constitutionally incapable of addressing might-have-beens, at least in respect of their own fates. Indeed, as noted in Chapter 1, it was to become a nice theological point as to whether or not God thought counterfactually. Leibniz, we saw, famously maintained that God's mind housed worlds that might have been. The Jesuit theologian, Luis de Molina, and even more so his so-called neo-Molinist successors, attempted to square the circle of providentialist predictability and the unpredictability of the exercise of free will divinely granted to human agents, by positing a God who not only could entertain counterfactual thoughts about his own creation, but who also, as omniscient being, has foreknowledge of the counterfactual scenarios of thought, decision and action that humans will occupy. On the neo-Molinist view, God is the ultimate theoretician of all possible worlds *sub specie aeternitatis*.[5] Jesus too has his (puzzling) moment with counterfactuals when, as reported in both Luke and John, he excoriates the inhabitants of Bethsaida and Chorizain for their failure to respond satisfactorily to his miracles with the argument that, if the miracles in question had occurred in Tyre, Sidon and Sodom, 'they would have repented long ago in sackcloth and ashes'. However, this is presumably more a rhetorical exercise in making a point (Bethsaida and Chorizain will not fare well on the Day of Judgement) than a genuine counterfactual. It is only under some very special belief-conditions that we can imagine Jesus working the same miracles in the mythical Old Testament city of Sodom.

## II

If God and Jesus can dwell in the counterfactual, what, however, of the angels (especially when weeping)? More pertinently, where is this recondite mini-excursus into the angelological supposed to be taking us? Some will doubtless have long guessed the direction of travel: way beyond the framework of mediaeval and early modern theology, into the early twentieth century and the famously iconic use of Paul Klee's *Angelus Novus* by Walter Benjamin as an allegorical backdrop to an elliptically complex theory of history that, among many other things, is implicitly yet indelibly stamped with the force of the counterfactual. Benjamin first saw the Klee painting at an exhibition in Munich in 1921, and it seems to have been a case of artistic love at first sight. He acquired it more or less on the spot, and it became a cherished companion to which he would gratefully return after his many travels, apart, of course, from the last journey, from which there was to be no return (committing suicide while escaping Vichy France and Nazi Occupation). In the retrospective context of Benjamin's end, Klee's angel can all too readily be cast as a prophet of doom, though the real story here is in fact how for Benjamin it became associated with a messianic (and counterfactually inflected) prophecy of hope. For Klee himself, a sense of doom-laden seems to have hovered over his own conception, with some, though far from clinching, evidence to the effect that his angel obliquely refers to Hitler.[6] Benjamin may more plausibly have had the Führer (as Lucifer) in mind when in 1933 – the year of the Reichstag fire and the Nazi seizure of power – he described Klee's angel as having something of the 'satanic'. He may also have had in mind Schlegel's angels of death as metaphors for what presides over the destructive regime of modernity ('industry and utility', wrote Schlegel, 'are the angels of death who, with fiery sword, prevent man's return to Paradise'). However, the Benjaminian gloss that really matters is the celebrated passage in the 1940 text, *Theses on the Philosophy of History* (the angel is gendered male because the grammatical gender of the German word 'Engel' is masculine):

> A Klee painting named *Angelus Novus* shows an angel looking as though he is about to move away from something he is fixedly contemplating. His eyes are staring, his mouth is open, his wings are spread. This is how one pictures the angel of history. His face is turned towards the past. Where we perceive a chain of events, he sees one single catastrophe which keeps piling wreckage upon wreckage and hurls it in front of his feet. The angel would like to stay, awaken the dead and make whole what has been smashed. But a storm is blowing from Paradise, it has caught in his wings with such violence that the

angel can no longer close them. This storm irresistibly propels him into the future to which his back is turned, while the pile of debris before him grows skyward. This storm is what we call progress.[7]

Often quoted yet obdurately opaque, here we have Benjamin's enigmatic prose joining with Klee's enigmatic image to set many an interpretive hare running, as if itself a kind of obscure theological text to rival anything the mediaeval scholastics could have produced. For my purposes, Benjamin's angel of history serves as a herald angel, announcing some of the themes this book explores. I call it Benjamin's angel because of what his interpretation both adds and leaves out, thus transforming Klee's image into something distinctively his own (it has been termed, somewhat acidly, 'Benjamin's logo'). What is most noticeably neglected are the claw-like hands and feet of the original, evocative perhaps of a bird or beast of prey, and hence less an angel blown horizontally through space than one descending, on a downwards trajectory to becoming a theologically fallen one. The most prominent addition is what Benjamin places in the central foreground. The angel's eyes do not weep, they 'stare', with a gaze seemingly aghast but whose precise meaning depends on assumptions and inferences as to the object, if any, of the gaze. Benjamin's answer is 'wreckage' and a 'pile of rubble', an on-going accumulation of ruins produced by the storm that is history post-Eden. It is Benjamin's counter to the conventional, and comfortable, arrangement of history as an intelligibly ordered 'chain of events', the kind of account that rationalizes and secures the outcomes of victors' history as the ever onward march of 'progress'.

There is no rubble in Klee's picture. *Angelus Novus* is an early example of his oil transfer technique – a kind of tracing in which the contours of an original pencil drawing are reproduced in outline on a sheet of blank paper below it, underneath which is a sheet of paper smeared with oil paint (here black); in some cases including this one, water colours are added to the traced image.[8] The result is a mass of swirling brownish-black colour that loosely frames a central mass of yellowish colour. There is no trace of a depicted ruin. This is clearly an instance of Benjamin interpreting in the service of his own allegorical ends. But if the import seems arbitrary, it is not wildly so; while the colour swirls evoke nothing distinctly representational, there is in them a hint of the apocalyptic. In any case, all that concerns me here is the use to which Benjamin puts Klee's image, and specifically what is entailed by the re-baptizing of *angelus novus* as the 'angel of history'. The metaphorical tapestry woven around the latter notion is dense, but, along with storm, stare and debris, two further motifs stand out: wings and back. Klee's angel wings, paralysed by a force so powerful that they cannot be closed, are manifestly not Leonardo's angel wings, poised for the purposefully airborne and wind-driven as tokens of the humanist confidence in a future informed by the marvels of science. They are perhaps more akin to Dürer's, the latter a formative influence on Klee's graphic art, in particular the *Apocalpyse* series, in one of which four angels battle against the winds of havoc associated with the Four Horsemen. Klee's angel, on the other hand, is less a fighter than a victim, trapped by the storm rather than opposing it. He would like to oppose it, 'would like to stay' so as to 'awaken the dead and make whole what has been smashed', as Benjamin puts it. Instead he is blown helplessly towards a future of which, his back turned to it, he has no knowledge, what in *Berlin Childhood around 1900* Benjamin calls 'that invisible stranger – the future'. The angel's back is a blank as pure enigma. But there is also something else, a 'back to the future' of the kind entertainingly plotted in the popular movie of that name (it has to be a truly fascinating pastime wondering what Benjamin would have made of that film!).[9] This is the double take which breaks and supersedes the linear 'chain of events' by virtue of a back to the future in the temporal sense of returning to the past in order to carry aspects of it (those interred in the trashcan of the past) into an alternative future – the one excluded by the implication of 'historicist' thinking in sustaining the terms of winners' history as both narrative and fact.

A further detail here catches the eye, though it didn't catch Benjamin's. The gaze of Klee's angel echoes the frontal look of Byzantine art, but there is also the suggestion of an averted gaze. The shift from the frontal to the averted is a feature of much humanist painting, and is often linked by the art historians to the new-found autonomy of the human subject left to the privacy of his or her own faith or thoughts. In the Klee picture the suggestion seems to be less a turn to inward seeing than the glimpse of something else in the foreground but off-stage, to the side of the storm, something unexpected that perhaps takes by surprise, though whether as occasion of horror or hope we cannot tell. This is not a question for Benjamin either (he does not mention any indication of an averted look). What, however, he does claim to see, through the angel's eyes, are the 'sparks of hope in the past', ruins as the ashes and cinders of the incinerated aspirations of history's losers, in which a residual spark lies as a potential flashpoint. The flashpoint famously has the power of 'blasting [the past] out of context', where 'context' is the straight line continuum of the progress story that has the past where it belongs, safely buried. This is the location of the Benjaminian counterfactual.[10] It is where the might-have-beens of a past and the forgotten narrative of history's losers become the might-bes of a possible future, a hiatus or 'fold' in the relation of past, present and future where past conditional designations have the potential to morph into future-directed ones.[11]

Benjamin has two further metaphors for this. One is the brush, with which to 'brush history against the grain'. Brushing the 'running-on' course of things against the grain is what counterfactualism is fundamentally about, ruffling history backwards to then consider what experimentally happens or might happen going forwards. The second is the metaphor of the heliotropic, as history's turning to the sun that rises over an extinguished past: 'As flowers turn towards the sun, by dint of a secret heliotropism the past turns towards that sun which is rising in the sky of history.'[12] It is the scene in which the angel's impotent desire to reawaken the dead becomes possible, the scene in which we can say of the past what Faulkner said (though Faulkner had a quite different idea in mind): 'The past is never dead. It's not even past.' Benjamin's reawakened dead are perhaps close to Nietzsche's returning ghost as disturber of the peace in *The Uses and Abuses of History*: 'a matter of wonder: a moment, now here and then gone ... returns as a ghost and disturbs the peace of a later moment.'[13]

# III

This is heady stuff, and arguably calls for a mildly chastening postscript. Benjamin thought he had discovered in the disintegrated might-have-beens of loser-hopes some of the ingredients for a transformative revolutionary politics. Whatever one thinks, retrospectively or prospectively, of the latter, there is clearly here a more general issue of major importance for all counterfactualist endeavours involving the fate of dashed aspirations. Quite how major is an issue in its own right, often obscured by the polemical smog pumped out by hostile commentary that mistakes polemic for understanding. The issue arising from Benjamin's interpretation of the Klee painting should nevertheless be posted as a health warning. The warning is often especially required in connection with the role of counterfactuals in utopian imaginings, where speculations as to what might have happened (and might still happen, if in altered conditions and forms) gets confused with what one would simply like to have happened. It is the danger, potentially fatal, of wish-fulfilling preferences being injected into the analytical bloodstream and befogging the distinction between, on the one hand, the possible (future past and perfect conditional constructions of the possible), and, on the other hand, the mere fantasizing of the impossible. How and where one draws that line is a question in its own right. It is also important to note that the same point about wishful thinking applies, if in reverse direction, to dystopian 'realism', the version that has an interest in denying that there are superior alternatives to a status quo sustained by vested interests. We can think of this further in terms of the relation of counterfactuals to processes of remembering and forgetting. The object of remembering counterfactuals is not just what (allegedly) happened but also what did not though, under certain beliefs, might have.

Exactly how one remembers in this form depends to a large extent on whether the perspective is that of winners' or losers' history. The 'what-if' of winners is typically a self-congratulatory 'thank goodness' (we didn't take that path), whereas the 'what-if' of losers is very often a self-pitying 'if-only' (we had taken that path). Both attitudes thus hold traps, and lend support to the merits of 'forgetting', though this too can prove congenial to winners and subscribers to the linear Progress-narrative.[14] Benjamin's friend and colleague, Max Horkheimer, seemed to have caught a whiff of wishful thinking in the former's 'redemptive' theory of history with his objection: 'past injustice has occurred and is done with. The murdered really are murdered.' Benjamin, of course, did not, ludicrously, question that. Like Horkheimer, he too wrote that the past is 'done with' in the sense that what has happened cannot be made to unhappen. That's not what reawakening the dead meant, just as the averted gaze of Klee's angel is not a looking away in the sense of a denial. Yet the suspicion of a sentimental investment in losers and their shattered dreams can easily linger. One way of draining that from the relevant argument is by turning briefly to a thinker in no way tempted by utopian dreams and robustly indifferent to the seductions of Romantic nostalgia.

Claude Lévi-Strauss is prima facie an unusual bedfellow for Walter Benjamin. Yet there are many striking parallels. As far as I know, there are no angels in Lévi-Strauss's writings. There is, however, a recurring preoccupation with magical thought, in particular the strong contrast between science and magic, as part of his continuation of the anthropological tradition of Evans-Pritchard. In *The Savage Mind*, he remarks that the 'first difference between magic and science ... is that magic postulates a complete and all-embracing determinism'.[15] In his pertinently titled book (*The Language of Demons and Angels*), Christopher Lehrich glosses this as the distinction between the more modest 'determinism' of science interested only in the physical laws of causation, and the extended 'determinism' of magic, concerned with certain kinds of 'why' as well as 'how' questions (why did the lightning strike that person in particular and not the other person?), adding that 'in theory, such a logic cannot end short of divine omniscience, of a divine understanding of all things simultaneously and how they all intersect and interact'.[16] This, of course, implicitly attributes to Lévi-Strauss a view reminiscent of Leibniz, and Marcel Hénaff makes it explicit when he speaks of Lévi-Strauss having a 'kinship with Leibniz rather than with Kant'.[17] Leibniz's closed system of 'interconnectedness', of course, goes hand-in-hand with the sense of alternative 'possible worlds'.

This sense of the alternative informs the entire Lévi-Straussian project of fashioning a marriage of anthropology and philosophy of history in which the history of mankind – crucially, its entry into historical time – is cast as a nexus of crossroads and turning points, but where each turning point adopted proves to be a wrong one rationalized, under the banner of 'progress', as the right one.[18] It is broadly the bleak tale of the technological mastery of nature, not, as in Marx and others, the historically successive chapters of the brutal but triumphal human victory over the realm of necessity, but as the persistent theft of the human from man beginning, roughly, with the Neolithic transition from small to large societies and carrying through to the decisive changes wrought by the Scientific Revolution and its agro-industrial legacies. This is close to the Rousseau of the *Second Discourse*; but it also echoes much of what Benjamin outlines in the *Theses*, especially the latter's definition of 'progress' as 'the progression of the exploitation of nature' at once creating and masking a 'regression of society', which Benjamin will specifically associate with Fascism ('the technocratic traces which would later be found in Fascism'). For Lévi-Strauss there are no obviously available ways back (to the future). Mankind has made its bed (its Mephistophelian pact) and must lie in it. On the other hand, irreversibility is not proof of necessity (the inevitabilist teleology of historical causation that underpins the progress-narratives of history). A form – complex and difficult to describe – of 'contingency' rules, such that, at the crossroads, other paths not taken could have been.

Memory traces of the latter are the basis of 'a logical framework for historical developments' formally outlined in *Structural Anthropology* and later sketched in the closing paragraphs of *From Honey to Ashes* as a set of 'compossibles', which 'are not all confirmed by experience' and 'only some of which...have been actualized'.[19] The non-actualized possibilities, however, remain deposited in the collective psyche of mankind as counterfactual virtualities in a state of latency, repressed as the discards of progress, but impressed, indelibly, in the privileged cultural record of 'myth', the place where, beyond linear historical time, events are related 'simultaneously to the past, the present and the future'. And let us not forget that remarkable passage, with its finale quotation from Rousseau, in *Tristes tropiques*, the biographical memoir that is sadness incarnate in its long, disabused, melancholic contemplation of the unstoppable ravaging work of modernity: 'Nothing is settled, everything can still be altered. What was done, but turned out wrong, can be done again. "The Golden Age, which blind superstition had placed behind (or ahead of) us, is *in us*".[20] Part of the grammar of that is the grammar of the counterfactual.

# IV

Angels appear elsewhere in Benjamin's writings.[21] The one that matters for the purposes of this argument is to be found towards the end of *The Origins of German Tragic Drama*, the book which grew out of the postdoctoral thesis on which he worked not long after the acquisition of the Klee painting. An inquiry into the roots, nature and meaning of the German baroque 'sorrow play' in the sixteenth and seventeenth centuries, it is also a philosophical reflection on the emergence of the modern world under the sign of catastrophe, the moment when, in Benjamin's words, history 'loses the eschatological certainty of its redemptive conclusion and becomes secularized into a mere natural setting for the profane struggles over political power'. The baroque is both product and reflection of a world rent by violence (crucially, the violence of the wars of religion), where the relation of divine and human appears broken beyond repair, spawning 'visions of the frenzy of destruction in which all earthly things collapse into ruins' to join 'the realm of dead objects'. Angels in this context are seen as 'falling into the depths'. Alternatively (the example is the decorative embellishments of baroque architecture), they are the 'perilously soaring angels', perilous because without real support from an earthly 'below'.[22] Another Dürer image springs to mind here, as indeed itself a crossroads at which Benjamin and Lévi-Strauss could be said to meet, with Klee hovering over the rendez-vous: *Melancholia 1*. Benjamin was obsessed with it (as testimony to 'Dürer's genius of winged melancholy'); Lévi-Strauss was reading about it as he entered his tenth decade; and, as noted, Dürer in general was an important reference point for Klee's *Angelus Novus*.[23] Dürer's engraving has a forlorn angel, lost and homeless in a space encumbered with the instruments of science, mathematics and time-keeping that shape, measure and control the disenchanted world of modernity, while in the far distance there is a radiant mix of sea and heaven marking the realm from which the angel has been exiled.

Dürer spent two years in Venice at the beginning of the sixteenth century. Along with some of the other Venetian painters, the young Titian apparently looked long and hard at examples of his work; indeed Dürer himself remarked sourly in letters home to Nuremberg that they were 'stealing' from him. There are angels aplenty in Titian's oeuvre, but, unlike Dürer's melancholic being, they are vibrant and purposeful, strong presences in a world of colour and action, and often mediators between sky and earth as if part of a natural landscape. In his religious paintings, they have little in common with Dürer's evangelical taste for apocalyptic and eschatological endgames, and often seem closer to the more secular side of the Renaissance imagination. The painting to which I now turn is entirely secular and has no angels in it, but which, however implausible this might seem at first (or any) sight, I wish to offer as a distant companion to Benjamin's allegory of history. It is a late work with a somewhat curious compositional history, starting with the fact that it has two titles, *Allegory of Prudence* and *Allegory of Time Governed by Prudence*, neither of which seems to have been Titian's designations. There is also no record of it in the inventory of Titian's work compiled on his death. These are already indications of the painting's anomalous status. Indeed it is not even clear that it *is* a free-standing painting at all. In the 1920s Baron von Hadeln maintained that it was in fact a *timpano*, a form of decorated cover to protect a painting beneath. If the description is correct, it also delivers a fine irony: of a work whose material purpose is to shield another from the very thing the shielding picture is about – the wear and tear of time; about time, it becomes also an act of resistance to it.

It has also been the object of a great deal of interpretive scrutiny, centred on a structure made of three sets each of three motifs: first, the three human faces (from right to left, the face of a young man in right profile looking forward; the face of a mature middle-aged man looking out at the spectator; and the face of an old man in left profile looking back); second, the three animal heads (dog, lion, wolf, assigned respectively to the faces, dog to young, lion to middle-aged, wolf to old); third, the tripartite Latin motto that crowns the picture: *ex praeterito* (above the left face), *praesens prudenter agit* (above the middle one), and *ni futura actione de turpet* (above the right one). It is generally translated epigrammatically as 'from the past, the present acts prudently, lest it spoil future action'. The interrelations of the three axes yield superimposed levels of allegorical reference, typically numbering three in turn: an Ages of Man and Seasons of Life allegory; a more abstract meditation on the structure of Time (as Past, Present and Future); a moral allegory on the classical virtue of Prudence and the importance of practical reason for the sagely managed life. Greatest attention has been given to the emblematic animal heads, variously read according to the allegorical template that is foregrounded (in Panofsky's words, 'according to whether the element stressed was "time" or "prudence"'), and thus as varied inflections of the rhetorical trinity inherited from antiquity, *memoria, intelligentia, providentia*.[24]

Steeped in Renaissance emblematics, the scholars have had a field day with this, above all the incomparably learned Panofsky, ever the hunter of meanings and sources (the two sometimes effectively indistinguishable), who tracks the iconography back to representations of the Egyptian gods (specifically the netherworld god, Serapis) and sideways into contemporary sources on the arts of memory. In doing so, he opens a possible avenue of inquiry, unmentioned by him, in fact almost certainly unnoticed, perhaps for the very good reason that it probably exists nowhere other than as an imprudent figment of my own imagination. It is nevertheless down this imagined avenue that we come to the reason for the otherwise improbable pairing of Titian's painting with Klee's and Benjamin's interpretation of it. I call it provisionally the fourth-face hypothesis, pure folly perhaps (but then all sorts of interesting things start to happen when, in the footsteps of Erasmus, we examine Prudence from the point of view of Folly).

When Panofsky turns to contemporary sources, two figures of the Italian Renaissance stand out: Piero Valeriano and Giordano Bruno, both practitioners of the exotic and esoteric *ars memoriae*. In Valeriano's *Hieroglyphica* (his commentary on Horapollo's treatise) the wolf/lion/dog trilogy appears as the hieroglyphic *tricipitium* of the three basic modes of Time, but in the context of a more general view of the remembering mind as elastic, caught up in journeys, both cyclical and lateral as well as linear, entailing all manner of loops and digressions within a labyrinthine mosaic of detour and a vast network of symbolic correspondences. And then there is the amazing Giordano Bruno, prime candidate for having given the expression 'Renaissance man' its later meaning. Frances Yates confesses to not having 'fully understood' Bruno's ideas about time and memory. If not Yates, then who stands a chance with Bruno's extravagant, dementedly complex yet rigorously ordered systems clothed in vivid dramatic metaphors? There is the 'Wheel of Memory' and its spinning kaleidoscope of memory formation. And there is the 'Mansion', an architecture of incredible complexity, with different 'memory rooms' for different memory images, and home of an 'Encylopaedia of Everything', with secret corridors and surprising junction points, in splendid disregard for the simpler forms of straight-line time (the 'acentric labyrinth' is one name that has been given to it).

The emblems wolf, lion and dog also make an appearance in Bruno's investigations, but, Panofsky reminds us, as bearers of all-round bad news for the life lived in time. In the coda poem of *Eroici Furori*, the three modes ('the "then", the "now", and the "anon"') are but different manifestations of affliction and 'torture', a tissue of anguish made from the memories of past mistakes, the anxieties of negotiating the present, and the disappointment in store for future hopes destined to fail. In this meditation on the whips and scorns of time, the virtue of prudence is eclipsed by an emphasis on bitterness, regret and repentance. Titian's *Allegory of Prudence* is sometimes read in similar vein, as more allegory of the Christian vices, where the animal heads represent *luxuria* (lustful dog), *superba* (proud lion), *avarita* (rapacious wolf). Repentance certainly figures in the one 'Ages of Man' painting by Titian to bear that name and which has in the middle distance an old man holding two skulls, reminiscent of a repentant Jerome. Repentance, like remorse, belongs in the ethical and emotional registers of counterfactual reflection on how things might, or should otherwise, have been (in, for example, a world actually governed by prudence). In the Bruno poem, the sense of the possible 'otherwise', of the alternative outcome, is there, if at all, only by implication, and the scope for it is limited by the view of time as no-exit entrapment in suffering. There is, however, a further context, an intellectual correlate in Bruno's work as cosmologist and mathematician, where (in, for example, the dialogue *De l'infinito, universo e mondi*) he runs a prototype of plural and possible-worlds theory that is by its very nature deeply implicated in the structure of counterfactual thought-experiments.

If we were to carry the spirit of this back into the Renaissance arts of memory, and from there into Titian's picture about time,[25] we may find ourselves closer to being able to imagine (as distinct from merely hallucinating) a fourth human face, endowed with a look that speaks of dwelling on the might-have-beens as well as the has-beens of the past; the look not just of the preterite but also of the conditional perfect. There is, of course, a four as well as a three in the Ages-of-Man trope, though in this variant (for example, the early seventeenth-century painting by Valentin de Boulogne) the fourth is infancy (the babe, and any corresponding animal emblem, having no part in any counterfactual scenario). But there is also the related metaphor of the four seasons. Which three of the four would match the faces in Titian's picture – spring for youth, summer for maturity and winter for old age? If so, that would leave autumn, the season of reflective retrospect, and the slot for the putative fourth face signifying the perspective of the conditional perfect. I am not for one moment, of course, suggesting that this musing represents a Titian counterfactual, something he might actually have put into his picture but, for whatever reason, chose not to. There is no evidence that it was a compositional option, in terms of either Titian's own artistic thinking or contemporary artistic convention.

The path of art history is nevertheless strewn with counterfactuals. In the celebrated essay, 'History of Art as a Humanistic Discipline', Panofsky comes close to such thinking in connection with the question of 'intention', the artistic choices the artist consciously makes while composing: 'Now, "intention" can only be formulated in terms of alternatives: a situation has to be supposed in which the maker of the work had more than one possibility of procedure, that is to say, in which he found himself confronted with a problem of choice between various modes of emphasis.'[26] More generally, however, Panofsky's entire conception of art history and its place in a wider history of mankind is teleological through and through, a tale of civilizational advance in which an archive of 'monuments' and 'documents' is the cultural mechanism for the transmission of past to present and future understood as the handing on of a treasure house of experiences and values, crucially including Renaissance *humanitas* as the ground of the 'humanities'. It is a view that stands in stark contrast to Benjamin's famous statement in the 'Theses': 'There is no document of civilization which is not at the same time a document of barbarism' (a difference that may go some way to explaining why Panofsky was so dismissive of Benjamin and of his book *The Origins of German Tragic Drama*).

It has therefore been interesting to see other, more counterfactually inflected art histories coming into view. There is Geoffrey Hawthorn's account of late thirteenth- and early fourteenth-century Italian painting (Duccio, along with Giotto and Cimabue, the prime examples) as a 'crossroads' moment when the painters are juggling with multiple options and solutions, essentially for the tasks of a Christian art in culture where science and mathematics are moving increasingly centre stage for the understanding of reality. The experiments of the Siennese painters and the questions that subtend them are seen as a counter to the art-historical telos (Panofsky again one of its major exponents) that enshrines the Florentine triumph of 'perspective' as more or less guaranteed by some quasi-providential 'law' of history. At the crossroads, no future outcome for painting seems in any way foreordained, such that the victory of perspective might not have happened or at least not in the way it did.[27] And then, fast-forwarding, there is T. J. Clark's evocation, in his study of Picasso, of a 'modernism that might have been', in conscious opposition to the settled image of modernism as always 'an arrow pointing to the future'.[28]

This, however, is not the sort of context in which the compositional history of Titian's painting appears to have unfolded. The *Allegory of Prudence* is sometimes read autobiographically, bound up with the elderly Titian's reckoning with mortality as well as his bequeathing of a legacy both artistic and financial (he is the old man in the painting, his beloved son, Orazio, the mature man in the middle, and his adoptive grandson, Marco, the young man). This is the reading finally preferred by Panofsky, but not, as one might have expected, as a painting that anticipates a farewell to the world. For Panofsky, the focus is not on the old man ('under-painted' compared to the others), but on the man in the centre looking at us in a 'present' of eye contact along with his more abstract function as a representation of the category of *praesens*. This emphasis on 'presentness' even as, for Titian, age sets in and death beckons could be said to have some bearing on something to do with Titian's relation to

'Renaissance'. The term is, of course, endlessly discussed and debated, both what it meant to the period that claimed the label, and what it can be taken to mean in general: in short, both Renaissance and renascences. The standard accounts start from Vasari's *rinascita*, the formula which defines 'renaissance' as the recovery of a past (antiquity) for a modern present (but where *moderno* also includes projection to a future for which the present lays the foundations). Another version, however, is more radically present-centred, stressing the immediacy of a 'now' as the site of the 'new' (a 'spontaneous resurgence of culture as such' is how Panofsky puts it).[29] This version found a powerful echo in the work of the historian, Konrad Burdach (Benjamin engages extensively with Burdach's historical thinking in the 'Prologue' to *The Origins of German Tragic Drama*). 'Turned backward, they struggle into the future' is how Burdach, in an uncanny echo of Klee's angel, describes 'renaissances', all of them. It is their very definition; at home in neither the past nor the future, renaissances live and breathe in the present moment of a beginning-anew, a 'rebirth' unfolding in what Burdach calls the 'middle' place between past and future.[30]

The relation of Titian's career to (*the*) Renaissance can be made to fit this frame, as total absorption by the creative energy of a present concentrated in and on its own presentness. On this account, what would matter most in the autobiographical interpretation of *Allegory of Prudence* is its own midpoint, the allegedly confident middle face representing the present.[31] And yet, what of the avenue I mentioned as opened though unexplored in Panofsky's iconological exploration, the avenue that might lead to the hypothetical fourth face? As it happens, we can now discard it, not just because it is fanciful, but also because, having served its proleptic purpose in my argument, it is not in fact necessary to the idea the fourth face was to instantiate. Look again at the three faces and we may well find it in one of them. Which one? Most elections would probably plump for the old man's face, musing on a lost past, possibly with remorse. But perhaps this would be the wrong place. What of the middle face, that of the man characterized by the pride, dignity and vigour of the lion below him, who has pondered options and makes prudent choices?

Bracket the iconographical equations, and look once more at his look at us. As always with frontal portraiture, what is going on in and with the painting is not just the portrayal of a fixed look. It also involves situations and relations of look*ing*, the portrayed face looking at us looking at it. And such are the indeterminacies of the reciprocal human gaze, the fluid transactional space of painting and viewer cannot be contained by the 'this-equals-that' algebra of emblematics and their decoding by the iconologist art historian. Within this less stable, more supple interpretive frame, it is just as possible to see something closer to Bruno, not exactly his present as a form of 'torture', but certainly more than a trace of anxiety, apprehension and perplexity, the look of a man who knows already that he will eventually arrive at the stage of life (represented by the face to his left) that is very far from being a counterfactual-free zone. And if it is then said that this way with the mature man's face is inconsistent with the emblematic meanings of the lion head with which it is partnered, then look again at the latter. Can one reliably say of Titian's lion that he seems buoyantly game for life's challenges? For an emblem of vigour and command, our lion seems unpromisingly downcast, disconsolate even. Look more closely still, and isn't that a tear one can see just below the left eye? It's a standard highlighting device in oil painting, but, since emblematics and anthropomorphism go hand in hand here, why not incorporate the 'tear' into the sorts of things it normally signifies in the human realm?

The look on the middle face we can call the 'crossroads' look, where practical reason and prudential assessment are not always fruitfully to hand in deciding which fork in the road to take. *Allegory of Prudence* is sometimes juxtaposed with *Sacred and Profane Love*, which stages Titian's variant of the Hercules at the Crossroads story. Unlike Dürer's print (where what counts as the right choice – the path of virtue – is not only obvious but equally obviously chosen by Hercules), Titian's paintings suggest that both options have claims on us and, thus to choose one in preference to the other stores up counterfactual possibilities for the future, when the time comes to look back on options both elected and declined. At the time and the place – the 'middle' place – nothing, however, is transparently clear. There is a shroud of darkness, akin to Dante's 'middle' in the opening line of *Inferno*, the midpoint on the path of life where one finds oneself in a dark forest confronted with a question. And as later, in the sixteenth and seventeenth centuries, new life-worlds emerge, leaving behind earlier ones in which answers often seem to be given even before the questions are asked, the dilemma of the fork in the road will become increasingly beset by chronic doubt, or alternatively with its resolution left to chance subsequently rationalized as God's handiwork. We will see much more of this shortly. For now let us return to the theme of the 'seasons' of life, in connection with the figure of the arc of time as studded with *kairos* (the ancient Greek for 'seasons' of life as occasions of decision-making), to remind ourselves that the word also signifies 'turning points', both those embraced and those ignored or missed and thus potentially saturated with might-have-beens. We are at the crossroads moment of the next chapter.[32]

# 4 CROSSROADS: THREE TALES, THREE GAMBLERS

*In the afternoon they came to a crossroads, what else to call it. A faint wagon trace came from the north and crossed their path and went on to the south. They stood scanning the landscape for some guidance in that emptiness.*

**CORMAC McCARTHY**

*He fled, not from his past, but to escape his future. It took him twelve years to learn that you cannot escape either of them.*

**WILLIAM FAULKNER**

# I

'Where we're going,' says Doc in *Back to the Future*, 'we do not need roads.' Such are the conveniences of time travel. Normal travel, of the land-based kind (sea and air add special dimensions of their own[1]) cannot do without them. As nodes of exchange and transition, roads, along with ports and quays, are – according to the historian, Charles Seignobos – the essence of civilizations.[2] For symbolic and metaphorical purposes, cultures high and low draw on roads in all manner of different guises: the Parmenidean paths of inquiry and the Herculean paths of vice and virtue; the road to Damascus and the road to Calvary; the Way of the Chinese sages; Dante's *mezzo del cammin*; Beckett's back roads; Dylan's 'Highway 61'; Kipling's 'Road to Mandelay'; Mandela's 'Road to Freedom'; the Road *tout court*

(Cormac McCarthy's zero, as the trek through the dystopian landscapes of the End Time). The inventory can continue almost indefinitely down a listing road of its own,[3] but must, of course, include the road from Delphi and hence the Crossroads. In folklores and mythologies, both ancient and modern, the crossroads is often perceived as a liminal and spooky zone situated outside the safer spaces of the social world. Neighbour of the crooked path, it is regularly associated with notions of crookedness of one sort or another. In some cultures, it is the non-place for the burial of criminals and outcasts. In others, it is populated by spirits, ghosts and demons. Hecate, in Greek and Roman myth something of an outsider in the divine order as the 'fringe' goddess of magic and witchcraft, was also the 'goddess of the pathways' and believed to consort with dark chthonic powers at crossroad sites. These in turn were sites of various apotropaic practices (in ancient Rome honeyed cakes were often left at crossroads as offerings to ward off evil spirits). In the more codified and scriptural forms of religious thought and wisdom teaching, the crossroads is typically a figure for representing the challenges of the moral and spiritual journey on the 'road of life', whether as the Biblical prophet, the Chinese sage, or the Greek philosopher-mathematician.

In the Hebrew bible, the crossroads is a metaphor for the starkly confrontational declarations of the prophet, Jeremiah: 'This is what the Lord said: "Stand at the crossroads and look; ask for the ancient paths, and ask where the good way is, and walk in it, and you will find rest for your souls."' This is more than just advice; it is also a thunderous admonition delivered to the Israelites, who, in taking the wrong path, betray the Covenant: 'But you said: "we will not walk in it".' The Confucian and Daoist 'way' stands in a more equivocal relation to the image. The origins and composition of the word *dao* (or *tao*) have been much debated among linguists and philologists.[4] Originally understood as a 'compound ideogram', some claim that the sign of the crossroads figures, in part or in whole, in the structure of the word as one of its logograms (the term for 'characters', more precisely *hànzi* or 'Han characters'). That, however, appears to be a simplified reduction to the straightforwardly ideogrammatic of a more complex set of linguistic elements. The more nuanced account has the word *dao* (道) as the root of the word 導, which in turn means showing someone the way at the crossroads. The image or primary sense of crossroads is not as such shown in the word itself, but is derived from the concept of guiding someone on a walk. But whatever the linguistic features, the cultural cluster of ideas that gather around the crossroads image seem to carry a largely negative freight, in contrast to its crucial role in the Biblical drama of command, test and salvation. According to Herbert Fingarette's commentary, a key to understanding the symbolism of the 'Way' is to see it as 'a way without crossroads', without, in other words, the traps of 'crookedness' and the temptations of deviation. The true Way is mono-directional, the straight path of a continuous learning process whose end is the educative process itself.[5]

Third, there is the case of the Greek ypsilon (or upsilon). As a letter that can be both vowel and consonant, it inhabits an alphabetical 'between' space, neither unequivocally one thing nor the other, akin to the liminality of the crossroads it came to represent. When incorporated into Latin at the instruction of Emperor Claudius, it was known as the *sonus medius* and also called the *i graeca* to mark its foreignness (and indeed was used originally only for the spelling of foreign words).[6] Its geometric shape as a straight stem bifurcating into two forks of equal length was further deployed by Pythagoras to illustrate the paths of vice and virtue. This adaptation of the sign was echoed in Roman literature (in, for example, the satires of Persius) and picked up in early Christian moral thought, either sceptically (as in the writings of Lactantius) or more positively (as later in the *Etymologies* of Isidore of Seville), before travelling into the figurative world of the Renaissance.[7] In more esoteric sources, it was also known as the Furca Pythagorica and the Ypsilon Cross. Here the relevant number is two, the model of the crossroads as *bivium* representing a binary choice, most notably, of course, in multiple versions of the story of Hercules' Choice. But, by taking into account the path which leads to the twin forks, it could also be modelled as a *trivium*, incorporating the talismanic number three that will haunt the crossroads as a place of darkness and evil (Hecate herself was often portrayed as three-headed, famously howling at the crossroads in Virgil). The number three also haunts the greatest crossroads story of them all: the story of Oedipus. 'Trivium! Crossroads! Remember this word!' is the injunction in respect of a junction which Stravinsky has the Speaker utter in his opera-oratorio based on the Oedipus story. We might also like to imagine it inscribed, along with the sign of the Ypsilon, on the portals of a Delphic temple of the Counterfactual.

While there is thus considerable historical and cultural variation in the symbolism of the crossroads, it remains fundamentally the suspensive location where the traveller pauses and deliberates (and perhaps panics or at least shivers) before possible alternatives – of both routes and futures, those possible alternatives, the 'paths' both literal and figurative that will feature as part of the life journey and those that won't but might have. Strictly speaking, the 'cross' in the crossroads (as either an × or a + sign) evokes the number four, in, for example, the Euclidean sense of four directions made from two sets of two intersecting lines that share a common 'empty' intersection point.[8] But if mathematically empty, existentially it is super-charged, the crossing point as a crux, of dilemma, decision and destiny. No other space even begins to compare as the natural home of the counterfactualist, to which she can return in imagination over and over to dwell with the ghosts of her own what-if's. There are, of course, brisk ways of dealing with these hauntings. One is simply to get on with it, armed with the don't-look-back attitude of a Yoga Berri; famously a bearer of bad news for the oracles industry ('it's hard to make predictions, especially about the future'), he also has some mischievously disingenuous advice to offer: 'when you come to a fork in the road, take it'. But just how useful can this breezy confidence be when there is a more than one fork? Which one do I take, Oedipus might ask, meaning simultaneously which to take and, by definition, which not to. And what difference would that make could be a follow-up question from Teiresias.

In a 'fate' culture, the answer is likely to be none, in the sense that the eventual outcomes will always be the same whatever road you take. In more modern cultural settings, the answer may also be that it doesn't matter which you take, not, however, because the outcomes will be the same (they won't), but because difference is of the very essence of the adventure of 'choice' and the freedom of the road. This is the world celebrated by Walt Whitman's 'Song of the Open Road', 'healthy, free, the world before me' that unfolds along the 'long brown road ... latent with unseen existences' where everything is a crossroads of sorts, joyously embraced as the 'cheerful voice of the public road, the gay fresh sentiment of the road'.[9] In other modern settings, however, arrival at the crossroads will be a source of puzzled introspective wondering and an occasion of 'anxiety'. Here is Yves Bonnefoy, in *L'Arrière-pays*:

> I have often experienced a feeling of anxiety at crossroads. At such moments it seems to me that *here*, or close by, a couple of steps away on the path I didn't take and which is already receding – that just *over there* a more elevated kind of country would open up, where I might have gone to live and which I have already lost. And yet at the moment

of choice, there was nothing to indicate or even suggest that I should take the other route.[10]

This is more reminiscent of the mix of curiosity and longing sometimes associated with the 'stretching' effect of early modern Dutch landscape painting, in which roads are 'seen' to continue beyond the horizon towards the tantalizing vista of a potentially glimpsed otherness, in a manner such that the unseen becomes a constitutive part of the painting. Whitman's open road can also be said to run backwards to a past, a literary one, for example, the adventures of the earlier picaresque hero. Fielding's amiable tale of the foundling discovered at a crossroads is, we might say, the modern's very different way with the theme of the abandoned child from that of the Theban baby destined to die on the mountainside, but who instead grows to walk from Delphi to the crossroads of Phocis.

The cultural history of the crossroads symbol is thus one of continuities and discontinuities. Part of the history, alas, describes a pattern where an earlier abundance and depth of meaning eventually give way to sheer banality. Apart from Bone's world-wide hit, the rap song 'Crossroads' (which captures something of the ancient sources with, in the music video, its evocation of a soul-gathering Reaper figure), today it is little more than a journalistic cliché recycled to cover virtually everything every day of the week. Barack Obama tells us the 'world is at a crossroads'. So too, it seems, are China, North Korea, Europe, the Euro, Brexit, American healthcare, the car industry, emerging markets investors, crypto technology, and the 'planet' (at the time of writing all recent news media headlines). France has both a radio programme and a supermarket chain called 'Carrefour'. The former makes sense, the latter is baffling (until learning that the first store was opened near a crossroads in the suburbs of Annecy). France, however, also has the wonderful road sign, *Nombreux Carrefours*. It is confusing at first to unfamiliar drivers (known to evoke thoughts of an unusual form of roundabout, akin in some respects to the branchings of a Calder mobile), but which I can now never pass without thinking of it as a redeeming mini-allegory of the numerousness of the crossroads motif itself.[11] As an attempt at getting some purchase on these variations, and more specifically on what they entail for culturally relative understandings of counterfactual possibility, I sketch three 'road' stories running from antiquity via the late middle ages to the early modern period, under the headings: Oedipus walks to

Thebes, Petrarch zigzags up Mont Ventoux, Ignatius of Loyola rides to Montserrat.

## II

If ever there were a refutation of the belief (enunciated by Ratcliff in Faulkner's *The Mansion*) that 'God is a gentleman and wouldn't bollix up the same feller twice with the same trick', it has be the story of Oedipus, above all as told or staged by Sophocles. The story begins in Thebes. Twice. It is where the play opens, with Oedipus the king and solver of Sphinx riddles imperiously flaunting his powers in getting to the bottom of the unexplained curse that lies over the city he rules. But it begins also in Thebes with the history that pre-dates the time of the play itself, as Oedipus's birthplace, where he himself begins though without knowing that until the end. The Thebes to which Oedipus goes is not just a place, but also an irony-laden time, a future seized in order to escape a past (his upbringing in Corinth) but which in fact is his past (the pre-Corinthian one). The story thus describes a loop, its ending the recovery through discovery of this other beginning (where he 'comes from' in the sense of his biological origins). From the rubble that his life becomes, eyes that opened at birth are blinded as a consequence of 'seeing' that to which he was blind ('he that came seeing, blind shall he go'). Thebes is accordingly primordial, in more senses than one. It is also but one coordinate of both a traveller's geography and a symbolic constellation centred on a junction point, the crossroads of Phocis, where the road from Delphi bifurcates, one way continuing to Thebes, the other branching to Daulis (or Daulia). From the point of view of the walking Oedipus, the crossroads can be thought of as a *bivium*, where purpose and direction converge on a binary choice between Thebes and Daulis, though the possibility of returning to Delphi to get a proper answer to the question he asked would surely count in some very close possible world as a seriously meaningful third option (indeed it is one of the great mysteries of the story that it does not seem to occur to him).

Returning to Delphi is certainly Laius's purpose, driven by the gnawing wish to acquire further information in respect of what he was told by the Oracle many years previously ('if you have a son, he will kill you', or, in the blunter no ifs-and-buts version, 'your son will kill you'). And once we factor in the road not from but to Delphi (the direction of travel from

Laius's point of view), we conjure a *trivium* (the word, remember, that we must 'remember', because everything hangs on it), the place Oedipus himself pointedly describes in terms of the number three, as the 'silent crossroad in the forest clearing ... where three roads meet'. The poor relation of the crossroads scenario is the road to Daulis. Rarely discussed because on the face of it there is apparently nothing to be discussed, it is for that very reason a source of fascination, its intriguing quality directly a function of its redundancy. It is the insignificant partner in the *trivium*, and yet one that, as Michael Wood puts it, 'lingers in the narrative', as if posing a question that no-one actually asks but non-vacuously could.[12] To see why, we need to consider a more complicated picture of the topographical facts, one that yields, minimally, not one but two crossroads on the road from Delphi. The Phocis crossroads is the second one. The first is a diagonal intersecting the Delphi road described by R. Drew Griffith as follows: 'One road runs roughly east–west from the Gulf of Corinth through Delphi to Thebes. The road is intersected at an oblique angle by a road to Daulis to the north-east. This second road continues in a south-westerly direction beyond the intersection to Ambrossus and hence to the sea' (i.e. the Corinthian Gulf).[13]

This account is partly borne out by scholarly cartography of ancient Greece.[14] This would mean that, setting off on the road from Delphi, Oedipus would have not two but four options. At the first crossroads he encounters there is a choice between going north-east to Daulis and going south-west to Ambrossus. Further along, he would come to the Phocis crossroads, where the choice is between either Daulis, though on a different road, or Thebes.[15] These proliferating options provide a field day for counterfactual speculation. Perhaps for this very reason, scholars in the actual field can be curiously categorical in rejecting them as trespassers. The road to Ambrossus is dismissed out of hand by Griffith as even remotely pertinent ('this continuation is not mentioned by Sophocles, is irrelevant, and should be ignored'). It should indeed be ignored (by Oedipus, that is), but for precisely the opposite reason. For Oedipus it is all too relevant as but a hop across the Gulf to Corinth, the place to which he has sworn never to return. This, however, is not the reason adduced by Griffith. For him it is 'irrelevant' because 'not mentioned' by Sophocles. That begs a key question. Is it irrelevant because unmentioned, or the other way round? If the latter (unmentioned because irrelevant), then, since Daulis *is* mentioned, what of its potential 'relevance'? One conventional answer to that question is equally categorical: 'there are no grounds at all for supposing that the road not taken by him, the one to the tiny village of Daulia, was a real possibility.'[16] Sophocles' play is, of course, a literary fiction, and what in these terms will count as a 'possibility' will fundamentally depend on the dramatist's literary purposes. Nevertheless, the assertion that the road to Daulis is not 'a real possibility' is pure assertion, its vulnerability a direct effect of its absoluteness, compounded by the tendentiously anachronistic description of Daulis as a 'tiny village'. That is doubtless what it would be for us, but from an ancient Greek point of view it was a 'town', and one moreover with a certain standing. The fact remains that Sophocles does mention Daulis, and this has to prompt the question why. Is it to make up the talismanic number three, while remaining merely the name of a town at the end of a road that is of no importance precisely because not taken? But just the act of saying that it was not taken is also to say that, without demonstrable impediment or pronounced disinclination, in principle it could have been taken (in at least one later re-telling it *is* taken).[17] There is, of course, one major impediment; it is called 'destiny'. Michel Foucault said brilliantly of Oedipus that 'his destiny was in his feet, under his feet' (rather than to be read in the stars), and that, of course, includes where the feet are to take him (to Thebes).[18] But in situ and from Oedipus's point of view, it doesn't quite look like this.

Laius has a reason for going somewhere in particular (to Delphi). Oedipus, on the other hand, has no reason for going anywhere in particular; his only purpose is negative (not to return to Corinth). He has been given a grim prophecy, but of Thebes he has been told nothing at all. Indeed, he later reflects at Colonus: 'I did not know the way I went. *They* knew; they, who devised this trap for me, they knew!'[19] Irrespective of the prophecy, we can speculate about preferences for Thebes that Oedipus might more ordinarily entertain (for example, drawn by its prestigious reputation as, in the words of the Chorus, 'the City of Light'[20]). On the other hand, Thebes was much closer to Corinth than Daulis (though not as close as Ambrossus).[21] Given what he believes in respect of his parentage, Daulis would be the safer option by virtue of being further away. Daulis, however, has its own off-putting legendary baggage, as home to the Thracian king, Tereus, who is served the flesh of his son, Itys, by his wife, Procne, as revenge for the rape of her sister, Philomela. Since Sophocles wrote a play about Tereus (of which however only fragments survive), we can perhaps assume some awareness on his part of the ironically inverted symmetries (a son slain by a mother and eaten by a father in counterpart to the tale of a father slain by a son who goes on to procreate with his mother).²² But that is a point about Sophocles, not about Oedipus. We are told nothing of the latter's knowledge or feelings on the subject of Daulis, just as we know nothing of any informed preferences that might make him decide in favour of Thebes. We can say that he 'chooses' to go to Thebes, and in a self-evident sense of the term that is indeed what he does. More generally, the question of 'choice' and 'agency' is front and centre of ancient tragedy, provided one avoids the anachronism of back-projecting onto it modern notions of 'choice'. The question of 'choice' at the Phocis crossroads is, however, a special case. The options are not pondered; no 'motives' are involved; it does not, in Vernant's phrase, 'consist in taking council with oneself'.²³ For all Oedipus knows at the time, ending up in Thebes is a matter of pure chance, which is indeed how he himself subsequently describes it ('I who came by chance'). In that sense, Thebes or Daulis are for Oedipus equally meaningful or meaningless options; the toss of a coin or equivalent (typically a shell in ancient Greek gambling) could readily decide the issue.²⁴ What if it were to come down in favour of Daulis, and what might this entail? Is it that everything would come out the same way, consonant with the prophecy and despite everything Oedipus does to prevent its fulfilment? Or is it 'destined' to come up heads however tossed (where heads = Thebes), but Oedipus is not to know that either (it is actually the least of what he does not know). Or is it the juncture at which a redundant loose end becomes what Wood calls a 'loophole', a breach in the story into which the counterfactual makes an appearance, however shadowy, and however much what we take to be the belief-world underpinning the conventions of Sophoclean tragedy would seem to banish it to the realm of the unintelligible (as perhaps inadmissible).

The list of counterfactual speculations that swirl around the Oedipus story is in fact quite long. Some are 'internal', in the sense of articulated by a character. The majority are 'external', prompted by the musings of reader or spectator (questions of anachronism naturally arise here in respect of the historical location of the latter; where a modern spectator might see an alternative possibility an ancient Greek might not have). The most flamboyant are to be found in re-tellings of the tale. In one such tale, Laius, a canny and well-informed king, knowing that oracles can bring terrible news, decides not to go to Delphi. What follows? Lots, anything, nothing? And if something, how to map it? Or what if Oedipus submits to what he thinks is his destiny, returns to Corinth, kills Polybus and sleeps with (a willing) Merope. This is the premise of Dare Clubb's play, *Oedipus*, with however a sensational kicker: when Oedipus asks Merope to marry him, she refuses, on what would normally qualify as unusual grounds but which here simply show respect for the will of the gods and the prediction of the oracle: 'I can't. I'm not your mother.'[25] To these we can add less extravagant examples. As previously noted, Oedipus could have returned to Delphi to demand an answer to the question he asked (more grandly still, the oracle could have supplied it first time round). Once king of Thebes, he could have left the plague to take its course; could have dropped his inquiry into Laius's murder; could have desisted from interrogation of the reluctant Theban herdsman. Indeed he is urged first by Tereisias and later by Jocasta to leave well alone. Tereisias himself twice affirms a counterfactual in respect of his own presence: wisdom consisting in discretion, if he had not momentarily forgotten what he knows, he would not have come to the palace, a remark followed by 'had you not called me, I should not be here'.

Then there are Oedipus's own 'what ifs', most notably in the twice expressed view that, if he had been left to die on the hillside, 'less ruin had I brought on me and mine', a thought further developed in a manner that wipes out the entire prophesy ('I had not then come and slain my father. Nor then would men have called me husband of her that bore me'). Whether these count as true counterfactuals is moot. They reflect less a view of options than a wish, that is, they are less 'what ifs' than 'if onlys', expressions of regret, anger, and despair mixed with futile lamentations; they resemble more complaints than expressions of a genuine belief that things could actually have been otherwise. As for the others (the 'external' ones), there is also the problem of limits, given that backwards extension in time can go on indefinitely (the potential downside, we have seen, of all counterfactual antecedent-switching).[26] Thus, Laius could have heeded the first consultation at Delphi and resolutely refrained from copulation. Cadmus, the founder of Thebes, could have ... and so on, and on. In any case, they are all fruitless. Fate decides ('Fate whose all-powerful sway weaves out the world's design', as the Chorus has it in Aeschylus' *Eumenides*), and 'fate' is often (especially in Aeschylus) synonymous with 'curse', a malediction that is both inescapable and ultimately incomprehensible, an enigmatic flaw at the heart of being.

What seems to preclude all these options, in both the Oedipus story and the ancient Greek world generally, is what, in *Shame and Necessity*, Bernard Williams calls the Greek 'sense of prearranged necessity'. The precise wording here is instructive. 'Sense of' is less committed, more hesitant than 'belief in', and takes us towards the shape of a paradox to which Williams gives the interesting name of 'modal bewilderment'. To be modally bewildered suggests a confused relation to the counterfactual, at once evoking it without invoking it. It is a logico-grammatical summary of what it is simultaneously to gesture at a meaningful alternative while ensuring that there is nowhere for a meaningful alternative to lodge. Williams illustrates the paradox with two Sophoclean examples: Ajax and Oedipus. The former presents the (for us, but for us only?) unmanageable thought that there might have been a way out of Ajax dying on the day fixed by Athena precisely because there was one (strenuously enjoined by the Chorus), except that there wasn't. There couldn't be one because Athena had determined that Ajax will die on the day in question. On the other hand, the option presented by the Chorus (his brother keeping him in the tent all day), and the retrospective counterfactual it sustains, cannot simply be ignored. Similarly, we can run a thought-experiment that counterfactually assumes that Laius and Jocasta do not get rid of their son at birth, but keep and raise him. 'Can we say that, if he had stayed at home, he would still have grown up to kill his father? Perhaps we can,' writes Williams. But equally, this deviation from the standard plot line can 'perhaps' mean that he doesn't kill his father, in which case his parents can't keep him after all; the principle of 'prearranged necessity' demands that he be sent away if that is a condition of fulfilling the prophecy and the will of Apollo. In order to ensure that Oedipus kills Laius, the story has to 'kill speculation about alternatives'.[27]

In short, while the counterfactual may have the appearance of pressuring the view that things had to turn out the way they did, in fact their purpose or effect is paradoxically to tighten the principle of necessity it notionally questions. These are the paradoxes of a culture in which, at least in its archaic forms, 'counterfactual thought runs into the ground even more readily than it does ordinarily'.[28] But, while that may be true, 'readily' is not the same as 'conclusively', just as 'sense of' is not the same as 'belief in'. It is intrinsic to the paradox that it can proceed in reverse; out of, as well as into, the ground. If this is a universe of thought and representation geared to 'the suppression of possibilities', why would a key expression of that outlook – tragedy – also be visited by something called 'modal bewilderment'? What is there here, in the register of 'could', 'might' or 'would', that is bewildering? Perhaps then the gearing of the (infernal) machine can also open up where it is supposed to close down. It is not that there is no place for thinking the alternative, but – a very different point – that whatever and wherever that place is, it remains shrouded in darkness, in 'the obscurity involved, for us as much as for any ancient Greek, in thinking determinately about what might have been'.[29] This is why the whole business around the question of fate, chance, choice and agency is 'bewildering'. Once the modal genie is out of the bottle, it is very hard to get it back in again.[30]

The bottle is that chronically unstable intermediary that is supposed to be the unmediated voice of the divine, and thus the reliable source for the credibility of a necessity-governed order, namely the Oracle. 'Sweet is the voice of the god that sounds in the Golden shrine of Delphi,' intones the Chorus, to which Creon adds the virtue of clarity ('I will tell you what Apollo said and it was very clear'). The view that oracles were in reality unclear, treacherously deceptive, because characteristically equivocal, does not hold for all or even the majority of the cases we know of. But among those that most detain us, many are either ambiguous or amphibological.[31] The oracular utterance is, we might say, the verbal cognate of the physical crossroads, built to branch out in multiple interpretive directions at the moment of consultation. In these cases, the decision as to which direction is the correct one rests with the terminal moment of the prophecy's fulfilment rather than the inaugural moment of its utterance. The latter is thus less about the future than (in Wood's felicitous summary) 'about what used to be the future', a kind of verbal time machine built for travel to a future past. It claims to foretell but in practice backtells, serving up as tautological 'proof' that what happened had to happen the fact that it did happen. Since hindsight is the property which ensures that the oracle is (nearly) always right, it is what most efficiently responds to the imperative that it *has* to be right. But along with ex post adjustment of prediction to outcome, the oracle could also operate as a hedging mechanism, holding alternatives in reserve in case they were needed to 'explain' the outcome in a manner consistent with the forecast. That kind of flexibility meant that in effect they were able to say that such-and-such will happen, but may not, or vice-versa. In short, oracles traffic in what might have been as well as in what will be.[32]

This brings us back, with the walking Oedipus, to the crossroads and the fork which leads to Daulis. The latter is surplus to requirements; indeed its absence would simplify matters in rendering a further counterfactual otiose (the one centred on timing: what if Oedipus had arrived at the crossroads before Laius did?). This, more generally, is tantamount to saying

– it has been said more than once – that the crossroads itself is surplus to requirements, at once unnecessary and undesirable (as a pointless circumstantial complication).[33] This does not, however, mean that the crossroads lacks significance, just that one has to look for it elsewhere. There are several places one can go looking. Stephen Halliwell directs us to one, with the argument that, as the foully evil place Oedipus cannot recall without a shudder of dread, it has less to do with Apollo's decrees than with the more primitive powers associated with Hecate in popular mythology (he also notes that Potniae, where Aeschylus locates the crossroads, was connected with Hecate).[34] Another interpretation – the one to bring into focus here – has the crossroads as the jewel in the crown of Sophocles' obsession with the number three ('a thicket of threes' is how one commentator has described the play).[35] Daulis is simultaneously the trivial yet non-trivial term of the *trivium*, trivial because there is no compelling reason to take it and yet non-trivial because, being there, it could have been taken and there is no reason not to. It is the material form of a question mark in the form of an implied modal, hovering over the story as a kind of mute beckoning to an alternative outcome (escape from the grip of the curse on the house of Cadmus). This is the thought about Oedipus's story that is both absurd and irresistible.[36]

# III

When wandering with Petrarch, there is likely to come a moment when you light upon the splendidly named Dionigi da Borgo San Sepolcro. 'The Ascent of Mont Ventoux' is dedicated to him. Of deep Augustinian persuasions, he was Petrarch's confessor in Avignon, a scholar and a teacher, who wrote a commentary, now lost, on Seneca's plays (Seneca's letters were a major influence on Petrarch) and taught some of the works of Boccaccio. Did he, one might ask, include the latter's *Misfortunes of Illustrious Men*, which has a chapter on the Oedipus story from the point of view of Jocasta? In any case, it seems reasonable to assume some familiarity with the story on Petrarch's part. Then imagine a truly outlandish form of 'magic realism' or a Calvino-style tale in which Oedipus and Petrarch meet on the road and briefly converse. Petrarch says something he will later commit to writing (in *Familiares*, the title he gave to his first collection of letters): 'There is nothing worse for a traveller than not to know where he is going.' Some version or other of 'it takes one to know one' might be the response here. They might also find themselves swapping notes on the topic of crossroads and the problem of 'choice', though with considerable divergence on the terms in which the problem is to be understood. Oedipus walks to lose something (his fate), Petrarch to find something (himself). They would, however, surely find common ground in the experiencing of their respective lives as riddle-strewn.

A letter of 1340 is written from what Petrarch calls 'this craggy place', his home in the Vaucluse, the area of France dominated by the so-called *géant de Provence*, Mont Ventoux, whose slopes, paths and summit are the setting of the second of my three vignettes. In it Petrarch speaks of being on the receiving end of two other letters, the upshot of which is that 'I find myself at a critical crossroads, and do not know which way to turn'.[37] The cause of this conundrum was itself strictly occasional, with Petrarch delightfully (and delightedly) caught between two prestigious invitations (one from the Senate in Rome to be crowned poet laureate, the other an invitation from the University of Paris; he chose to go to Rome). In context, the expression 'critical crossroads' can be little more than a mildly jocular conceit around an enviable choice of honours and recognitions. If we are also invited (we sometimes are) to view it as striking a more profound note, that is unlikely to survive other, more dyspeptic applications of the 'critical' (for example, Gibbon's witheringly sarcastic take on the belaurelled Petrarch). On the other hand, the 'critical crossroads' is a key Petrarchan theme, in relation to both deeply felt personal dilemmas (where not knowing which way to turn often resembles a permanent spinning in the wind), and his historical moment. In European cultural and literary history, there are few associated more routinely and in so many ways with the image of the crossroads than Petrarch. He is quintessentially a 'crux' figure, at the junction of the middle ages (he was the first to describe them as the 'Dark Ages') and Renaissance humanism, between languages (Latin and Italian), looking back to antiquity while opening a path to the modern (one of the 'first truly modern men', in Burckhardt's famous description).[38] What it means to call Petrarch 'modern' is, of course, much debated (Burckhardt specifically linked it to Petrarch's alleged 'receptivity' to the natural world). Petrarch looked backwards as much as forwards, and when he famously said 'I am alive now, but I would rather have been born at some other time', the counterfactual drift of the implied 'if only' is difficult to locate in time – back to classical antiquity or forwards to a fully post-mediaeval world? (Most bets would be on the former.) For present purposes, 'modern' is to be taken here as marking the emergence of a sensibility geared to inwardness, perplexity, and – central to the role of the counterfactual at the Petrarchan crossroads – the play of 'chance' (genuine or staged, we shall never know) that takes place at the summit of Mont Ventoux.

Petrarch was a prodigious traveller, with a pronounced fondness for travelling on foot, and Petrarch the walker is also a figure who seems to face many ways.[39] There is perhaps a proto-humanist homage to the philosopher Peripatetics of antiquity, an echo of the late mediaeval pilgrim (Chaucer claimed to have met him in Padua), and a foretaste of the Romantic 'ramble', walking for pleasure in communion with Nature (Petrarch claims to have walked to the top of Mont Ventoux simply for the sake of the walk, though, as we shall see this is manifestly disingenuous; what most appeals is the view). He is in fact closer to the spirit of Romanticism as one of the inventors of the introspective walk later cultivated by Rousseau in the *Rêveries d'un promeneur solitaire* and Wordsworth in the *Prelude*. Petrarchan introspection in part corresponds to what he called 'care of the mind', something of a classical virtue tinged with Christian self-examination,[40] but which could also become so wrought that it often resembles what in the Romantic period would be described as a ravaging malady of the soul. The full title of his most 'confessional' work, the *Secretum* is *De secreto conflictu curarum mearum*. The key term here is 'conflicts', anguished, intractable and perhaps irresolvable, the stage of the self as enigma because incurably divided.

The walk for which Petrarch is best known was notionally upwards, but, to be more precise, was more a mix of the upwards and the sideways (the mix important to the allegorical purposes to which the account of the walk was put). This was the ascent of Mont Ventoux on Good Friday 1336 in the company of his brother, Guerardo, and two servants, and recorded in the form of a nearly 6,000-word 'letter' in Latin addressed to Dionigi. Questions of 'authenticity' have always swirled around its status as an epistolary record, and there have even been doubts as to whether the walk actually took place. In the text itself, Petrarch improbably claims to have written it immediately after the descent, before dinner at a nearby inn in Malaucène. He may have sketched a draft, elaborating it much later for publication in the *Familiares* and many years after the death of Dionigi, who thus becomes more a dedicatee than an addressee. There seems now to be a consensus view of it as, largely if not entirely, a 'fiction' in disguise. This would seem, at least to the secular mind, the only way to make sense of what happens at the summit.

The walk pivots on the different paths taken by Petrarch and Guerardo. The brother strikes out more or less straight to the top, whereas Petrarch opts for a zig-zag route of detours and loopings. Although neither involves a crossroads, the spatial differences and journey rhythms yield a set of terms that stand for, or can be mapped onto, inward dispositions: steep/level, narrow/wide, direct/circuitous, easy/difficult, fast/slow. Petrarch's digressive rhythm is moralized as a sign of 'laziness' in contrast to his brother's steadfastness, but then, in a characteristic Petrarchan twirl, is paradoxically tweaked: the 'easy' way becomes the 'long' way and thus the more 'difficult' ('I wandered about hollows in the mountainside looking for an easier long way round and ended up in profound difficulties').[41] Exhausted, he pauses, his thoughts switching 'from corporeal to incorporeal matters', thoughts of the 'life we call happy ... and narrow is the way, as they say, that leads to it'. The 'easy' path of lower earthly pleasures' is contrasted with 'the journey of the spirit which keeps me sighing day and night'. The metaphorical 'summit' of the latter is then assimilated to the actual one and the effort required in getting there ('these reflections stirred me mentally and physically to get on with the remainder of the climb').

'The Ascent to Mont Ventoux' has been described as 'one of the great texts that oscillate indecisively between the epochs, namely between the mediaeval period and modernity'.[42] Before rejoining Petrarch at the summit, we can capture a sense of this oscillation by means of a detour of our own, via three figures who can be said to preside over Petrarch's journey of body and soul. One is explicitly present, namely Augustine, and we shall return to him later. He serves as Petrarch's near constant companion, interlocutor, and foil, above all in the *Secretum*, that cross between a confessional dialogue and a scholastic debate in which Augustine participates in the construction of the Petrarchan self as a kind of inner tribunal. The other two are unnamed (one of them arguably repressed). The first and more readily accessible in the strands of Petrarch's text is the Hercules of the Two Paths (of Vice and Virtue). An object of suspicion throughout early and mediaeval Christianity for doctrinal reasons (principally to do with the theology of *dea virtus* according to which only Christ can represent God's principle of true Virtue), the story is sometimes said to have been rescued by Petrarch and sent on its way to its place of centrality in the Renaissance. He wandered freely in the ancient sources, to the point where, in the unfinished chapter on Hercules for Book 2 of *De Viris Illustribus* (*On Illustrious Men*), he confessed to feeling 'as if entangled in the windings of a labyrinth'. There were, he also said, 'many Herculean men', but his own interest unfolded on broadly two fronts. In the epic poem, *Africa*, and guided mainly by Livy, Petrarch associates Hercules with Scipio Africanus, the exemplary hero of the Roman republic and embodiment of manly civic virtue.[43] In the more personal *De vita solitaria* (*On the solitary life*), the focus is more on Hercules in a coming of age parable. Here Petrarch resurrects the story recounted in Xenophon's *Memorabilia* and retold by Cicero, while importing both the symbol of the Pythagorean ypsilon as representing a *bivium* and relatedly the image of the crossroads (neither the ypsilon nor the crossroads have any place in the ancient versions).[44] In *De vita solitaria* Hercules hesitates and then chooses the right path: 'hesitating long and hard as though at a parting of the ways, he ultimately spurned the way of pleasure and took possession of the path of virtue.' But for Petrarch the hesitating ('long and hard') counts as much as the deciding. On the inherited scene of virtue embraced is superimposed a scene of question and doubt. This is one of the major forms in which the Hercules story will travel into the later Renaissance, and reflects one of the ways in which we can speak of Petrarch as 'modern'.

The third figure, altogether more obscurely present, is Dante. In the entire Petrarchan corpus, Dante is a near blank. Petrarch claimed (stretching the credible to breaking point) not to have read the *Commedia* until sent a copy in 1351 by Boccaccio with a letter urging him to read it. Eight years later he wrote in turn to Boccaccio to repudiate any affinity with or imitation of Dante. Many things lay behind this insistent distancing. One explanation is that he simply did not know what to do with Dante. Part of the difficulty turned on a perception of differing agendas in a form of culture war (humanist as against mediaeval, Latin as against vernacular). Less disinterestedly, there was doubtless the fear – an acute case of 'anxiety of influence' – of being eclipsed by the 'illustrious' predecessor that Petrarch, fuelled by the desire for laurel-garlanded fame and glory, least needed.[45] This is one of the two worldly vices with which he is charged by Augustinus in the *Secretum*.[46] The other is carnal desire, and very possibly the real nub of his difficulty with Dante, the shorthand name for which is a proper name: 'Beatrice', and the complex legacy her place in the *Commedia* transmits to the question Petrarch carries with him nearly everywhere, including on the climb to the summit of Mont Ventoux, the question of 'Laura'.

For someone so caught up in a drama of carnality and spirituality played out symbolically in various 'crossroads' scenarios ('do I go this way, do I go that?'), it would be truly astonishing if Petrarch had not been struck by the famous opening line of the *Commedia*, with Dante on the 'road of life' wandering into a 'dark forest where the straight way was lost' and doing so at the road's 'middle' point, with all its connotations of a time of 'crisis'. Dante issues from the forest onto the slope of a mountain, takes the upward path towards the light, is blocked by three beasts (the emblematic wolf, leopard and lion), is rescued by Virgil who acts as his guide down into the circles of Inferno, then upwards once more through *Purgatorio* (also figured as a mountain),[47] and finally ascending to the blissful realm of *Paradiso*. For this last stage of his journey he has a new guide, the radiant Beatrice, all lustful desire for her not so much denied as distilled and sublimated. The parallels with Petrarch's story are obvious, but it is the difference that is fundamental. Dante described Beatrice as 'the glorious lady of my mind'. Laura too dominates the Petrarchan mind, as a construction that Petrarch sought to anchor in the ideal of *otium* (peace of mind) he found in Cicero, but which constantly escaped the realm of mind to return to the agitated and 'infernal' realm of the body, as if he were locked in a prison from which there is no escape. There was, however, one other escape route to try, though it also proves to be blocked. This takes us back to Mont Ventoux and to the strange drama that takes place at its summit.

Of the two invisible travelling companions accompanying Petrarch on his walk, Hercules is readily identifiable in the tracks and traces of the text (specifically in the resonances of the distinction between the 'steep' and the 'easy' paths). Dante is elusive as if but one of his own shades, the unwanted and uninvited ghost that nevertheless hovers over the scene. The other companion, however, is fully visible, explicitly named and given an active role as potential liberator from the prison-house: Augustine. At the summit Petrarch admiringly takes in the spectacular view, while also conscious that this is but worldly distraction, pleasure in material things. This thought also brings to mind an earlier and still unresolved struggle:

> It is not yet three years since that vile perversion of the will that did have total control of me and reigned alone and unchallenged in every chamber of my heart found a contrary side of my will rebelling and resisting its power. Since then my thoughts have been a battlefield on

which the two sides have been joined in a wearying struggle for control over the divided man that I am, and the struggle still goes on unresolved.

The object of this still unresolved struggle is, of course, a fourth unnamed travelling companion, or perhaps more accurately a very heavy piece of psychological 'baggage': Laura. The 'rebellious opponent' is someone who has been listening carefully to Augustine. And, perchance, Petrarch has with him a pocketbook copy of the *Confessions*, given to him by Dionigi. He takes it out. What follows is an act of emulation, the repeat of a precedent, and the form of which is literally a bookish roll of the dice. Petrarch does with the *Confessions* what, in the *Confessions*, Augustine tells us he did with the Bible that was to prove the vital turning-point in his 'conversion'. Petrarch also opens his book randomly: 'I opened it ready to read whatever presented itself.' It would, of course, have been a 'coincidence' too far (with perhaps more than a hint of the stage-managed that in fact hangs over the entire narrative of the Ascent) if Petrarch had opened the *Confessions* at the point where Augustine recounts having blindly opened the Bible at St Paul's *Epistle to the Romans* with its exhortation to abandon the works of the flesh. He will indeed shortly refer us to this passage. The actual 'coincidence', though less too-good-to-be-true, is nonetheless a handy one: the *Confessions* falls open at the page where Augustine speaks of the folly of admiring 'earthly wonders', included in which – this is the stress point of credibility – are mountain peaks. Looking around him at spectacular mountain tops and enjoying the view is an index of what Petrarch must renounce. But the true, and impossible, object of renunciation that underlies this censoring of innocent visual pleasure is, of course, Laura, never reducible to but always implicated in the more powerful currents of carnal desire.

The descent takes place in thoughtful silence, Petrarch reflecting on the vanity of 'looking in the outer world for what could have been found within'. However, the reflection is not at all the same as a resolution. When at the inn he sits down to compose his account for Dionigi, he speaks not of focused resolve but of 'these vain and wandering thoughts' that may one day become 'coherent'. The Augustinian experiment at the summit of Ventoux is not a 'win'. In the *Secretum*, however persuaded he is by Augustinus, Franciscus remains elsewhere, in this world, here below with Laura: 'I cannot get beyond it.' In the poem 'I'vo pensando', which opens the second part of *Rerum Vulgarium Fragmenta*, the complex struggle with 'desire' is centre stage, closing with a citation from Ovid's telling of the Medea story in Metamorphoses, in which it is difficult not to hear also a downcast allusion to Hercules's choice: 'I can see which is the better, but still incline towards the worse.' 'Incline', of course, is not 'choose'. It's the position of hesitation, and, unlike Hercules (at least prior to Carracci's painting), of being congenitally unable to choose.[48] For all its insistently uplifting notes, 'The Ascent of Mont Ventoux' ends inconclusively, a quest narrative without a safe haven, or a spiritual journey whose central dilemma finds no solution, neither Dante-esque sublimation nor Augustinian repression. Both offered models of a Christian answer to the problem of desire; neither works. This is perhaps one of the things that makes Petrarch 'a modern man', as someone who, despite his Christian faith, is at the edge of immersion in the secular though unable fully to assume it. He is the self-interrogating sceptic stranded at the crossroads, the doubting subject lost in an endless soliloquy. He is 'modern' as an 'identity' never sure of its ground, always unfinished, forever a process of searching and making.

In connection with the repeat throw of the dice at the summit of Mont Ventoux, there are two things we perhaps most carry away from the tale of the ascent, both of which have a bearing on what it means to call Petrarch 'modern'. One has to do with the repeat, the other with the throw. The emulation of Augustine repeats not only a precedent but also one which itself repeats a precedent (as Petrarch notes, Augustine's moment with the Bible echoes St Anthony, though the latter case turns on what Anthony hears at Mass, not on what he randomly finds in a book). The particular point here meshes with a larger one, namely the sheer wealth of learning that Petrarch carries with him wherever he goes. The 'Ascent' is no exception. Where *Oedipus Tyrannus* has been called a 'thicket of threes', the 'Ascent', drenched in erudition, has appositely been called a 'thicket of learned strategies and references'.[49] The impressive learning, tokens of a nascent humanism, can however also be seen as a burden, a weight of knowledge that can befog the mind rather than clear it. You can read too much (Augustinus accuses him of just this: 'What good has all your reading done you?'), and think too much. In its more elaborated forms it becomes a thick overlay of sophistication, weighing on, inhibiting and ultimately paralysing the self of decision and action, what much later Hegel was to diagnose as the Unhappy Consciousness of the moderns.

Second, the throw: if you don't know which fork to take (or do know but can't make the decision to take it), why not toss a coin, roll the dice, or open a book in the way one might arbitrarily take a card from the deck face down? Petrarch seems to have felt a certain uneasiness in respect of this apparent gamble on chance. 'As God is my witness' is how he announces the place in the *Confessions* he has stumbled on. Indeed, not just a witness, it seems, but Augustine's words as also the implied agent of the preordained: 'I couldn't believe they had come up by chance. What I had read I thought had been addressed to me and to no-one else,' a belief buttressed by noting that this is what both Augustine and St Anthony believed of what they respectively read or heard (thus strength in authoritative numbers as a counter to the random numbers of the gamble). There are several frames of reference Petrarch could have drawn on to sustain this belief in providential intervention, for example, the practice of the *sortes virgilianae* (one commentator has explicitly compared the Mont Ventoux episode to them), equivalents of which were to be found in the divinatory use of other sacred texts including the Bible.[50] This in turn might suggest something akin to the oracle, although in the unfinished *Rerum memorandarum* Petrarch dismisses oracles from the point of view of the Christian critique of oral utterance as demonic (while also trying to rescue the Apolline 'voice' for purer things).[51] Or he could have gone by way of Fortuna, especially since one of the dialogues between Reason and Joy in *De remediis utriusque fortunae* (*Remedies for Fortune, Fair and Foul*) is devoted to Gambling. Joy likes gambling, especially when she wins. Reason, on the other hand, brings to it the denunciatory energies of a hellfire preacher. Gambling is a 'gaping cesspool', affording the 'dismal pleasures of a filthy and corrupt mind'; the gaming table is the 'kingdom of all vices', and its 'inventor' is 'some creature from hell'.

It is no surprise then that Petrarch goes out of his way to dissociate what he does with the *Confessions* from any association with a punt on Lady Fortuna. But this is exactly what it is, and Petrarch knows it. This may explain why he hedges by converting his gamble into a one-way bet with a guaranteed spiritual win: after telling us that he opens the book 'ready to read whatever presented itself', he immediately adds 'which I knew, of course, could only be something expressing pious thoughts and religious devotion'. It is, however, only under certain belief-conditions that this could possibly be true. Suppose that, at this decisive crossroads moment of the Petrarchan pilgrimage, he had instead opened the *Confessions* at the page where Augustine reports having prayed in connection with the renunciation of carnal appetite: 'Lord, make me pure, but not yet." And if Petrarch had landed on this passage rather than the one urging Pauline denial of the flesh? This is the counterfactual that subtends Petrarch's game of chance, one moreover that would leave Petrarch in the place that almost comes naturally to him, suspended in the deferral of the 'not-yet'. It suggests an alternative descent from the summit of Mont Ventoux, lost in a very different kind of silence, brooding on Laura, but perhaps also, as the true first of the early humanists, on the fact that the Greek gods themselves were not averse to gambling.[52] In the meantime, debates about Fortuna and Providence had a long post-mediaeval life ahead of them, in the religious and secular thought of the sixteenth century. It is here that we come to our third 'crossroads' story, that of Ignatius of Loyola, where the die is not a book but a horse. An irrelevant but appealing footnote is one we could imagine as immensely agreeable to Joy in the guise of an erudite man of the turf: in the late nineteenth century, a thoroughbred called Petrarch won, in the space of three years, the 2000 Guineas, the St Leger, and the Epsom Derby.

## IV

Along with Petrarch, Ignatius of Loyola is one of the great walkers of early modern Europe. But whereas for Petrarch walking was inspired by the ancient association of walking and thinking allied to the difficult task of the 'care of the mind', for Ignatius it was part of the fiercely self-punishing regimes of a radical form of Christian spiritual hygiene that included fasting, abrasive clothing, flagellation, and walking's opposite (seven hours a day on one's knees praying). For the lay reader this can be hard to take. However anguished the Petrarchan agonistics of the soul, they are usually leavened with a kind of sweetness; weeping over Laura for example (in the *Canzoniere*) is mitigated by proximity to the sweet waters (the 'chiare, fresche e dolci acque') of the Fontaine du Vaucluse. The terms and tone of the struggles described by Ignatius of Loyola in his autobiography are very different, often plain repellent, body and soul wallowing in what to the secular mind resembles a masochistic drama of ecstatic abjection.[53] When, in Chapter I of the *Autobiography* (narrated throughout in the third person), Ignatius speaks of the 'desire of penance', we should give special weight to the term 'desire'. It seems to be insatiable, and will return throughout. Whatever Ignatius inflicts on himself, it is never enough; like a criminal repeatedly revisiting the scene of his crimes, he always comes back for more. Nowhere is this more visibly the case than in connection with the formal rituals designed to relieve him of the burdens of sinfulness: confession and absolution. These also are but preludes or halfway houses, invariably accompanied by the nagging worry that he has not confessed to everything; however detailed his list of transgressions (these can include 'thoughts' of bread or 'visions' of meat when fasting), in the farthest recesses of his contaminated soul there is always another sin lurking, to be rooted out, exposed and expunged. In Montserrat, he spends three full days writing out his confession and 'with great diligence and care had tried to make sure it was complete'. But apparently he has not tried hard enough: 'yet he always felt that he had forgotten something in his confession, and this caused him much anxiety.'[54]

Thus we enter another Ignatian torture chamber, whose principal instrument is the prospect of confession without end, a task at once inexhaustible for Ignatius and exhausting for his confessors, constantly brought face to face with the apparent inefficacy of the powers of absolution with which they are charged. There were times when his priestly interlocutors were understandably exasperated, and we can only sympathize when one confessor, anticipating unedited endlessness, both sensibly and self-protectively 'commanded him to confess nothing of his past life except what was very clear and evident' (another 'bade him break his fast', for the very good reason that otherwise there would be no Ignatius to confess). The command is naturally obeyed – for just two days during which he finds himself happily 'free from scruples'. 'On the third day', however, 'the remembrance of his sins came back to him. One suggested another, until he passed in review, one after another, all his past sins.' No surprise, of course, if 'he then thought he ought to repeat his general confession'. Mercifully for all concerned, he has an illumination, the consequence of which is that 'he resolved never again to speak of his past sins in confession. From that day he was free from scruples, and felt certain that it was the will of our merciful Lord to deliver him from his trouble of soul.' This was to become one of the foundations of Ignatian spirituality and one of the guiding principles of the *Spiritual Exercises*, linked to the view that thoughts of our sins are often sent by the devil and thus best cleared from the mind and consigned to oblivion. In the shorter term, however, it is no surprise if this determination also does not survive for long. When he falls seriously ill in Manresa, 'he cried out to some noble ladies who had come to visit him, and asked them, for the love of God, to cry out aloud the next time they should find him near death, "O sinner!" and "Remember the sins by which you have offended God."'

The *Autobiography* is itself that cause's greatest fan; it never fails to 'remember' and is often manically inventive in devising ways of satisfying 'the desire of penance'.[55] But where this leaves the 'will of our merciful Lord' in the shaping of Ignatius's journey has to remain a question if – as his report illustrates over and over – the very last thing that has been 'delivered' is permanent release 'from the trouble of his soul'. We are told that 'he felt certain' that this was God's work, but what can be the grounds of certainty when so often the least enduringly reliable thing in Ignatius's own self-description is what he 'felt' at any one time of vision-based emancipation? One of the standout features of Ignatius's story, the one which sheds most light on his obsessions and compulsions, is the sense of uncertainty. The path as road to a life in Christ may be a salvational bed of nails, but it is also strewn with doubts, as if each trial and each crisis were a crossroads moment at which a decision has to be made, and then explained and justified after the event. Reference to divine guidance occurs at several of the key turning-points of Ignatius's story and is absolutely crucial in connection with the decisive journey recounted in Chapter II of the *Autobiography*. This is the journey – not on foot but on horseback (in some versions a mule) – from his native Loyola to Montserrat, and where, at a crossroads, the horse plays a crucial part in a tale of vocation and providence that has nevertheless all the appearance of being the embodiment of pure contingency.[56]

The back story, narrated in the opening chapter, has Ignatius's swaggering career as a high-born soldier – rambunctious, womanizing, violent – come to an effective end when, seriously injured in the siege of Pamplona, he is repatriated to his native Loyola, where, after agonizing surgery and a long convalescence, he undergoes a spiritual conversion. Hitherto 'the heart of Ignatius was enthralled by the vanities of this world', especially the 'empty desire of gaining for himself a great name' nourished by the 'military life'. While convalescing, he asks for his favourite reading matter, 'some romances' (tales of the chivalric warrior-knights). Instead he is given a Life of Christ and a Lives of the Saints. His thoughts continue to wander, sometimes to 'holy things', sometimes to what 'he had been accustomed to dwell on before'. The latter include images of 'an illustrious lady' and the wish to 'please her, with all the chivalric-erotic undertones that a taste for the 'romances' would imply. The former gravitate to ideas of 'divine mercy' and visitation by another set of images, an 'image of the Blessed Mother of God with the Infant Jesus'. Although unstated, there is a theological subtext here that has much to do with the struggle between Reformation and Counter-Reformation. Where Luther accorded primacy to the ear ('the only organ of the Christian'), for Loyola it is 'visions' that are paramount; there are many recorded in the *Autobiography*. This one, we are told, proves crucial in ridding Ignatius henceforth of 'the least motion of concupiscence'. He further speculates that this spontaneous and enduring effect points to divine intervention, the visitation described as a gift from God ('we may suppose' it 'to have been a divine gift'). But Ignatius then adds a rider, a qualification that will take us to the very heart of the dilemma at the crossroads. It may be inferred that this is God's gift 'though we dare not state it, nor say anything except confirm what has already been said'. Not daring is partly a function of humility, but also a function of uncertainty. On several subsequent occasions in the *Autobiography*, Ignatius will invoke the 'will of the Lord' as if this self-evidently explains and justifies what befalls him. As we approach the critical juncture of Ignatius's narrative, we would do well therefore to remember this moment of hesitation before the 'dare' of assuming knowledge of God's plans for us (if any).

Ignatius's convalescence in Loyola can be described as the first 'crossroads' experience of his story, reflected in the oscillation between the two kinds of images and visions and issuing in the resolve to undertake the journey to Montserrat, where he will give up his life as a soldier to become a priest, subsequently the founder of the Jesuit order and ultimately a saint. The journey in turn brings two further crossroads moments, one mental, the other physical. While on the road, Ignatius encounters a Muslim traveller (a 'Saracen' in the text), characterized as 'an event that occurred during this journey to show the manner in which God directed him'. They enter into a conversation 'in the course of' which 'mention was made of the Blessed Virgin'. The 'mention' rapidly modulates into oddly abstruse theology: the 'Saracen' has no difficulty with the Mother of Christ having 'conceived without detriment to her virginal purity', but, for reasons that are unexplained, has a very hard time crediting that 'after the conception of her divine Son she was still a virgin'. Ignatius tries to argue him out of this impasse (the grounds of his own case also unexplained[57]), but the Saracen 'was so obstinate in holding this opinion that no amount of reasoning on the part of Ignatius could force him to abandon it. Shortly afterward the Saracen rode on, leaving the pilgrim to his own reflection.' This creates an instant dilemma for Ignatius. He is still nominally a soldier, and a Christian one. The traditional duty of a Christian soldier, exemplified by the mediaeval Crusades, is to avenge all insults to the Virgin Mary by putting the 'infidel' to death.[58] He 'consequently felt impelled by a strong impulse to hasten after him and slay the miscreant for the insulting language he had used'. But then, as if caught in indecision at a moral crossroads, Ignatius hesitates: 'After much internal conflict with these thoughts, he still remained in doubt, nor could he decide which course to follow.' If the reader catches echoes of the Hercules story here, that would make perfect sense (despite misgivings in Rome and orthodox Catholicism, the story was much used for educational purposes in the Jesuit schools). Not being able to decide is also, and crucially, the tenor of what follows, at the physical crossroads. This is the passage on which the entire story pivots:

> The Saracen, who had ridden on, had mentioned to him that it was his intention to proceed to a town not far distant from the high road. At length, wearied by his inward struggle and not arriving at any determination, he decided to settle all his doubts in the following novel way: he would give free reign to his horse, and if, on coming to the crossroad, his horse should turn into the path that led to the destination of the Moor, he would pursue and kill him; but, if his horse kept to the highroad, he would allow the wretch to escape. Having done as he decided, it happened through the Providence of God that his horse kept to the highroad.

'It happened... that the horse kept to the high road.' A sentence in this form would normally be one way of saying that this was how the cards fell, 'it happened' as happenstance. But reinsert the key missing words ('through the Providence of God') and we have the cards dealt by an omniscient Dealer, who knows in advance how they will fall, who has indeed stacked the deck to secure a particular outcome, namely the taking of the 'high' road which is also the 'right' road. The sceptic might say that, however sincere Ignatius's beliefs, this has all the air of a rigged narrative, but if so, it is in a highly unusual form. Compare the turning-point moment with a further instance of the citing of divine will. Much later in the *Autobiography*, Ignatius tells of his abortive project to do the Lord's work in the Holy Land. Here above all is where God's calling is heard loud and clear (Ignatius has previously spoken to his confessor of 'his great desire to go to Jerusalem, and to do everything for the greater glory of God'). Once there, 'he decided to remain in Jerusalem'. This decision is, however, countermanded by representatives of the Holy See. There is thus a quandary: it is his duty as a Christian to remain; it is his duty to obey the orders of his Church superiors. There is no obvious way to adjudicate this conflict. On the other hand, to defy his superiors would be awkward. The dilemma is once again resolved from above: 'God did not wish him to remain in Jerusalem' and 'since the Divine Will would not suffer him to remain', he leaves. But if that looks like convenient rationalization providing safe passage out of a tight spot, at least the 'decision' to leave is nominally taken by Ignatius himself.

This is not what occurs at the Montserrat crossroads. Or rather Ignatius does in fact 'decide', but in the paradoxical form of a decision not to decide, delegating the question of how 'to settle all his doubts by giving free reign to his horse'. One is reminded here of the Confucian saying '(deciding what not to do) is as important as deciding what to do', except that here, in a gesture of paradoxical negation, what is decided not to do is to decide oneself. Ignatius's horse thus assumes his master's agency, but in what sense can a horse be said to 'decide', especially at a point that is to have such momentous consequences, not just for Ignatius but for the future of the Catholic order. There were, of course, precedents, although the ones that spring immediately to mind deliver a discouragingly mixed message. There is the Biblical example of Balaam in the Book of Numbers, whose ass is allegedly guided by Jehovah on the road to Moab, but, as himself a diviner, Balaam could be said to have had a vested interest. The source closest to hand was deeply implicated in the 'romances' Ignatius enjoyed but has now abjured: Cervantes' Don Quixote, happy with 'leaving it to his horse's discretion to go which way he pleased ... believing that in this consisted the very being of adventures'. In context, 'discretion' is wonderfully discreet, but 'adventures', however represented, is not really the category Ignatius most needs for his tale of pilgrimage and initiation. The Don's horse is a gamble on waywardness in choosing the way, a surrender to the adventitious pleasures of chance and contingency. Ignatius's travels can afford themselves no such pleasures (or comical debacles). His horse is the centre of a structure of decision-making thrown into radical confusion. As exercises in transcendentalist explanation go, this one looks more than a little exposed to the charge of making it up as you go along. Ignatius himself calls this 'novel'. A far stronger description comes from a present-day contemporary Jesuit priest, informing us that during his noviate he and his contemporaries were wont to refer to this episode as the moment when Ignatius 'fleeced' God.[59]

Ignatius had powerful reasons for believing what he did, and we have none at all to question the depth of those beliefs. The concern here is more with the structural features of a narrative, its critical turning-points and, more particularly, its negotiation of a dilemma that unfolds at a crossroads. Further light can be shed on this from one of the past masters of the structural analysis of narrative, albeit that his Ignatian preoccupations have to do with the 'language' of the *Spiritual Exercises* rather than the story-telling twists and turns of the *Autobiography*. In *Sade, Fourier, Loyola*, Roland Barthes proposed to effect a translation of what, delightfully if obscurely, he calls a 'theophany' into the terms of a 'semiophany', a uniquely Ignatian orchestration of signs, symbols and interpretations as the music of a distinctive sensibility. I take three points from it. First, the centrality of the 'binary', the omnipresent sense of 'alternatives' and bifurcation points; second, an 'indifference' vis-à-vis outcomes, a passive surrender of self and will to the 'virtuality of possibles', with a particular reference to what Ignatius's disciple, Jérome Nadal, reported of Ignatius's relation to 'decision-making' (his one 'inclination' was to 'incline to nothing'); third, a 'problematic of the sign', which Barthes sees as related to the 'mantic' arts of ancient divination and the mediaeval *sortes*. The episode with the horse in the *Autobiography* relates meaningfully to all three of these features of the Ignatian writing landscape: a binary choice of roads to take; a yielding of decision by the horse's owner to the horse; the interpretation of it as a 'sign' from God (in the age that has been described as that of the 'Lutheran crisis of the sign'). These are also, of course, the attributes and attitudes of the gambler, taking a chance on chance: the acceptance of the either/or binary as win or lose; the submission to whatever the wheel or the dice or the toss of the coin will yield; the obsession with 'signs' as the substance of superstitions regarding 'luck', good or bad.

The gambler can also be left with the thought that if he had put it on red rather than black he would have won (or lost). Which, of course, brings us back to the 'what-if' of Ignatius at the crossroads: what if, in the moment, the horse had 'chosen' to take the other path? Is this for Ignatius even a coherent thought? Does the counterfactual – any counterfactual – have a place here other than as a threat to the providential order? Playing counterfactually with Providence is to play with fire, and very possibly hellfire.[60] Where Ignatius's future is concerned, his course is set:

to Montserrat and all that will flow from it. There is no alternative on offer, and any suggestion of modal bewilderment would be merely a betrayal of the true faith. Providentialism rules out conditionality as a potentially blasphemous questioning of God's designs. There can be no 'ifs' here. God is invoked to close the door to them, but not before the syntax of Ignatius's own prose opens the door with his own conditionals, in the double 'if' construction: '*if*, on coming to the crossroad, his horse should turn into the path that lead to the destination of the Moor, he would pursue and kill him; but, *if* his horse kept to the highroad, he would allow the wretch to escape.' Here, the 'ifs' tie a knot of syntax which the 'Providence of God' is supposed to untie. If the horse had taken the other path (call it the 'left' road after the example of Hercules), Ignatius would have found and (probably) killed the Muslim. This would have been the wrong road, but why? Surely this outcome too would be governed by God's foresight and will; it cannot therefore be the 'wrong' one, except that it is because the right one is the road that leads to Montserrat. The only (theologically risky) way out of this impossible double bind would be to view taking the other road as an instance of sheer bad luck, the unhappy consequence of a horse allowed to follow its own nose, and the contingent cause of an outcome that Ignatius would surely have lived to regret (assuming that in that circumstance he were to remain recognizably 'Ignatius'). We are on the cusp of the some of the issues informing the next two chapters.

Before we go there, it is time to recall what earlier I suggested needs to be remembered whenever Ignatius invokes Providence: the qualification 'though we dare not state it'. Ignatius in fact 'dares' and 'states' time and again. Theologically, the dare is suspect, even forbidden, because of the risk of hubristic usurpation, claiming to know the mind of God on the back of an inference from an alleged 'sign'. It is also the dare of the risk taker as gambler. In extremis, it is the gamble of faith, what permits the move beyond a paralysing doubt. But it is the doubt itself which gives rise to the dare in the first place. That is what the hesitation both before and at the crossroads in the *Autobiography* is about. It also needs saying yet again that the sincerity of Ignatius's beliefs is not the issue. But the fact that Ignatius did not doubt his faith did not mean outright hostility, either on his part or more generally within the Jesuit order he created, to the instruments of doubt, even some of those associated with certain Reformers or Reform sympathizers. We have already noted the recourse in Jesuit pedagogy to the Hercules story (normally as stage adaptations in the Jesuit schools), after its long suppression by the Church as a heterodox rival of the doctrine of *dea virtus*. In addition, there was the insistence on the value of teaching grammar as the foundation of securely treading the other great path (not of virtue but of inquiry), grammar as the basis of right reason and clear thinking; in some Catholic quarters this was deemed to be so dangerous as to warrant campaigns to prohibit it.

Most importantly, there was the guarded openness to some of the ways of thinking of the 'prince of the humanists', Erasmus. Ignatius himself passes that way. In Chapter VI of the *Autobiography* he finds himself in Salamanca, where he is interrogated by a Dominican monk who 'pressed him, giving as a reason that many were once more thrusting forward the erroneous doctrine of Erasmus'. Ignatius's response to this is to refuse to respond, just as the decision at the Montserrat crossroads was not to decide. One reason given was a reluctance to acknowledge the Dominican's authority to question him.[61] But it is not unreasonable to surmise that there were others, including what Ignatius knew that Erasmus knew about the experience of the crossroads dilemma, namely the sheer intensity of vacillation along with the imperative to decide. One has to choose of course, that is the moral of Erasmus's deployment of the Hercules story in the *Enchiridon*. But what it is truly like for Erasmus to be 'a man at a crossroads' is best described in his *Adages*: 'I am at the crossroads of decision. This is applied to those who are of uncertain mind, hesitating as to which alternative to choose.'[62] For all its heated fervour, the *Autobiography* is similar when speaking of what it was to be caught in the perplexities of the crossroads drama. Ignatius's text is not just the story of his 'conversion'. It is also one of many stages on which, at the threshold of the modern world, the 'doubting' subject of the sixteenth century appears. This is very different from Oedipus's story. At the Phocis crossroads, Oedipus doesn't find himself torn, hesitant, undecided, and if we can call him a 'gambler' of sorts, it is as one who is not so much hesitant before as indifferent to outcomes (the road to Thebes or the road to Daulis), since there is no obvious reason for him to prefer one to the other. More generally, until he is unsteadied, and finally unhinged, by what Jocasta tells him of the circumstances of Laius's death, 'doubt' is fundamentally alien to his overweeningly self-confident stance to the world. With both Petrarch and Ignatius we are in another kind of story altogether, both culturally and generically.[63]

As for the mute yet eloquent horse, when Ignatius gets to Montserrat, after 'a long time in prayer' and (once again!) 'writing a general confession of his sins', he 'begged and obtained leave' not only 'to hang up his sword and his dagger in the church near the altar of the Blessed Virgin', but also 'to give up his horse'. Too much should probably not be read into this beyond the obvious symbolic gesture of Ignatius's renunciation of the soldier's life. But a thought lingers: bet once and win is one thing, but best not to push your luck, if that is what it is. One may end up uncomfortably close to the gambler in the movie *A Bronx Tale* and his plaintive counterfactual: 'if it hadn't been for bad luck, I'd have had no luck at all'.

# 5 LOOKING BACK: FROM METANOIA TO BUYER'S REGRET

*When I try to analyse my own cravings, motions, actions and so forth I surrender to a sort of retrospective imagination which leads the analytic faculty with boundless alternatives and which causes each visualized route to fork and re-fork without end in the maddening complex prospect of my past.*

**VLADIMIR NABOKOV**

*One looks back at one's youth as to a cup that a madman dying of thirst left half-tasted.*

**W. B. YEATS**

## I

To go back to the opening sentence of this book, if when reading 'we pass forks in the road and forget them, concentrating in memory only on the single road we took', this also applies (perhaps indeed for the most part) to how we live, driven by the 'will', as either the whiplash of desire or the sheer need to survive, down the 'single road' we have taken or that has been prescribed for us. But, even for the most driven (with special exemption for those who combine ego-powered thrusting and insufferable self-satisfaction), it is not the only way we live. There is also remembering as well as forgetting, and memory's treasure trove of counterfactuals in the recalling of the life already lived. For the philosopher or the historian, counterfactuals typically raise analytical questions, with a strong pull towards abstraction (they are indeed sometimes characterized *as* 'abstractions'). But for the actors involved, they also have a psychological and emotional life, tied to the human registers of retrospect, the forms and shades of attitude, feeling and mood that can inflect our reckonings with the past, as we look back to a fork in the road not taken and reflect on how things might have turned out had it been. Under certain (rarely satisfied) conditions, this can be a survey governed by the dispassionate gaze, where the decisions and actions that have set the course of a life also become an object of analytical attention and a matter of coolly rational assessment. Appraisal of this kind is especially attractive to those of Stoic persuasions and partisans of the view that the past, however painful or unsatisfactory, is inalterably done and dusted, there to be assumed not re-imagined. Most human beings aren't like this. Some may be smugly indifferent to counterfactually entertained alternatives, secure in the imperviousness that stems from the thought that the world has treated them well, and that this happy outcome consorts with the natural order of things as their legitimate due. This unpleasant customer is a different animal altogether; he has nothing in common with the Stoic's commitment to the disciplines of *askesis*.

Someone who did, as a sort of twentieth-century soulmate, is the Sparrow. There would have to be something gone seriously awry in what it is to be human not to be moved by Piaf singing 'Je ne regrette rien'. One reason we are moved is because of the courage defiantly shown in the face of adversity and tragedy. But another is because both the song and the singing implicitly speak of regrets so profound that, without the fortifying courage, they might unhinge and overwhelm. Alongside this, then, consider someone else who, so he told us, sang 'Je ne regrette rien' – in the bath on the night Britain was forced out of the European Exchange Rate Mechanism. The triller was the former Chancellor of the Exchequer, Norman Lamont, and his moment in the bath was relayed around the world to explain how happy he was now that the government was no longer hobbled by a monetary policy he himself had fully supported (at least as an 'anti-inflation' tool).[1] He didn't last long in the post thereafter. Buried in these contrastive tales of song and regret is more than one lesson, but primarily that there is clearly regret and regret, as well as different modalities beyond the merely smug for its alleged absence (gratitude is one such, according to Cicero the basis of all the virtues).[2] There is also a different relation to the counterfactual elements of regretting. Piaf evokes them in abundance, as a tacit substratum to the 'no regrets' stance (tacit because the whole purpose of the song is to keep them under wraps). Lamont's little ditty evokes no such thing, merely weeks of political sweat and panic buried in the fog of the politician's bright complacency. One presumes his buoyancy did not survive the immediate aftermath of his political demise, and that with this perhaps the coarser form of counterfactual paradox raised its dispiriting head ('I do regret so publicly regretting nothing, I could have held on to office').

When it comes to hindsight evaluation of the course of our own lives, most of us inhabit the counterfactual domain in one or more of the registers that are here provisionally gathered under the umbrella term 'Regret'.[3] They include (this list is far from exhaustive): sadness, nostalgia, guilt, shame, remorse, repentance, reproach, anger, complaint, and that very special case, sorrow. Which dominates in any given scenario of retrospect will naturally vary according to circumstance, temperament, and in many cases cultural and social pressure. A basic contextual differentiation will typically distinguish between the personal (so-called 'agent-regret') arising from direct involvement in what is regretted, and the impersonal, whose relation to the regretted event or state of affairs is more remote. The classic borderline case is the driving accident example cited by Bernard Williams in connection with the role of 'moral luck' in our lives and the kinds of reactions we have when the luck in question turns out to be bad luck. Agent-regret can bear on the agent's actions in one of two quite distinct ways: the ethically or the egocentrically focussed, my sense of something done of which I am ashamed and my sense of something done which was a bad practical call in terms of my own interests. There is also the important distinction between 'on-balance' and 'all-in' regret, though distinctions of any kind may fade to insignificance in the light of Kafka's sweeping view: 'Whatever you decide, you will regret.' It is also here that the 'should have' modal finds its natural, though unsettled, home.[4]

Stoics (and saints) to one side, for most of us the landscape of retrospect is an emotionally and morally complicated place, strewn with all manner of counterfactual traps. At its most dangerous, it is a veritable minefield, some of the explosives threatening to blow up the ground on which a sense of the 'self' stands (of which more in the following chapter). It is the place where standing at the crossroads poised for decision is commonly succeeded by wandering in a maze littered with signposts to blind alleys, in the company of 'shoulda' as perhaps the blindest of Roth's blind mice, the ethically neuralgic point on the grammatical map of regret, and a reminder that the cup of recollection from which one drinks is all too often a poisoned chalice. Travelling in one direction – inwards to self – it hooks up with 'remorse' as moral regret for one's role in bad outcomes, a positive value in Christian ethics, a disaster according to Nietzsche ('adding to a first act of stupidity a second').[5] But moving in another direction (projected outwards to non-self as complaint and blame), it locks onto and feeds the belief that life cruelly dealt me the wrong cards, fuelling the conversion of the counterfactual 'what if' into a plaintive 'if only'.

## II

In so far as we can track it, regret is also not uniformly the same thing when viewed historically and cross-culturally. Let us return to the time and place of our first crossroads scene, in ancient Greece, and its vocabularies for the regret-laden backwards look. There is no term in Classical Greek that corresponds exactly to our modern sense of the term 'regret'. This raises the sort of question familiar to the anthropologist, an instance of which is furnished by Caroline Humphrey in respect of her study of a source from thirteenth-century Mongolia: 'Can we (should we) recognize regret in another culture, especially when, as is the case with the thirteenth-century Mongols, there is no indigenous term that corresponds exactly to the English word?' Her own answer to the question is affirmative; we can recognize it, provided the investigation attunes itself to 'the range and subtlety of Mongolian understandings of regret', and also to how these changed historically.[6] Lexical differences or absences, in other words, do not necessarily, or even generally, entail deep conceptual differences or absences, still less conceptual incommensurability, such that one set of ideas is 'untranslatable' into the terms of another set. On the other hand, this does not mean that passage from one to the other is without difficulties or blockages, and, since translation is often our only gateway, there is always the risk of misleading back-importation from one lexicon to another.

In a translation of Euripides' *Trojan Women*, for example, Andromache says to her mother: 'One who falls from happiness to tragedy is driven with regret and memories of blessedness.' The original term translated here by 'regret' is *alatai*, literally meaning 'roam' or 'wander', and hence much closer to ideas of the 'distraught' and a mind 'wandering' in the sense of the expression not to be 'in one's right mind'. 'Regret' doesn't even begin to carry the weight of this. Similarly, in a translation of Homer's *Odyssey*, when Odysseus meets with Epicaste in Hades, he speaks of the 'cruel punishment of the gods' inflicted on Oedipus as including 'the tortures of remorse'. The question of the place of 'remorse' in the Oedipus plays (and Greek tragedy generally) is a much debated one. Although Oedipus's feelings about himself and his (unwitting) crimes bear some resemblance to what we understand by 'remorse', the relation is complex, and only with very considerable difficulty assimilable to later moral notions. In any case, as a translation of *The Odyssey*, 'tortures of remorse' is a clear case of anachronistic transfer from one culture to another. Homer's term is *algea*. In Greek mythology, the *algea* were the spirits or *daimones* of physical and mental suffering, bringers of pain, distress and grief in the triple guises of *lupê*, *ania* and *akhos*. The *algea* are also invoked by Antigone at the moment of her extreme anguish at the end of *Oedipus at Colonus*. They are the presiding figures and terms for the language of woe in the face of the unendurable and the irremediable that are indelibly part of the ancient Greek tragic consciousness.[7]

This is not, however, only a question of infelicitous (and thus potentially rectifiable) rendering, but also of real semantic gaps in which something is destined to get lost in translation. Imagine, frivolously, a time-travel counterfactual in which Edith Piaf is tele-transported back to ancient Greece, with the mission of teaching the Stoics modern French so that they would be able to understand her famous song. It is far from clear what her listeners might have made of it, in all manner of ways of course, but crucially in terms of understanding what precisely she meant by 'regrette'. Classical Greek has two terms associated with some of our uses of the term 'regret': *metanoia* and *metameleia*. The match is imperfect, and that should not surprise us, especially from the point of view of the standard (if controversial) distinction between 'shame cultures' and 'guilt cultures' that informs much discussion of the difference between ancient and modern societies. On the other hand, it is not a case of radical disjunction; both terms were to have a long and fertile afterlife in religious and secular thought post-antiquity, indeed through to the present day, if as appropriations that almost certainly would often have astonished the ancient Greeks.

The primary meaning of *metanoia* is 'afterthought' or 'change of mind'. Changes of this kind can readily involve regret at the second thoughts not having been the first ones, and often involve considerations of practical reason without any particular moral dimension, indeed often in flagrant indifference to it.[8] In his *Cyropaedia*, the lesson Xenophon draws from detailing the successes of the Persian king, Cyrus, is that they compel us to 'change our opinions' on the alleged impossibility of 'ruling men', an eminently pragmatic question if ever there were one. More bluntly, when he also has Cyrus himself declare an afterthought while reflecting on bad strategic decisions, it is emphatically in the style of the mafioso version of regret: 'I am not sorry that I killed your son, but that I did not kill you as well.' These are instrumental assessments linking opportunism and opportunity costs. Where miscalculation or surrender of right judgement entails missed opportunity, *metanoia* often partners with *kairos*, in the sense of the latter as the 'opportune moment' for decision and action. Where the moment is seized, it must be governed and guided by *metis* (skill, cunning); or where missed, skill is needed in exploiting the afterthought for useful future ends. Alternatively, the afterthought comes stamped with the bitterly regretful taste of the 'too late'. The counterfactual aspect of this latter relation is forged by the link to a third term, *pothos* (yearning or desire). This was normally associated with nostalgic longing for something one once had but has lost (usually a young lover), but could also involve something not had in the first place, a looking back with longing at the missed opportunity as a desired might-have-been (a relatively rare state of mind given the typical attribution of outcomes to the will of the gods), or as the wish for better foresight at some future fork in the road.[9]

On the other hand, *metanoia* can also acquire an ethical hue and evoke meanings akin to repentance and remorse, sometimes in unexpected places. One such is Thucydides. He is the ancient historian whom we especially associate with historical realism and impatience with the might-have-beens of history, in contrast to his predecessor, Herodotus, who posits a grand-scale counterfactual in the form of asking what would have happened if Athens had not pitted its navy against the Persians (the answer is that it would have lost the war).[10] Thucydides, by contrast, we think of as someone who looks to the facts while turning his back on the counter-to-fact.[11] Yet here he is, on an aftermath as the occasion of an afterthought. It concerns the Athenian treatment of the rebellious Mitylenians: the leaders 'in the fury of the moment determined to put to death not only the prisoners at Athens, but the whole adult male population of Mitylene, and to make slaves of the women and children'. The determination is, however, followed by major second thoughts:

The very next day there was an immediate change of mind [*metanoia*], and they began to reconsider the savage and extreme decision to destroy an entire city rather than just those directly responsible. When the Mytilenaean delegation present and their Athenian sympathizers became aware of this, they got the authorities to reopen the question. They were not difficult to persuade because it was obvious to them that most of the citizens wanted someone to give them the opportunity of discussing the matter again.[12]

An earlier translation (by E. P. Dutton) has 'repentance' rather than 'change of mind' for *metanoia*. Strictly speaking, this is once again a mistranslation, but far less so than some of our earlier examples. It is quite clear from the passage that the 'second thoughts' here are not merely pragmatic (the military value of killing and enslavement), but also express a moral repugnance (the cruelty of the Athenians' actions). These sorts of views and feelings were sometimes associated with the term *metameleia*, more commonly translated as 'remorse'. But this does not appear to have generally been one of the more impressive of the ancient virtues or even a virtue at all. In his *Ethics*, Aristotle took a dim view of it as unbecoming to any man of standing, a sign of weakness, vacillation and inconstancy. Elsewhere, its ethical colouring tends either to the wan or to the garish. Though sometimes connected to ideas of atonement and deliverance (a fragment attributed to Democritus states that 'remorse for shameful deeds is the salvation of life'), its drift was passive rather than active, referring more to the pains consequent upon, in Plutarch's words, the 'shame from pleasures that are contrary to law and uncontrollable'. Plutarch's metaphors for these pains are 'stings', 'wounds' and 'ulcers', inflicted by memories of the 'wicked action' that 'shames the soul with confusion and punishes it with torment'. In *The Republic* Plato used the term *metameleia* in a similar way, to designate the mental prison house of the 'tyrannized soul' in the 'tyrannized city', compulsively driven 'by the gadfly of desire' and 'full of confusion and remorse [*metameleia*]'.[13] Imagined in *Laws* as the punishment that consists in the wrong-doer being brought to 'loathe his wrong', *metameleia* is a hellish condition, indeed not unlike some of the circles of Dante's *Inferno*, or even Sartre's *Huis Clos*. In so far as some notion of counterfactual 'regret' is in play here, it is in the form of self-punishing lacerations from within an inescapable condition.

The picture, for us, of how exactly the terms *metanoia* and *metameleia* functioned in ancient Greece remains blurred, a zone of indistinct boundaries and shifting meanings, in part, of course, as an effect of our distance from that world, but perhaps also reflecting intrinsic uncertainties over the whole place of regret and related concepts in the ancient stance towards a human life lived, or for that matter a divine life lived (the gods, we recall, can be both quarrelsome and regretful mind-changers). One of them, Hades, god of the Underworld, is also sometimes billed as the god of Regret. How that came about is obscure. It does not seem to have been a classical idea, but a later invention. The association almost certainly has something to do with being the guardian of a domain populated with regretful shades and the special status of the afterlife as a place for post-mortem afterthoughts (Achilles the most famous of them, apparently regretting the short warrior life lived for 'glory' as against a longer one as a mere slave). Back in this life, one thing that most scholars seem to agree on is that the use of the terms *metanoia* and *metameleia* does not reflect later forms of 'inwardness', and that more specifically we should not view them through the 'Christian lens' of more strongly developed notions of 'remorse' and 'repentance'. They appear to have more to do with the external than the internal, with action rather than introspection, status rather than soul. In some contexts (Aristotle), they are seen as status-negative, in others they enhance status, but often as public performances intended for an audience and bent to a practical purpose. Such expressions of 'regret' and related feelings is a feature of many cultures (for example, they are central to the thirteenth-century Mongolian case cited earlier).[14] As we shall see, they also have a part to play in our own society, albeit differently inflected, above all in publicly stated 'regret' by politicians anxious to secure a *metanoia*-free space for conceding 'mistakes' in a way that minimizes damage to electability.

## III

From early Christianity through to modern times, and in contexts combining ideas and themes from both religious and secular thought, the semantic and cultural adventures of *metanoia* and *metameleia* are manifold, carrying over some elements from the ancient world while also generating new meanings, usages and associations. Of the pair, *metameleia* is very much the junior partner in this history. In the Greek New Testament, it (or a grammatical relative, usually verbal) appears around half a dozen times, compared with around fifty instances of *metanoia*.

Crucially, it is the term that in the Vulgate is translated as *paenitentia* (sometimes spelled *poenitentia*) in connection with the story of Judas, whose 'remorse' is famously of the wrong sort, as a collapse into despair and in ending with suicide, the antithesis of a true 'repentance.'[15] *Metanoia*, by contrast, was to be the key term for a true but active repentance, a turning of the soul towards both the future and God, in a convergence on the goal of salvation. The counterfactual (regret at what I might or should have done then) is subordinated to a future 'turning' to what I should and will now do. Its centrality was stressed in the Gospels by Matthew and Luke (commenting on Peter's sermon), as by Paul in the Epistles. In the late fourth century, John Chrysostom, Archbishop of Constantinople, will devote some of his homilies to Paul's Epistles while codifying the 'five pathways' to repentance. More or less contemporaneously, Augustine, in the *Confessions*, models his conversion as a Pauline *metanoia*, although, of course, the terminology is now Latin and hence the relevant term *paenitentia*. The stage is more or less set for that other famous conversion over a millennium later, the visionary *metanoia* of Ignatius of Loyola and the subsequent incorporation into the *Exercitia Spiritualia* of the conception of *paenitentia* as a relation between contrition and self-administered pain.

The Renaissance brought some of the issues informing these religious preoccupations into the realm of ethical and political thought as well as into the iconographic schemes of visual representation. Machiavelli's didactic poem, 'Tercets on Fortune', features *Kairos* (with the now more familiar name of *Occasio*) and *Metanoia*, the former signifying the pathways to fortune between the spinning wheels of circumstance, while the latter awaits you, ready to strike with the regret-laden in the event that skill or luck deserts you. There was a conscious echo here of Ausonius's *Epigrams* (with which Machiavelli was familiar), where *Metanoia* is described as: 'a goddess to whom even Cicero himself did not give a name. I am the goddess who exacts punishment for what has and has not been done, so that people regret it. Hence my name is Metanoea.'[16] There are also parallels in Renaissance painting and drawing, most notably Vasari's sketch which has the personified *Metanoia* as the shadow companion of *Occasio*, not joined back to back as if Siamese twins, but so close as to suggest that each is the flip side of the other; the commitment to seizing the kairotic moment is in part the anticipatory knowledge that we shall regret not having done so. Machiavelli's poem might also be said to have planted some of the seeds for the emergence of what has been termed 'political *metanoia*', whether in accounts of the arts of statecraft or in republican conceptions of the polity, all the way through to the eighteenth century, above all in puritan America and the confluence of the religious and the political in the image of the City on the Hill.[17] In short, across a variety of sources – literary, pictorial and political – the Renaissance identifies in *metanoia* an energizing power which, beyond its religious settings, fuelled secular aspiration in the sphere of civic life and the project of the formation of the good citizen.

The question of how to understand 'repentance' and its relations with 'regret' and 'remorse' was, of course, not a settled one. There were many complications and challenges, over some of which wars, both literal and doctrinal, were fought. One such in the later middle ages was the Cathar 'heresy'. The Cathars had an interesting way with the doctrine of repentance, interesting because its implementation was itself at once kairotic and metanoiac, a question of timing, good or bad. The key moment in the life of a Cathar was the *Consolamentum*, simultaneously a moment of penitence and renunciation (of the pleasures of the flesh, principally the eating of meat and sexual relations). As the condition of passing after death into paradise, renunciation once performed was definitive; there was no going back, relapses strictly forbidden. Timing was thus crucial. Since, bar suicide which would send you straight to the flames, the moment of your death was beyond your control, if you opted for the safe bet and renounced early, you were henceforth condemned to a possibly long period of abstemious misery. The optimal moment was as close to death as possible, but if you risked all on that play, you could leave it too late and so miss the boat to paradise, presumably with *Metanoia* as your sad companion whispering 'if only'. All this gambling with salvation, not to mention other heretical beliefs, was naturally intolerable to orthodoxy, and dealt with by interrogation and annihilation on the part of the Papacy, the Inquisition and the French monarchy. No-one seems to have expressed any regret, let alone repentance for this brutality. Interrogated Cathars, on the other hand, sometimes did in respect of the beliefs that brought this reign of terror and destruction. Béatrice de Planissoles, the chatelaine of Montaillou (one of the centres of the heresy) was questioned by Jacques Fournier, the Bishop of Pamiers, acting for the Inquisition. She concluded her deposition (in Occitan; the proceedings were recorded in Latin) by combining expressions of both 'regret' and 'penitence': 'I have great regret at having heard these heretical remarks and more to have believed these heresies, and I am ready to undergo the penance which My Lord Bishop would like to impose on me for this.' Assuming sincerity on her part (there was, of course, much feigning in order to escape the rigours of the Inquisition), the meanings of the term 'regret' (*redic* in Occitan) would have been close to 'grief' and a close relation of 'penance'.[18]

This, however, was a local affair. What really mattered for changing religious conceptions of *metanoia* were the insurgent theologies of the Reformation. The initial groundwork was linguistic in character, for the most part the endeavours of the early humanist scholars in the comparative analysis of biblical translation, pre-eminently the philological and textual investigations of Lorenzo Valla (otherwise best known for his exposure of *The Donation of Constantine* as a forgery) in respect of the Latin Vulgate (the *Collatio Novi Testamenti*). Armed with his knowledge of the Greek versions, Valla's annotations for *paenitentia* clearly reveal that he had *metanoia* in mind as the textual bedrock for the interpretation of 'repentance': he suggested *mentis emendatio* ('amendment of mind'), while interestingly *metamelomai* is glossed as 'to feel regret' and is associated with feelings of 'frustration'. These were not just technical matters, but scholarship in the service of substantive questions, above all in relation to the distinction between true and fake repentance that will concern so many thinkers throughout the sixteenth and seventeenth centuries. Two key figures above all relied extensively on Valla's work: Erasmus, the loyal Catholic but whose probing mind brought him close in his early career to some of the views of the Reformers, and the Protestant firebrand, Luther.

Erasmus's recovery of the Greek New Testament (*Novum Testamente omne*) was published with the Latin text of the Vulgate on facing pages, a procedure that today would seem innocuous, but in its time was provocative. The resurrection of the Greek meant a return to a status quo ante, and provided a benchmark for interpreting the Latin Vulgate which, along with accumulating layers of interpretation, dogma and practice, had held sway throughout the Middle Ages and came together in the creation of what has been called 'clericalized Catholicism'. This enabled Erasmus to juxtapose *metanoia* and *paentitentia*, and then to ponder what follows. What follows is considerable, largely by way of contrasting the verb forms *metanoiete* and *paentitentiam agere*, a contrast which, beyond questions of grammar and lexicography, engaged with questions of doctrine embedded in institutional practices over the many centuries of the Catholic Church. The mediaeval doctrine of *paenitentiam agere* turned on the meaning of *agere* as 'performance of an action' as by an actor, referring specifically to the priestly ministry as standing in for Christ, enabling and guiding the various forms and stages of the sacrament of repentance, namely confession, absolution and penance as self-punishment or 'good works'. This came to be seen by many as so much accumulated paraphernalia, where 'action' was not the internal cleansing and correcting actions of the soul, but was wholly attached to externals – of speech, rituals, and 'performances' in the less reputable sense of the mechanical or the feigned. To the questioning eye, it was a form of institutional corruption of the original religious meanings of *metanoia* that reaches its nadir with the spread of the use of 'indulgences' as a way of reducing punishment and enhancing the chances of salvation, often in exchange for cash payments (*poena* as penalty after the fashion of a parking ticket). This was the background to Erasmus's quiet adoption of one of Valla's other Latin suggestions for *metanoia* (the simple *resipiscte* for 'change of mind').

In the meantime, Calvin preached the virtues of *metanoia* as both change of mind and spiritual conversion (a turning of the soul). In England, Tyndale insisted – to the intense annoyance of Thomas More – on translating *metanoia* as 'repentance' rather than 'penance', the former as the inwardly focussed as against the focus on institutionally directed practices of confession and absolution. At Oxford, Jewel and his mentor, the self-exiled Italian, Peter Vermigli, developed their own explanation and defence of the reforming affirmation of *metanoia*, drawing on Augustinian sources and construing it as a sacred 'conversion of mind' rooted in a form of 'internalized spiritual cognition' akin to the inward experience that brings us before the 'presence' of Christ in the moment of the Eucharist (that endless topic of theological controversy).[19] Above all there was the towering figure of Luther, who in the *Ninety-five Theses* threw down the gauntlet in denouncing the practice of 'indulgences'. In his famous letter to von Staupitz on why he wrote the *Ninety-five Theses*, Luther appealed to the Greek sources (elsewhere having acknowledged a scholarly debt to both Erasmus and Valla) for his view of the proper alternative. In particular, Luther's strategic use of the term 'disposition' had an echo in Erasmus's *Enchiridion*, his version of a Christian manual, in which he wrote of the 'disposition of the soul' as crucial to all scenarios of repentance and redemption.

> *Poenitentia* (or *metanoia*), therefore, means coming to one's right mind and a comprehension of one's own evil after one has accepted

the damage and recognized the error. This is impossible without a change in one's disposition and [the object of one's] love ... Then I progressed further and saw that *metanoia* could be understood as a composite not only of "afterward" and "mind", but also of the [prefix] "trans" and "mind" (although this may, of course, be a forced interpretation), so that *metanoia* could mean the transformation of one's mind and disposition ... Continuing this line of reasoning, I became so bold as to believe that they were wrong who attributed so much to penitential works that they left us hardly anything of *poenitentia*, except some trivial satisfactions on the one hand and a most laborious confession on the other. It is evident that they were misled by the Latin term, because the expression *poenitentiam agere* suggests more an action than a change in disposition; and in no way does this do justice to the Greek *metanoein*.[20]

In their reflections on the question of 'repentance', Erasmus and Luther rarely invoke the notion of regret. Erasmus uses the term to critical and satirical ends in his *In Praise of Folly* (which in turn inspired Du Bellay's collection of poems, *Les Regrets*), and in one place 'Moria' speaks in a manner of which we shall soon be seeing more ('no-one regrets their own temperament'). But for the most part, the term or its equivalents are reserved by both Erasmus and Luther for occasional, though far from casual, autobiographical reminiscence: the older Erasmus regrets some of his earlier writings including the *Encomium Moriae* ('I wish I could undo everything and start all over again'), while Luther comes to rue his more incandescent attacks on the Catholic 'indulgences' in the *Ninety-five Theses* in light of the conflagration they triggered ('I regret having given birth to them'). The subtending counterfactual of the older Erasmus's expression of regret is a question to which I return in the next chapter.

## IV

Elsewhere, however, a link between 'repentance' and 'regret' was repeatedly established, albeit as a highly flexible relation subject to varying interpretations, and where in some cases the point of making the link was then to rupture it or at least to have the two terms tug in different direction. The intention was to capture tensions, ambiguities and instabilities of one kind or another, above all along the frontier of the religious and the secular. We can get a sense of this from three exemplary moments, all French, one in the sixteenth century, two in the seventeenth, and in the form, respectively, of an essay, a letter and a maxim. Their authors are, in sequence, Montaigne, Pascal and La Rochefoucauld. Despite their many differences (Pascal expressly selected Montaigne as one of his principal sparring partners, aiming for a straight knockout), they have one thing in common: when they examine the issue of repentance, they all do so, in one form or another, in relation to the term 'regret'. They do so in pursuit of different agendas, but share an interest in bringing a theology into close contact with a psychology centred on human motives for action and belief. This combination of the philosophical and the psychological, the religious and the secular, placed a bomb beneath the ground of received opinion.

The essay by Montaigne is, self-selectingly, 'Du repentir' ('On repentance').[21] One of the late *Essais*, it is vintage Montaigne, packed with erudite reference and switching argumentative focus as it unfolds, in a kind of Montaignian *metanoia* of the practice of writing as a process of pure mind-changing. Its opening paragraph sets a hare running with a characteristic view of the imperfect self as flux and change ('I am unable to stabilize my subject'), but with a regretful counterfactual wrapped around it: 'I give an account of Man and sketch a picture of a particular one of them who is very badly formed and whom I would truly make very different from what he is if I had to fashion him afresh.' But no sooner is the hare released than it is crisply despatched: 'But it is done now.' The backward look and the accompanying counterfactual fantasy are pointless because what is 'done' – me – is done. The general drift of the essay is not to dabble counterfactually, but to show us someone who has in fact a marked aversion to the idea of 'repenting' and who tolerates regret only in its modest forms, largely on the grounds that, in connection with anything that fundamentally concerns or implicates us, we cannot really mean it when we repent or regret, since to do so in the ways demanded by religious and moral authority would require us ceasing to be who and what we are. Montaigne recognizes only himself as the relevant authority in the matter; he is his own adjudicating tribunal ('I have my own laws and law-court to pass judgement on me, and I appeal to them rather than elsewhere').

Montaigne sets out his case for this sceptical view in relation to two fundamental themes: power and identity. One reason the counterfactual rapidly bites the dust is because of limits on our power to have been or to have acted in a significantly different manner. I can, for example, regret some of the small things of myself and my life that are within my power to modify (certain habits, for example); or, more extravagantly, I can, in a manner of speaking, 'regret' not having been an angel or Cato. But I can neither truly regret nor meaningfully repent what is not within my power to alter. Anything else is a futile 'if only' wish fulfilment masquerading as an option for myself that never was and never will be one:

> As for me, I can desire to be entirely different, I can condemn my universal form and grieve at it and beg God to form me again entirely and to pardon my natural frailty. But it seems to me that that should not be called repenting any more than my grieving at not being an angel or Cato. My doings are ruled by what I am and are in harmony with how I was made. I cannot do better: and the act of repenting does not properly touch such things as are not within our power – *that* is touched by regretting.

The tacked-on phrase at the end of this canonical passage points to a characteristic double-take or apparent paradox at the heart of Montaigne's conception of 'regret'. On the one hand, it is a modest human attribute, concerned with the small things. On the other hand, its scope is huge, in so far as it can be linked to a desire that is itself huge (to be or have been other, 'entirely different'). But since this desire is a wish for something impossible and thus meaningless, regret is in fact but the sad remainder of that impossibility, a residue with which the psyche might play as if with a toy. It serves not the rationally grounded sense of actual options, but pure fancy, as counterfactual narrative with no anchorage in reality. The vast scale of its freedom to roam across the universe of the 'possible' is merely an index of its wanton abandon. In other words, the constraints of which Montaigne speaks are also connected to questions of identity. I can undergo metanoiac 'changes of heart' ('ravisements'), even 'vigorous' ones, or show repentance for transitory, contingent sins, those that steal upon me to take me by surprise, because they are not typically part of me. But the sins that arise in and from the 'proper domicile' of the self cannot plausibly be an object of repentance: 'Provided that he listen to himself, there is no-one who does not discover in himself a form entirely his own, a master-form ... I am virtually always settled in place, as heavy ponderous bodies are. If I should not be "at home", I am always nearby.'

Some of this, of course, is 'cosy' Montaigne ('at home'), but the force of what he is claiming can be felt in the categorical refusal to repent of 'sins' that belong to the psychological shape of the 'master-form' of the self,

> those sins which are rooted in our complexions and indeed in our professions and vocations ... I cannot conceive that they are rooted so long in one identical heart without the reason and conscience of him who is seized of them being constant in his willing and wanting them to be so; and the repentance which he boasts to come to him at a particular appointed instant is hard for me to imagine or conceive.

That said (i.e. settled), there is nevertheless one fissure in Montaigne's sanguine stance, that very strange moment when his composure abruptly modulates to the viscerally intense. After dismissing repentance as normally insincere because inconsistent with our natures ('I do not know any surface repentance, mediocre and a matter of ceremony'), he adds a caveat: 'Before I call it repentance it must touch me everywhere, grip my bowels and make them yearn – as deeply and as universally as God does see me.' Repentance that takes hold of the entrails and bowels looks like a version of repentance all the way down ('everywhere'). It's a startling moment, with more than a hint at something overwhelming or shattering. The moment, however, is brief, a hiatus. Montaigne does not pursue its implications, most notably the likely impact of such an experience on the measured (in both senses of the term) master-form of the self. Perhaps sensing trouble ahead, he judges it wise to leave well alone, drop it, and resume the more low-key conversational tone. As for 'regret', Montaigne concludes with the categorical statement that basically he has none of any real import, and with that no time for counterfactuals: 'If I had to live again, I would live as I have done; I neither regret the past nor fear the future.'[22]

Most of this would have been, indeed was, a red rag to the existentially agitated Christian, Blaise Pascal. Along with the so-called 'pagan' in Montaigne that so upset Pascal, there was also the whiff of provincial complacency that can be caught in the Montaigne who takes up abode in the comfort of his 'at home', as a thinker for whom the idea of being at ease with oneself occasionally appears to trump all other considerations. Yet, apart from temperamental dispositions, there were compelling historical reasons for Montaigne's scepticism, arising from the turbulent sixteenth-century conjunction of religion, politics and war, a time when dramatic acts of repentance, both forced and feigned, dividing nations and tearing families apart, were commonplace. And the question of inauthentic or incomplete repentance also exercised Pascal, if from the very different point of view of the austere doctrines of Jansenism and an 'at home' within the forbidding precincts of Port-Royal. Largely because of his Pauline and Augustinian affiliations, Pascal's theological and religious perspective has what has been called certain 'elective affinities' with some of the positions of the Reformers. This is especially evident in the context of the attack mounted on the Jesuists in the *Lettres provinciales*. Here Pascal intervened on the vexed question of the relative merits of 'attrition' (penalties) and 'contrition' (inner repentance) in relation to absolution and remission of sins.

The distinction was not, of course, Pascal's own, nor was it exclusively Jesuit, but a standard theological one, the point of debate and contention being whether attrition was a sufficient condition for absolution. Richelieu's diocesan catechism, issued when he was bishop of Luçon, held that it was. Saint-Cyran's objection to that view is one reason why Richelieu was hostile to Jansenism. Pascal's intervention, in Letter 10 of the *Provinciales*, was based on the specific worry about the insufficiency of attrition, namely if and when performed primarily from fear of the adverse consequences of having sinned, whether as divine punishment in the afterlife, or in the here and now as the 'temporal' inconveniences that flow from our sins (such as ill-health or financial loss); in short, 'attrition' conceived solely from 'fear of penalties'. Against this is set true 'contrition', as a 'turning' of the soul towards the 'joy of having found God which is the real principle of our regret at having offended him, and of our whole change of life', as he puts it in one of the letters to Charlotte de Roannez. The emphasis on conversion as involving a divinely inspired 'whole change of life' echoes the spiritual 'turning' movement of the biblical *metanoia*, an idea also expressed in the *Écrit sur la conversion du pêcheur* where the 'conversion' is also described in the metanoiac terms of the soul coming to see things in an entirely new way.

A notable feature of Pascal's vocabulary in his discussion of repentance is the recurrence of the term 'regret'. Instances in the *Provinciales* are numerous, for the most part in connection with man's sinful nature and the question of absolution. Where Montaigne brings 'repentance' and 'regret' into the same space, it is only to prise them apart and keep one at arm's length from the other. In Pascal, 'regret' is more a synonym or very close equivalent of repentance, whether of the complete or incomplete kind. Its precise use is importantly a function of syntax, 'the regret that ...', the restrictive relative serving discrimination of kinds, broadly between the good and the bad, those that are pure of heart and those that are contaminated by self-interested considerations. In itself, however, the term 'regret' is both neutral and powerful; its status in any given case is more a question about the motives that drive it. However, a somewhat different note can perhaps be heard, if but quietly, in the well-known letter to Charlotte de Roannez on our proper relation to time past, present and future (Pascal's religious take on the great topos of the Renaissance):

> The past ought not to trouble us, since we have only to feel regret for our faults; but the future ought to concern us still less, since it is wholly beyond our control, and since perhaps we may not reach it at all. The present is the only time that is truly our own, and this we ought to employ according to the will of God. It is in this that our thoughts ought chiefly to be centred. Yet the world is so restless that men scarcely ever think of the present life and of the moment in which they are living, but of that in which they will live. In this manner we are always living in the future, and never in the present. Our Lord has willed that our foresight should not extend beyond the present day. These are the bounds within which we must keep both for our safety and for our own repose.[23]

There is something about the context in which the term 'regret' appears here that suggests a certain self-distancing from it. It is not an implied criticism, not even an equivocation, and there is certainly nothing of Montaigne's disdainful relegation of regret to the realm of the insignificant. Pascal seems to be faithful here to Augustine's distinction between bad and good regret, the latter clearly the intended reference in what he writes to Charlotte; regret in the service of the good is itself a moral good. The real point, however, concerns what regret both accompanies and governs: the past. The past is of little consequence, the only relation to it that has any point at all being concern for our faults. Pascal's main purpose, however, is to devalue the past (and even more so the future) relative to the present. This also puts pressure on the term that defines one of our principal relations to the past; in that sense, even where genuine, it is 'mere' regret alongside the glory of a present 'that is truly our own' when submitted to the 'will of God'. There appears to be an implication that, if we spend too long in the past and thus in the state of regret, we are guilty of the wrong 'turning', our heads, like those of Dante's soothsayers, fixed to stare backwards. In the qualitative contrast of temporalities, regret, even as a moral and religious term implicated in a genuine repentance, seems to lose some of its force. Just as the counterfactual built around Cleopatra's nose is itself a reflection of the meaninglessness of history on which it comments, so 'regret' is a futile turning away from the only 'turning that matters' (that of the soul towards God).

La Rochefoucauld brings to the question of repentance and regret the brevity of the maxim, indeed in the form of a single sentence (which needs to be quoted in the original French in order to catch its lapidary elegance): 'Le repentir n'est pas tant un regret du mal que nous avons fait, qu'une crainte de celui qui nous en peut arriver.'[24] English translations vary, many of them scratching the gem-like brilliance of the original. Arguably the best is the slightly old-fashioned: 'Our repentance is not so much regret for the ill we have done as fear of the ill that may happen to us as a consequence.' Espying macrocosms in monad-like microcosms, especially a twenty-odd word sentence, is one of the more hazardous moves of intellectual history. On the other hand, its brevity is deceptive; that is part of its point. Insinuated into its epigrammatic tautness are various significant displacements, which gesture towards a larger picture in which words, concepts and cultural understandings meet as if in a historical fulcrum. One is contextual, another lexical. The first involves the transfer of a religious set of concerns to a thoroughly worldly setting. There is a religious backdrop, biographically located in a circle of friends of Augustinian persuasions, and some with Jansenist sympathies (the *Maximes* have been called a 'companion piece to Pascal's *Pensées*').[25] But unlike Pascal, where it is omnipresent, any religious backdrop here recedes into the background and is kept at a distance. Theology gives way to psychology, in the form of a naturalist anatomy of human motive and the scrutiny of conduct in society (more exactly, in social groups such as the modern nobility versed in the refinements of sophisticated social interaction and complex calculation in settings such as the court and the salon). In La Rochefoucauld's velvet-gloved hand, the maxim is like a rapier thrust into a social body dedicated to games of flattery, seduction, concealment, deception and self-deception that are governed by an overarching rule – what La Rochefoucauld calls *amour-propre* or 'self-love'.

The second displacement is lexical and concerns the internal relations of 'repentance' and 'regret'. The maxim drives a wedge between the two terms. In this, La Rochefoucauld resembles Montaigne, except that the wedge serves a different semantic outcome, more akin to Pascal's distinction between the genuine and the fake. Substantively, regret ('for the ill we have done') is placed where it never is in Montaigne's essay, in pole position, as in effect a synonym for (true) repentance, whereas the word 'repentance' itself is consigned to the sphere of the inauthentic and the self-interested, a mere cover story behind which is hidden a real motive ('fear' of bad outcomes, or, in short, egotism). It is precisely here, however, in these semantic displacements and reversals, that the deceptive simplicity of the maxim gives way to the opening of a Pandora's box. One commentator has pointed out that very many of the maxims stage a formally simple 'equation' (after the manner of $x = y$).[26] Here it is repentance equals fear (of the 'ill that may happen to us as a consequence' of the 'ill we have done'). The equation conjoins the terms at either end of the maxim ('repentir' and 'crainte'). But in the middle, sandwiched between the two, is the key that unlocks the box: the term 'regret' taking the place of (true) repentance and thus yielding a second implied equation: $z = x$ ('regret' equals 'repentance').

We thus have two equations as a set of reverse mirror images: in the first case, repentance equates with self-interested fear; in the second case regret equates with repentance for our sins. This may be, interpretively speaking, to dance too elaborately with or around La Rochefoucauld's proposition. But it may well also remind us that how we read it has as much to do with the literary genre of the maxim as with a consistent moral philosophy or a developed theory of human nature. In La Rochefoucauld's hands, the seventeenth-century maxim is refashioned from being a small-scale dissertation (on rules of conduct and suchlike) into a composition, a rhetorical structure that plays with antitheses and inversions, and often destabilizes as much as it stabilizes. It has been claimed more than once that the heart of the La Rochefoucauld maxim is paradox. That is probably excessive, but there is one instance of the paradoxical that, in relation to the maxim before us, demands our attention: 'Our virtues are usually only vices in disguise.' This is in fact a pseudo-paradox, in that its actual meaning is not that virtues are vices but that they often provide masks behind which vice lurks (Molière showed us how on the stage). There is also a get-out clause in the adverb 'usually', but no guidance on how to apply it.

Transposing this logic back to the maxim before us, we could therefore end up with a truly mind-bending paradox, according to which it is not after all true that 'regret for the ills we have done' is a true repentance; it may be the mask of yet another vice, in addition to the cowardly 'fear of consequences'. But, if so, that would make of the aphorism itself something like a silent mask in its own right; positioned to speak to how it stands to the maxim which declares virtues to be 'usually' disguised vices, it remains mute. Perhaps it is an exception to the 'usual' rule, but we are not told, so perhaps it isn't. As readers, we are left wandering in a hall of mirrors where all the reflections are perhaps masks and disguises, and all is deception or self-deception; this after all is a world in which, as La Rochefoucauld puts it in another saying: 'We are so accustomed to disguising ourselves to others, that in the end we become disguised to ourselves.'[27] His maxim on the topic of repentance and regret could then come out resembling not a water-tight and truth-telling aphorism, but a house of cards, liable to collapse as the elegant antithesis and the supporting inversion disintegrate, with the entire structure at risk of disappearing into the quicksands of what, in yet another maxim, is said to dominate our natures and our condition, that supreme artist of mask and disguise – rampant self-love (*amour-propre*), radical, pervasive, incorrigible, and wholly indifferent to others except in so far as they can be instrumentally used for our own ends: 'We are so prepossessed in our favour that often what we take to be virtues are only vices that resemble them, and that self-love disguises from us.' Regret may be one of them.

In the early modern period, 'regret' is often centre stage in accounts of our relation to past choices. But in that centrality there is also an unsteadiness, movements from a 'strong' sense of the term to do with genuine contrition, to 'weak' senses bound up with the limitations of who and what we are and our inexhaustible capacity for rationalization and self-deception. The unsteadiness has a historical context: theological disputes, wars, the emergence of secular society and worldly cultures, and with the latter new forms of secular or quasi-secular analytical inquiry. This in turn made for a proliferation of meanings and uses for the term 'regret', along with a process of fracturing and a weakening as it is called upon in connection with so many different types of experience, setting and interaction. We can get some idea of what, in snapshot form, this looked like by consulting Furetière's *Dictionnaire Universel* (first published in 1690). This was a landmark text, enmeshed from the word go in controversy, in institutional, religious and political terms. News of the project elicited fury within the Académie Française (which felt its own monopoly as guardian of the language in the business of dictionary-making was under threat). The Jesuits at the Collège Louis le Grand meanwhile copied the

1701 edition to make one of their own, savagely edited with the removal of all 'Protestant' elements. As ever, 'definitions' could touch sore spots and trigger claims to authority over the 'meaning' of words.

For the word 'regret', the third edition of Furetière's *Dictionnaire Universel* (which appeared in 1708 with revisions and additions by Basnage de Beauval) gathered up most of its current meanings, on a spectrum from the superficialities of polite discourse ('mes regrets, Madame') through mere annoyance at the loss of something once possessed, to things of the mind altogether more profound, mainly of Stoic and Christian provenance. Interestingly, however, many of the illustrative quotations indicate disapproval; Saint-Evremond, for instance, is cited, according to whom regret is strictly for the weak-minded (an echo perhaps of the ancient Greeks). There is one anomaly: the plural form *regrets*, which is initially defined as 'lamentation' and 'woe' (*doléances*). We find here a trace of Old French *regreter*, *regrater* which, like Old English *greotan*, derives in part from old Norse *grata*, 'to weep' (the meaning still active in modern Danish, *graede*). The meaning survived into the later Middle Ages, for example in the *Lais* of Marie de France and in Villon's 'Regrets', where the sense of 'regret' is very close to 'lament' for what is irretrievably lost. But in Furetière what remains of this is but a flicker of meaning, soon extinguished as the definition continues by going on to specify *regrets* as both pointless ('inutiles') and superfluous ('superflus'), in short a fairly emphatic association of the term with the relatively non-serious. As for the verb form, *regretter*, in what appears to be an echo of Montaigne (although he is not cited), every single definition and source cited designates feelings and attitudes devoted to the relative trivia of life (the nearest it gets to an exception is itself a close call: 'on ne saurait trop regretter une bonne femme, quand la mort nous l'enlève'). All this seems to point to a lexical and cultural history that, despite 'strong' uses (principally in theological contexts), unfurls what Montaigne set in motion or brought to the fore – a progressive sapping in the early modern period of the force of the term 'regret', an etiolation that will become even more marked in the enfeebled usages of our own time.

# V

In the nature of things, we cannot 'know' for sure, if indeed at all, what inwardly transpires in another person, especially when it comes to matters of 'conscience'. This is one reason why the theologians and moralists of the early modern period found themselves struggling with the question of regret and repentance. How was a listener or a reader to distinguish between the fake and the genuine when access to the private realm of motive could be only a matter of inference? There is, of course, a copious history of public professions of regret, sometimes linked to apology and acts of penitence. As previously noted, the ancient Greeks often construed such displays as involving a loss of status and prestige. This, it seems, was also one of the widespread reactions to the public penance (at first at his Attigny palace in 822 and then again 11 years later in the St Medard church in Soissons) of the Frankish king, Louis the Pious (son of Charlemagne), for the death of his rebellious nephew, Bernard. Since Louis wasn't nicknamed the 'Pious' for nothing, adding profusely and gratuitously to the list of his confessed sins, there is reason to believe that there was an element of genuine piety involved. But it was clearly also an instance of how, in a polity scholars have termed the 'penitential state' ideologically framed by the principle of 'accountability', a Christian monarch could – in emulation of Theodosius – use public display as an enhancement of royal authority. It does not, however, seem to have played well with the barons, many of whom saw it as a dilution rather than a strengthening of power. Theodosius's public penance (for the Thessalonica massacre) was not in fact voluntary but undertaken at the insistence of Ambrose, and was unquestionably bound up with the new relation between Church and secular rule at a time when Nicean Christianity had become a state religion. As for the spectacular abjection of Henry II for complicity (which he always denied) in the murder of Thomas Becket, the jury is still out on the question of motive; most historians are agreed that, given the numerous crises Henry had to deal with, it certainly did his political interests no harm. On any rational assessment, the odds are very long, in the vast majority of documented cases, on 'sincerity' being a component of the performance, but there is no point in placing a bet since, given that we can never know, we can never collect.

'Accountability' as regret-speak is, of course, also part of the ritual culture of contemporary politics and public life.[28] Here we are almost certainly on much safer ground in laying serious intellectual cash on a punt with the moral bookies. Bankers forced to explain themselves before parliamentary committees have in recent years drenched us with avowals of regret, even 'profound' regret, for financial havoc, as the prelude to denying all responsibility for the behaviour of a 'market' alleged to be 'beyond their control'; duty done and then it's back to the bonuses. Ministers, both current and former, have refined the arts of regret-speak so as to be able to apologize while disclaiming intent (if you were offended by what I said, I'm truly sorry, but it's not my fault if you misinterpreted my words). The generals and their spokespersons issue statements of regret in the wake of civilian casualties (pre-sanitized as 'collateral damage'), in a manner that combines the euphemistic and the evasive (euphemistic as the politer version of 'stuff happens', and evasive as deflection of responsibility). Finer still, is the adjective 'regrettable', more impersonal and free-standing, a predicate intrinsic to the action without reference to the notionally regretting agent. These are the fleshless bones thrown to appease stirrings of moral unease, the cadaverous neighbour to the 'no comment' style of the public relations machine. Grudging and generally incidental to the incident in question, expressions of regret are themselves a form of collateral damage for the machine itself; too many of them and it might self-destruct from having tried too hard.

Contenders for the top spot in the shameless are numerous. But, when it comes to mixing it conceptually and lexically, there is arguably none to compare with François Fillon, former prime minister and candidate in the 2017 French presidential election. Fillon's profile combined elements of the neo-Thatcherite conservative and the devout Catholic with roots in the rural communities of *la France profonde*. First, there was the 'Jewish Question', his opaque reference in late 2016 to an unspecified time when 'we fought the drive by Jews to live in a community that did not respect all the rules of the French Republic'.[29] His strangled response when called upon to explain himself contained the term 'regret', but not for anything he said; what he regretted was the deformation of his meaning by others ('I therefore regret that some people dared to twist what I said'). This disingenuous clarification of a remark in which several caught a whiff of Vichy did not prevent the 'Question' coming back to bite him, when some months later a campaign aide posted an image of rival candidate, Emmanuel Macron, as the archetypical 'Jewish banker' of the 1930s.

Then there was the scandal that erupted over the use of a large amount of taxpayers' money to pay large sums to his wife and children for what were allegedly non-jobs. Fillon, while insisting he had done nothing illegal, expressed 'regret' at his 'mistake' in not having caught up with the contemporary French public's 'mistrust' of using their money in this way. It was reported as a 'calculated act of contrition' that 'may have swayed enough conservatives to keep his limping campaign afloat'. 'Calculated' steers the statement more in the direction of the political equivalent of an 'attrition', based on fear of the negative consequences of the revelations for his candidacy, precisely the distinction that so exercised Pascal in *The Provincial Letters*. This, however, was not the only occasion when the language of Christian contrition appeared during the campaign. There was also the extraordinary tour de force of turning another, even more resonant, term not only against a rival, but on its head. When Macron made a speech in which he said that France had a lot to answer for in connection with aspects of its colonial history in Algeria ('a crime against humanity'), Fillon responded as follows: 'This dislike of our history, this continual *repentance*, is unworthy of a candidate for the presidency of the Republic.' 'Repentance' is an unusual term to find in a context such as this. This is what the sixteenth- and seventeenth-century theologians and moralists wrestled with as the term for a transformation of the soul, real or feigned, in respect of past sins or wrongs. Fillon, the good Catholic, turned it inside out by making it part of a vocabulary of insult to describe a statement by a rival as a stain on the honour of the Republic and its highest office. 'Regret', perhaps, might pass muster, as a euphemism that commits one to little, but 'repentance' is another thing altogether, an unacceptable slur on a 'people' and its 'national history'.

During the intensive media coverage of Fillon's doomed shot at becoming President of the French Republic, no-one, not even in France, seems to have thought of La Rochefoucauld. Though distinctively seventeenth-century in tenor and tone, the *Maximes* are happily portable. La Rochefoucauld, we saw, uses inversion to position 'regret' as a lever for the exposure of (fake) 'repentance'. Fillon went one stage – in fact several stages – further, all the way to somewhere in lexical outer space where the dictionary is rearranged in such a way that, when applied to a political rival, a keyword undergoes a major semantic perversion. Fillon's use of the term would presumably have left Pascal not so much stunned as frankly baffled. La Rochefoucauld, on the other hand, we can imagine taking his anatomical scalpel to it with considerable relish, especially, when cornered, Fillon once more tried to brave it out with a mangled and table-turning reference to that other consecrated term, 'conscience': 'I've examined my conscience ... I wouldn't wish anyone to have to do the same in such circumstances. I call on members of my political family. It's for you now to examine *your* consciences.' Now let's please move on and seize the moment of opportunity, there's an election I want to win.

'Moving on' – the kairotic companion to modern public regret – is a very long way from Hannah Arendt's belief in the complementary acts of 'forgiving and promising' as the means of an authentic 'turning' from a past of error and harm to a future of reparation (another and nobler version of a political *metanoia*). No-one seems to have been exceptionally dismayed by this performance; it's all part of the way we live now. Moving on, however, turned out to be moving in short order to a quick political death. La Rochefoucauld's other maxim comes to mind: 'Le soleil ni la mort ne se peuvent regarder fixement' [Neither the sun nor death can be looked at steadily].

## VI

In the wider culture of everyday life, 'regret' is everywhere and yet taboo. We wallow in it and yet fear it. As essentially a thing of the media, we also trivialize it. Here's a headline for our times: 'Why the Kid Who Got Jeremy Corbyn Tattooed On His Back Won't Live to Regret It.' It is hard not to warm to this by virtue of its (unintentional?) ambiguities as to whose back gets tattooed and the fate that might await the kid. While the decision involved is scarcely on the scale of Croesus's to go to war, this sentence at least has the merit of bearing some resemblance to the interpretively open form of the ancient oracle. Most of the rest is a swamp, the scene of an extended, technologically mediated, me-me selfie dedicated to nostalgic yearnings, with political correlates in flaunted returns to past 'greatness'. The culture has generated various reactive movements, ways of dealing with regret, loss and yearning (the modern forms of *pothos*). Two in particular stand out: FOMO and YOLO.

The first (Fear of Missed Opportunity) hijacks *metanoia* in order to partner her with *pronoia* in the attempt at bringing metanoiacs, pronoiacs and paranoiacs together as a fraternity in the shared experience of anticipatory regret over the prospective missing of various trains, forms of the great party to which I have not been invited or of whose whereabouts I have not been told. The ailment is often contracted from contact with exciting posts on social media by successful party-goers, though ironically the main source of our acquaintance with sufferers is their having posted richly documented symptoms also on the very same media. It is the contemporary version of Vasari's *Occasio and Metanoia*, the gaze of the latter fixed on the moment when Occasio slips away from us, only less beautiful, packaged for consumption in throw-away wrappers. YOLO (You Only Live Once), on the other hand, is a recipe for 'millennial' living, packaged in wrapping paper decorated with quotations from Nietzsche. Yoloists offer prophylactic antidotes to Fomoist pronoiac neurosis, indeed to actual or anticipatory regret of any kind. They are a breezily cheerful counterpart to fretful anxiety and pining (and count members from the political classes, those who see bright futures in reckless decisions, while heaping contumely on purveyors of 'doom and gloom' and 'whingerama' addicts). As 'the rallying cry of a Millennial culture tired and frustrated with the burdens of the economic crisis', YOLO can offer you valuable tips on such matters as dietary regimes for looking after your body, or advice for the 'Modern Man' in respect of online dating ('living a life of regret is totally unnecessary' in contrast to 'a life spent rising through your life purpose as a man, while also being successful with women').[30]

Along with the agony aunts and newspaper advice columns for dating, there is also lavish backup assistance from branches of the self-help industry, along with varieties of psychotherapy ('merchants of hope', in Ernest Gellner's phrase, peddling the narcotic called 'positive thinking') and the odd professional media 'philosopher' devoted to feel-good messaging. Assistance includes use of the therapeutic distinction between 'upward' and 'downward' counterfactual thoughts in the face of 'unfortunate events' (the direction a function of whether the counterfactual has alternative outcomes as either worse or better). To this can be added the startlingly tautologous insight that if we didn't try to compare actual and alternative outcomes, we would be less prone to regret (YOLO naturally prescribes comparatist abstinence). To all this we must also add inputs from the fields of neuropsychology and cognitive science, much of it serious experimental research, with forbidding titles such as 'Outcome representations, counterfactual comparisons and the human orbitofrontal cortex. Implications for neuroimaging of studies of decision-making.' Similarly, as perhaps good news for Fomoists, there is the view, developed by the cognitive scientists, Smallman and Roese, to the effect that 'counterfactual thinking facilitates behavioural intentions', an approach echoed in Kahneman and Tversky's description of 'regret' as a 'counterfactual emotion' and their application of 'possible-worlds' semantics to the cognitive mapping of regret scenarios as a basis for regret-management and what is now called 'choice architecture'.[31] And, as good news for Yoloists, there are the Perfectionism Lab and the Optimism-Pessimism Lab at the University of Michigan, whose director, Edward Chang, has characterized 'regret' as 'practically un-American'.[32] If, like Murphy at the Magdalen Mental Mercyseat (in the Samuel Beckett novel), we remain impassive before pitiless therapeutic bombardment on behalf of either the Fomoist or the Yoloist cause, there are two other options. One is radical, a return to R. D. Laing's 'anti-psychiatric' use of the concept of *metanoia* in connection with his notion of the 'self cure' and the perilous existential journey out of solitude and mental chaos to relation with others and the exercise of autonomy. The other is simply, but understandably, weary, namely the telling counterfactual reflection of a fictional psychotherapist, no less, played by Gabriel Byrne in the series *In Treatment*: 'I just found myself wondering what my life would have been if I hadn't gone down this path, if I hadn't become a therapist.'

Although one lives inside neurosis while the other claims to have transcended it, what Fomoists and Yoloists have in common is their location at different points on the shared map of the modern regretting outlook known as 'buyer's regret' (a variant, with hints of soul-torment akin to victims of *metameleia* in Plato's *Republic*, is 'buyer's remorse'). The expression 'buyer's regret' also has many metaphorical extensions, a sure sign of its colonizing power over how we 'deal' with one another. One such is post-purchase political regret. This description of the mind-changing voter is of a piece with similar metaphors in the language of politics. Political parties no longer represent (movements, interests, classes); like stockbrokers, they propose an 'offer' to an electoral class of voters seen as a group for whom a policy is a 'sell' (hard or soft, cheap or expensive) while omitting to add that there is a hefty 'spread' between the offer and the sell prices. But while the figures of speech stretch across the political and social body with tentacular reach, it is important to stick with the literal meaning and the basic link to the exchange relation of buying and selling. Buyer's regret is consumer *metanoia*, a challenge to which modern commerce has risen with the policy of the 'return'. Once upon a time a purchase was a purchase, protected only by the 'guarantee' (normally against defects or violations of the trade descriptions act). Now, however, it can be subject to the fluctuating wishes and preferences of the after-thought, though this can be blocked by the contractual hitch and thus become the typical occasion on which regret becomes remorse and a version of torment sets in ('if only, if only').

Running across the contemporary landscape of regret is the attempted construction of a cost–benefit calculus for estimating relative 'opportunity costs', the value that shopper's *metanoia* can place on a botched transactional *kairos*. Fomoism, as the inverse of buyer's regret, is exceptionally powerful in this context, the fear of non-buyer regret taking hold as a consequence of being too late for the snatched 'bargain' (an anxiety ritually exacerbated by the annual pandemonium appropriately known as Black Friday). Acute fomoist anxiety is also known to haunt the 'investor community', the kairotic anticipation of a future regret that will ensue from missing out on a smart-looking IPO (this converts fast to its opposite when, post-purchase, the stock subsequently heads south). Indeed, it seems that, in the marketplace, fomoist fears are in fact outweighed by sensitivity to 'loss aversion' (sophisticated statistical models have been devoted to comparing the two attitudes – fear of missing out and fear of losing – with a view to delineating patterns of 'investor psychology'). These are some of the forms of what we can call 'capitalist' regret, characteristic of advanced economies with an intricate system of the division of labour, competitive markets, unequal distribution and a plurality of 'choices' along with myriad possibilities for their subsequent classification as the 'wrong' ones. Such a world is intrinsically saturated with counterfactual possibilities (and moreover not confined to the regretting kinds; there is also the jubilatory kind where the counterfactual takes the downward form of 'if I hadn't queued all night for the Black Friday bargain-fest…').

More generally the expression 'buyer's regret' and the various life-contexts to which it applies introduce us to the idea of an 'economics' of the counterfactual (as distinct from the important role of counterfactuals *in* economics as a discipline).[33] When the calculation delivers negative 'if-only' outcomes, regret can rapidly become grievance and a demand for 'compensation', from hard cash to psychic comforts supplied in exchange for cash. Freud left compensation to us, accomplished through the compensatory work of the unconscious, above all in dreams. Now our fantasies and desires move in the transactional circuits of commercial society. As with some other keywords of our time, 'compensation' has been abused either to reduce its meaning to rubble or to redirect it to a meaning for which it was not designed (bankers once received 'salaries', then the socially more upmarket 'remuneration', and now 'compensation' as if for an injury they sustained while squandering other people's money in the global casino). But while the principle of compensation for opportunities lost as well as injuries sustained has its distinctively modern calibrations, there is also an ancient lineage for compensatory adjustment, bound up with various offshoots of the semantic history of *metanoia* via

Latin cognates such as *poenitentia*. The history is often linked to etymologies, some of them, however, of doubtful reliability. They include an association of the language of second thoughts with notions of 'weighing' and thus calculations of relative 'values'. They also include associations with more primitive notions of debt, penalty and pain. Latin *poena* – a derivative of Greek *poinē* – was often used to signify compensatory payments and notions of 'blood money' (widespread in the *Iliad*), as well as producing the term *subpoena*, which was subsequently to enter the discourses and practices of law and legal systems.

Counterfactuals are central to the structures of legal reasoning and often a theoretical topic in the philosophy of jurisprudence. In *The Problems of Jurisprudence*, Richard Posner has commented on 'the heavy but largely unremarked reliance that the law places on determining counterfactuals. Counterfactual conditionals pervade our thinking about causes and effects. Often they are unproblematic,' before then going on to specify the respects in which they are often the reverse, by virtue of having to imagine eventualities (possible worlds) which have never existed.[34] The problems can be severe in the field of tort law and the assessment of liability on the part of the tort-feaser. In connection with the following three cases of litigation involving a claim to compensation, we might need more than the given protocols to make sense of them. In one case, a practising lawyer sues his alma mater (Oxford University) for 'damages' to his career as a consequence of not having been awarded a first-class degree, the actual result in turn allegedly the consequence of unsatisfactory tuition in one area of his course. A judge rules that there is a prima facie case to be heard and thus is fit for trial. On the other hand, unpacking it as a counterfactual yields some serious difficulties. How, in such a case, does one counterfactually assess, first, the hypothetical substance of the antecedent switch (the quality of the teaching he would have received in the relevant part of the degree course) and, second, the probability percentages of the perfect conditional consequent (would have secured a better degree outcome and hence a better career, and hence a better life in some sense or other of the term)? All of this is far from clear, especially given the temporal distance between his time as a student and his pressing of the claim (aged 38). It is no surprise that the plaintiff lost.[35] The peculiarities of the case are, however, small beer compared to those of the second – that of the teenager who won the Euromillions lottery and sued the lottery agency for 'negligence' in having ruined her life, ruination being the consequence of her having come into the possession of so much money. This 'if only' counterfactual takes buyer's, or rather gambler's, regret to an unfamiliar place – where one sues for not having lost. We do not appear to know in what 'compensation' for not having lost might consist. It also throws new light on the news that AI has developed an algorithm for a programme called 'Using Counterfactual Regret Minimization to Create Competitive Multiplayer Poker Agents'.

The stand-out example of the three, however, concerns one Lawrence McKinney from Memphis, Tennessee, who was released after 31 years in jail for crimes he did not commit because he could not have committed them (DNA evidence surfaced that proved he could not have been at the scene). The authorities evidently gave the matter of 'compensation' some thought, since they came up with the offer of a princely seventy five dollars. Naturally, McKinney's lawyer pitched for a round million. Apart from basic issues of natural justice, or indeed as part of them, a fundamental question here concerns the precise nature of the tort requiring compensation. What here is the object of compensation: the exiguous, liberty-deprived life he had in prison, or, counterfactually, the better life he would have had outside prison? How to place a 'value' on either? McKinney's own reported statement certainly nails the backdrop to the appropriate counterfactual question: 'I don't have no life, all my life was taken away.' In such circumstances, there may come a moment when we feel for Woody Allen's predicament. On the subject of his own autobiography, Allen broaches, with a fair degree of equanimity, the theme of how to handle 'the many regrets in my life' ('that's OK. It's conflict and excitement. It would be nice to write that out'). But it could just as easily end by throwing in the autobiographical towel with the more intriguing, endgame reflection: 'my one regret in life is that I am not someone else'.

Montaigne, we saw, gives regret and repentance short shrift, from an insistence on being and remaining the person he thinks he is. Woody Allen mounts the horse of regret and rides off in absolutely the opposite direction. Montaigne occasionally toys with counterfactuals, but as if playing idly, and not for long, with an innocuous and inconsequential bauble. Woody Allen projects himself into a possible world that consists of nothing but counterfactuals. In the ordinary run of things, wanting to be or to have been someone else is innocuous enough (the young girl who wishes, regretfully, she were or had been a princess is unlikely to be bothering either the psychiatrist or the philosopher). But if one presses just a little harder on Allen's remark (and sidelines its probable status as a gag), it can start to spawn an awkward question: whether, in the envisaged possible world, he is still also Woody Allen while being someone else. If he isn't, then whoever 'someone else' is, he (or she) would not appear to be someone whose identity is governed by the first-person pronoun 'I' with which Allen's sentence begins. An even more extreme example of this type of existential regret we meet in the next chapter, but not at all as a gag. It is not the wish to be or to have been someone else, but the wish not to have been anyone at all; that is, the wish never to have been born. The wish never to have been born we can call an 'identity crisis'.

# 6 NOT, NEVER OR FOREVER BEING ME

*It is one of history's great counterfactuals: if Boris Johnson wasn't Boris Johnson and Michael Gove wasn't Michael Gove, would Boris Johnson and Michael Gove be able to sort out the mess Boris Johnson and Michael Gove have made?*

**TOM PECK**

# I

The well-known Keynesian *metanoia* ('When the facts change, I change my mind. What do you do?') is memorably challenging as a riposte to less nimble opponents intent on charging Keynes with inconsistency. While probably apocryphal, it has not proven especially controversial. One thing that would presumably occur to no-one to suggest is that Keynes's change of mind also entailed a change of identity, such that the John Maynard Keynes with the new views was in some important sense a different individual who happened to have the same name. This preposterous straw man goes up in smoke at just the hint of a spark. Nevertheless, once despatched, it leaves the way clear to head towards more interestingly murky waters. How do things stand when the change of mind engages deep, self-defining matters of belief (loss or acquisition of an identity-sustaining religious faith, for example)? And what ensues when the frame of reference is not the factual but the counterfactual, especially in the mode of regret, along with an array of possible wishes in respect of how things might have been otherwise? How do such considerations stand to cases that involve names (technically the branch of modal logic concerned with the relation of proper names and 'identity')? What, for instance, of the Saul who becomes Paul in the road-to-Damascus story, the crossroads moment when, in the received version of the story, the anti-Christian Jewish zealot is transformed into the committed Christian apostle?[1] And what of that other Paul, the painter Gauguin (curiously re-baptized 'Saul' by Vincent Van Gogh in a private notebook), who keeps his name but drastically changes his life when he leaves both his country and his family for Tahiti?

We shall return to this case in greater detail shortly, but the question it raises is, in a nutshell, whether regret of a certain kind (intense, 'all-in') for a decision of a certain kind (the radically life-changing) would mean not just wishing that one had acted and lived otherwise, but effectively wishing not to have been oneself. Adapting slightly a formulation of Bernard Williams (from and of whom there is a great deal more to come in this chapter), the question concerns the distinction between a different individual story and a story of a different individual. Running this distinction requires many of the discriminations we find in philosophical theories of the self. But it is important to note that in many ways it stands somewhat to one side of their normal concern with the principles of change, persistence and continuity, along with their variously exotic thought-experiments (from hypothetical tele-transportation to the imaginary torture chambers that await persons after hypothetical body swaps). Here, and as Williams further puts it, the basic questions that attach to counterfactually expressed regret, have less to do with 'identity over time' than with 'identity in relation to possibilities' and what in this connection will count *as* a possibility.[2]

The structural crux of the issue is a relation between standpoints and perspectives, the gap that intervenes between how things looked prospectively at the crossroads of decision and how they look in retrospect at a given point in time, the latter perspective in turn to be causally understood as the 'standpoint' of a 'later self' that, as Williams puts it in *Moral Luck*, 'will be the product of my earlier choices'.[3] It is the causal dimension of this relation between past and present perspectives that explains the potentially devilish work of the counterfactual, introducing a disturbance that ripples along the chain linking standpoint, narrative and, ultimately, 'identity'. At time point *t*, the agent (or the historian) looks back to a fork in the road not taken and considers how things might have been had it been taken. One inevitable consequence is that the retrospective point of view adopted at the same time point *t* will inevitably be different from that in which the imagined alternative is contemplated.

The difference is a function of everything that would have happened to the agent along that other road in life.[4] When, for instance, in the letter of 1530 Erasmus writes 'I wish I could undo everything and start all over again', he specifically had in mind his earlier works such as *In Praise of Folly*. This is but the rueful backwards look of an older man on his younger self (as we saw in the first chapter, one of the tropes of Renaissance painting), and it is unlikely that it was wholeheartedly meant. If, however, we take it seriously (that is, if we counterfactually imagine an Erasmus who hadn't written the *Moriae Encomium*), then one thing we can be sure of is that, whatever his regrets in 1530, they would necessarily have been different in some fundamental respects; by definition they couldn't include regret at having written *In Praise of Folly*, but might include an older man's regret at not having done so.

This may resemble mere game-playing with the counterfactual. Yet the potential disruption here is not merely playful. There is a disturbing consequential implication to Erasmus's wish 'to undo everything and start all over again' even being entertained. The ideas, and the writings that expressed them, were not like hats to be doffed and removed at whim, not merely contingent features of a 'career', but wound into the very core of his being, so fundamental to his life's project that an Erasmus without the early writings, without the *Moriae Encomium*, would arguably not have been 'Erasmus'. This puts pressure on the sustainability of the backwards-looking perspective and thus of the counterfactual thought experiment itself. Just how much pressure will depend on how substantial the divergence of the alternative path from the one actually taken proves to be, and more particularly the extent to which the different life both imagined and desired involves transformative changes of commitments, values and outlook (for example, *metanoia* as 'conversion' in its various forms).[5] At the outer limit, the disturbance is not just to standpoints, but also to the very fabric of the self. It is where, in the telling of counterfactual narratives about a life, Allen's 'someone else' incoherently looms as both their hero and their narrator. Time to return to Gauguin's story.

The story is told by Williams as a fable to illustrate what he terms 'moral luck'.[6] Gauguin, famously or notoriously, abandons his family for a life in Tahiti, a decision that, for him, is crucial to his becoming a certain kind of artist. The decision itself is a gamble (on 'luck') in that he cannot know in advance what the outcome will be: success or failure in the project on which he has staked all. How things eventually turn out for him as a painter shapes both his and our retrospective assessments of what by normal standards was a cruel decision; it is the point at which luck becomes an issue of 'moral luck'. If successful, Gauguin may properly feel some 'regret' at the pain inflicted on his deserted family, but not 'all-in' regret at a decision on which he apparently gambled everything in order to become the great painter he allegedly is.[7] It is probably fair to say that, although intriguing, this is one of Williams's shakier contributions to moral philosophy. The ground projects that govern a life may indeed, in some circumstances, override rigidly fixed systems of 'morality', but the particular form of that argument here can all too easily come out as a vindication of the sweet smell of success trumping all other considerations. There is a very great deal of evidence to suggest that Gauguin was quite simply moral shabbiness incarnate ('cynical, cheap, and utterly self-centered' is Adam Gopnik's entirely reasonable description, in a discussion of his relationship with Van Gogh to which we come shortly).[8]

For present purposes, the interest of the Gauguin tale turns on the implications of the counterfactual (at the crossroads of his life Gauguin might have acted otherwise). These implications have been lucidly analysed by Meir Dan-Cohen. 'Suppose', he writes, 'that the alternative to going to Tahiti involved becoming a bank-teller in France. For Gauguin to wish that he had pursued this option would be to opt for an impermissible, identity-disrupting counterfactual, which amounts to the incoherent wish that he were someone else'.[9] It is impermissible because 'conditions of personal identity set the limits on the counterfactuals about ourselves that we can intelligibly entertain'. Quite how they are set is a thorny question, and it is one of the strengths of Dan-Cohen's argument that the difficulty is fully confronted. Basic limits, however, are set by the special class of decisions that are deemed to be 'constitutive' and equally the special class of projects that are deemed to be 'defining' – broadly the bundle of values, priorities and urgencies that lock an identity in place, in a fashion that evokes the spirit of Luther's *hier stehe ich, ich kann nicht anders*. The condition under which a biographical or an autobiographical counterfactual appears to commit you to an effective 'identity-switch' is where the decision in question is 'constitutive'. It has nothing to do with external conditions of possibility (in these terms the option on Gauguin's staying in France and working in a bank was fully available to him), and everything to do with internal conditions of impossibility, impossible because of the kind of person one simply is.[10] Gauguin's decision is one he has to take and his project one he has to embrace because they are, in some very deep way, what make Gauguin

'Gauguin'. In these terms, counterfactual contemplation of an alternative path for him makes no sense, since, whoever might have taken that path, it could not have been Gauguin.

Not all decisions and projects are like this; in fact most are not.[11] The 'constitutive' and the 'defining' in the very strong form envisaged are typically associated with certain kinds of individuals, for example, warrior-heroes in the ancient world and pioneering artists in the modern world.[12] But even here there are grey areas and blurred boundaries. Take Van Gogh's story, and specifically the life-changing decision for the type of artist Van Gogh wished to be, namely the departure for Arles and the light of the Midi. Gauguin, of course, figures centrally in this story as Van Gogh's house companion, and most notoriously in the endlessly rehashed episode of the severed ear that ends with Gauguin fleeing Arles, Van Gogh's breakdown and his admission to the St Rémy asylum, from which he was briefly discharged only to be re-admitted, and where he was to paint the great pictures, *The Starry Night* and *Cypresses*. A question that might arise here is the extent to which what happens to Van Gogh is equally 'constitutive' of his 'project', but, if so, it is in a manner altogether less intellectually and ethically rigid than the framework in which the counterfactual is excluded from the Gauguin life story as incompatible with who and what Gauguin 'is'. Van Gogh wrote movingly to his brother, Theo, about the failed 'communitarian' venture with Gauguin and his admission to the asylum:

> Poor egotist that I've always been and still am now, I can't shake off this idea, which, however, I've already explained to you two or three times, that it's thus for the best that I go into an asylum right now. It will perhaps turn out all right in the end ... However, the fact that the idea of an association of painters, of housing them together, some of them, although we haven't succeeded, although it's a deplorable and painful failure – this idea remains true and reasonable – like so many others. BUT NO BEGINNING AGAIN (Van Gogh's caps).[13]

This captures many things. There are elements of regretful nostalgia for a lost communitarian possibility once deemed crucial to Van Gogh's conception of the artist, but also a refusal of regret and by implication of related counterfactual temptations. There are no dreams of rewinding the story and 'beginning again'; the asylum is the right place and entering it the right decision, not just for reasons of safety, but also as a place where he can now be himself, not the 'poor egotist that I've always been and still am now', but precisely the artist. The asylum is where, now, he can and will paint.

It is fair to say that this offers a far richer brew than the Gauguinesque allegory of moral luck turning on a single decision. Around the question of what it was for Van Gogh to have a core of being – the core of what it was to be the painter Van Gogh – there are regrets, hesitations and decisions woven into a skein made of twists and turns, protests and acceptances, imaginings of the possible and recognitions of the actual, a complex mix of both the backwards gaze and the forwards gaze. The example of Van Gogh certainly lends weight to Dan-Cohen's important point that it is not straightforwardly easy to distinguish between 'identity-preserving and identity-disrupting counterfactuals, and correspondingly to devise a threshold of regret beyond which it will have lost its subject'. The moral he draws is one we should heed: 'Whatever the distinction and the threshold, we should not imagine them as clear-cut. The most we can do in this area is post some warning signs alerting people to a broad and ill-defined yet significant danger zone, in which certain attitudes that are perfectly intelligible outside of it lose their coherence.' That is indeed the most we can do, but it is already a lot. As well as being a caution, it also leaves open a space for counterfactual assessments of past choices and decisions that do not send the self spiralling into its logical annihilation, where imagining yourself as having lived differently commits you to imagining yourself as no longer 'you'. On the other hand, the cautionary note constrains as much as it permits, limiting that space for the most part to choices that are relatively inconsequential for the sense of self, contingent matters of passing tastes, whims and so forth, neither 'constitutive' nor 'defining', more the small change of counterfactual evaluation. We will want later to consider the possibility of larger spaces for the perusal of the possible, including the thought that even the 'defining' can be re-defined and the 'self' not bound to a template that closes the door on the large-scale counterfactual understood as a threat to the foundations of the self's very existence.[14]

## II

The thinker who sought not only to close the door but also to lock it and throw away the key was Nietzsche, the philosopher who above all others repudiated the (substantive) counterfactual, especially of the regret-laden variety, as both incoherent and contemptible. His most famous 'character' arrives, accompanied by his followers, at the emblematic place of decision and object of retrospect: 'they came to a crossroads; then Zarathustra told them he wanted to walk alone.'[15] But it is not the place where one fork in the road will prove to have been the 'right' way, and the other the 'wrong' way, of the type that can later become the focus of regretful musings. Whichever is taken, it will be 'right' by virtue of having been taken. It is midday, the liminal 'great noontide'. Zarathustra declares the death of 'all the Gods' and the moment come when 'now we desire the *Übermensch* to live'[16]. The verb 'to live' in Nietzsche is, of course, no simple infinitive. It is one of the load-bearing terms of an entire philosophy of self and identity in which 'life' is its own self-justifying value. In *Thus Spake Zarathustra*, as elsewhere in his writings, the simplest of the Nietzschean formulae for 'life' as its own value is the unconditional 'Yes', unconditional in the sense that excludes all counterfactual conditionals, namely 'the eternal Yes to all things'. This, however, is but the beginning of a whole string of complications, along which, as we shall see, the counterfactual effects its own strange return, and whose endpoint will take us to a new and unbearable place for the reflection on regret and identity – the place where you are not 'someone else' but no-one at all, and where the ringing 'Yes' is met by a resounding 'No'.

The main source or context in Nietzsche's writings for the affirmation of the 'eternal Yes' is the obscure doctrine of the 'Eternal Recurrence', the claim that everything that has been, is, and will be forms a system of interconnected parts that repeats over and over in every particular, with no exceptions; remove one of the parts and all the others go with it. 'Let us think this thought in its most terrible form: existence as it is, without meaning or aim, yet recurring inevitably without any finale of nothingness: "the eternal recurrence".'[17] We are thus invited to participate in a thought experiment ('let us think this thought'), perhaps one of the most singular in the history of philosophy. The Recurrence is sometimes billed as a 'cosmological' doctrine, but, as Alexander Nehamas notes, in these terms the doctrine lacks elementary credibility given the conspicuous absence of any attempt on Nietzsche's part to supply even the rudiments of a 'proof'.[18] In these terms, it comes across as a weird form of unsupported determinism, an allegedly law-bound dispensation for the 'world', for which no actual laws are cited and which resembles nothing so much as a hellish recipe for the cosmic order in the form of an eternal Groundhog

Day. The interest of the Eternal Recurrence in fact has little to do with physics and everything to do with human psychology and 'ethics', in the very special Nietzschean (i.e. resolutely anti-Kantian) sense of the term. It is more a gathering point for a collection of notions centred on the question of 'identity', what irreducibly makes you 'you', or 'how man becomes what he is'.[19]

This is the subtitle of *Ecce Homo* (*Wie man wird was man ist*). The notion of becoming what you are appears to echo Aristotle's principle of entelechy, the process whereby a potential becomes actual as the consequence of teleologically driven processes in nature. This is not Nietzsche's world. You become what you are, not as pre-given essence purposively realized in process, but as the sum and stamp of everything that has happened to you and everything that you have done; 'you' are no more and no less than the web of connections that is your life, in turn part of the web of connections that is the world. Remove any one element from the web and it unravels, in the profound sense that it would no longer be your life and its subject no longer you. In this respect, Nietzsche's 'all-in' version differs from the Gauguin story. The latter involves a foregrounding and a backgrounding, a hierarchical structure of relevance inside which it concerns itself not with Gauguin's entire life but with only the critical turning point in the road of that life and the very special, indeed unique, decision that occurs at it. At the same time, however, the Recurrence is neither an ontology nor a history. It does not claim, or at least interestingly claim, that you literally repeat for eternity the same life inside the same body. It is, precisely, a thought experiment, in the form of a dare and a test: how much of your life can you affirm; anything short of everything means you fail the test. The most famous invocation of the Recurrence as a summons or challenge that has riding on it nothing less than the life/self equation is the moment in *The Gay Science* when the demon comes to visit with a startling message and an exacting question:

> What if some day or night a demon were to steal into your loneliest loneliness and say to you: 'This life as you now live and have lived it you will have to live once again and innumerable times again; and there will be nothing new in it, but every pain and every joy and every thought and sigh and everything unspeakably small or great in your life must return to you, all in the same succession and sequence – even this spider and this moonlight between the trees, and even this moment and I myself ... Do you *want* this again and innumerable times again?[20]

What matters here has little to do, other than rhetorically, with objective 'facts', and everything to do with a subjective attitude to a purely speculative eventuality. It is a question about 'wanting' wrapped around a supposition, and more specifically, whether you have the inner strength to will the recurrence. 'My formula for human greatness', he writes in *Ecce Homo*, 'is *amor fati*: that you do not want anything to be different, not forwards, not backwards, not for all eternity.'[21] Nothing to be different, neither prospectively nor retrospectively, this life, and only this life – these are the terms which the doctrine of the Eternal Recurrence bequeaths to Zarathustra's 'eternal yes to all things': 'Have you ever said Yes to one joy? O my friends, then you said Yes to *all* pain. All things are enchained, entwined, enamoured – if ever you wanted one time, two times, if you ever said "I like you, happiness! Whoosh! Moment!, happiness! Abide, moment!", then you wanted *everything* back!'[22] The Recurrence, though notionally it not only is but has to be about everything, is in reality centred on one thing – the vast and inescapable sea of suffering that is 'life'. This is what the Recurrence calls upon us to acknowledge and accept as that which we would willingly live and re-live, over and over. Wanting 'all back', uttering the 'eternal Yes to all things', is the same as all-in assent to the suffering, not as passive resignation, but as affirmation and as a counter to all-in regret. The Eternal Recurrence is Nietzsche's robust antidote for Eternal Regrets.

It is also the waste paper basket for shredded counterfactuals. Willing the recurrence as the eternal Yes has to mean, as Nehamas puts it, 'that no counterfactuals of the form "If I had done such-and-such instead of such-and-such, then I would have ..." can ever be true.'[23] But this is where our string of complication twists, to form a sort of Möbius strip that can turn things inside out, and where the very modes of argumentation deployed by Nietzsche the ardent anti-counterfactualist arguably make of him a counterfactualist *malgré lui*. This is not, to be clear, a critique of Nietzsche, an attempt to trip him up. There are many other ways of going about this should one wish to. We will probably also want to avert our gaze from the late formulations that so excited his Nazi-loving sister-editor of *The Will to Power*, such as 'the idea of recurrence as a *selective* principle, in the service of strength (and barbarism!!)'. The issue here concerns rather the place and role in Nietzsche's work of counterfactuals of different kinds, and in particular the dependency on the heuristic use of conditionals to mount an argument dedicated to despatching substantive counterfactuals of the kind cited above by Nehamas. The logical grid of the argument, especially in its use of the Recurrence, relies heuristically on three procedural 'ifs': (a) if one's life were to recur, the life would be the same in every respect; (b) if anything were different, then everything would be different; and (c) if different, it would not be your life but 'someone else's'.

For the most part, these are imported 'ifs', the ones standardly used by commentary to explain and clarify Nietzsche's thinking as extrapolations from what lies implicit in Nietzsche's mode of argumentation.[24] And then there is the fully explicit: the repeated appeals to the language of supposition ('suppose that …'), the rhetorical use of conditional and subjunctive forms ('would you not'), and the obsessive 'if's. There are times indeed when 'if' seems to be Nietzsche's favourite word, albeit as more the 'if' of hope and imperative than of the analytical counterfactual conditional.[25] Nevertheless they bathe in the atmosphere of the hypothetical, and on occasion become the 'what if' that routinely prefaces counterfactual speculations (most strikingly the 'what if' that inaugurates the cited passage from *The Gay Science*). In short, 'ifs' are everywhere. It has often been pointed out that Nietzsche's theories of causation rely on heuristic counterfactuals.[26] But so too do his ideas of self and identity, and most notably when the explicit thrust of those ideas is to banish the counterfactual. That does not, of course, render Nietzsche's argument inherently self-contradictory. There is a genuine distinction between a substantive and a procedural counterfactual, but it does suggest a certain strain in the relation between the substantive and the procedural.[27] If Nietzsche or his demon or Zarathustra can invite me to consider what 'would' follow 'if' I were to will my life to recur identically and forever, we are not terribly far, if any distance at all, from a counterfactual alternative to what my life currently, and abjectly (because unheroically), is.

One might also want, though more cautiously, to add to the mix a hint of the worst feature of counterfactual imagining: wish fulfilment fantasy, the very thing that, along with self-pity, Nietzsche's robust ethic of pure affirmation despises. In relation to the concepts of 'life' and 'self', the Recurrence, we have seen, is all about wanting and wishing, that is, it is about how Nietzsche ideally wants things to be. How he wants them to be is explicitly part of an anti-Christian agenda, the embrace of the 'this-worldly' and the rejection of the 'other-worldly'. His ideal type is the opposite of what in *Thus Spake Zarathustra* is called the 'pale criminal' who 'was equal to his deed when he did it; but could not bear its image after it was done'. The pale criminal is an archetype for, among others, the guilt-ridden, life-hating Christian, anathema to Nietzsche. Yet it was

Carl Jung who, in the notes for his seminar on Zarathustra, signalled some curious affinities. Nietzsche's demand that we will it all, the 'woes' as well as the 'joys', indeed the woes *as* joys, as suffering sublimated and stylized, may be said, suggests Jung, to recall, at a very general level of typology, the self-mortifying ecstatic trance induced by Ignatius of Loyola.[28] 'What if' thought experiments should perhaps carry a health warning: be careful what you wish for.

There is also something else. It is our final complication where Nietzsche's example is concerned, but one that takes us towards a trunkful of other complications. Nietzsche's 'Yes' has a historical setting that in turn serves as a model: the ancient world and specifically the pagan world of the tragic consciousness prior to the advent of Socratic rationalism and the reflective mind divided between reason and the instincts. The tragic consciousness of ancient Greece is the subject of *The Birth of Tragedy*, Nietzsche's first extended exposition, under the heading of the 'Dionysian', of the conversion of pain and suffering into the joyous acceptance of what will become Zarathustra's 'eternal yes'. This ancient mode of being is described from many points of view. One of them has it as a source of 'metaphysical solace', and one of the figures that instantiates it is the tragic Satyr:

> The metaphysical solace – with which, I wish to suggest, we derive from every true tragedy, the solace that in the ground of things, and despite all changing appearances, life is indestructibly mighty and pleasurable, this solace appears with palpable clarity in the chorus of the satyrs, a chorus of natural beings whose life goes on ineradicably behind and beyond all civilization, as it were, and who remain eternally the same despite all the changes of generations and in the history of nations.[29]

This is consistent with several features of what will later evolve into the doctrine of the Eternal Recurrence. There is, however, another, and very different, entrance made by the figure of the satyr in *The Birth of Tragedy*. This is the occasion when he is asked to speak of the best that can be, although in terms that *mutatis mutandis* might evoke Samuel Beckett's grim play in *Worstward Ho* with how to distinguish between the better and best worst and the worse and worst worst (the comparison is not purely random or arbitrary; Beckett will reappear shortly). This other satyr is Silenus, whose encounter with King Midas is recounted in the early chapters of *The Birth of Tragedy*. Midas asks Silenus what is the 'best'. Silenus's answer has nothing to do with the unconditional affirmation of the one and only lived life; the best is not the one life you have, but no life at all, and, if that is not possible, the second best is as swift an end as possible to the life you have. It is the definitive and literal life-denying No to the all-affirming Yes:

> An ancient legend recounts how King Midas hunted long in the forest for the wise Silenus, companion of Dionysos, but failed to catch him. When Silenus has finally fallen into his hands, the King asks what is the best and most excellent thing for human beings. Stiff and unmoving, the daemon remains silent until, forced by the King to speak, he finally breaks out in shrill laughter and says: 'Wretched, ephemeral race, children of chance and tribulation, why do you force me to tell you the very thing which it would be most profitable for you *not* to hear? The very best thing is utterly beyond your reach: not to have been born, not to *be*, to be *nothing*.[30]

## III

There is, however, in this formulation a point of language, which for the most part would normally pass unnoticed, but which, in the context of our questions, may give us pause for thought. For Nietzsche's original German 'nicht geboren zu sein', the above translation has, as do others, 'not to have been born'.[31] The alternative, and more literal, way of rendering this is in the present rather than the perfect infinitive form: 'not to be born'. The four-word match here is exact, although the word order, of course, varies and, more generally, the grammatical analogues between the two languages are not precise (not to mention the even wider gulf where ancient Greek is concerned). In ordinary usage, the two forms of the passive infinitive would normally be heard as expressing broadly the same thought, such that any pressing of the point of difference might come across as mere hair-splitting. Nietzsche's German is by no means eccentric, though the purist confronted with 'not to have been born' as a translation of 'nicht geboren zu sein' might maintain that the elision of 'worden' (the past participle of the auxiliary verb, 'werden') could be telling us something.[32] If there are any loose ends here, it is because of what, in relation to the possibility of counterfactual statements, can respectively be claimed of the two infinitive forms. 'Not to have been born' gets us, if unsteadily, to a counterfactual. While there are logical difficulties with the formulation, I can, bleakly, say 'it would be best for me not to have been born'. There are no comparable first-personal options for the present infinitive; other than under some rather unusual conditions in the amniotic fluids, as far we know; 'I' cannot say or think 'it would be best for me not to be born'.[33]

Silenus, however, can say it of everyone. The English translations of the ancient sources for the Silenus story (Aristotle, Plutarch, Cicero, etc.) oscillate between the two infinitive forms, but most commonly opt for the present infinitive 'not to be born'. This is indicative of a distinctive world view, the one Nietzsche tries to capture, in which what lies 'out of reach' is not just an option for Midas but any compensatory counterfactual for existence as such. Some appear to be of the view that Silenus's words are a denunciation, specifically a metaphysical and moral comment on the sheer awfulness of humans, with then an implied counterfactual of sorts (to the effect that the world would be a much better place if there had been no humans born into it). In one or two of the sources there are moments that suggest something along these lines. Aristotle, for example, has Silenus say 'for humans, the best for them is not to be born at all, not to partake of nature's excellence', which suggests the human as a flaw in the otherwise excellent design of the natural order. Cicero's Silenus, on the other hand, puts it all down to the work of fate (the 'rocks of life' and the 'fire of fortune'): 'Best by far not to be born, and not to come up against these rocks of life, but, if you are born, it is next best to escape as it were from the fire of fortune as quickly as possible.'

However, the notion that Silenus is singling out mankind as the incorrigible flaw in the world makes little sense of Nietzsche's invocation. In *The Birth of Tragedy*, Silenus's words are not a prelapsarian musing on a might-have-been without humans. There is no suggestion that the 'world' (of, say, flowers, trees, cows) would be better without the human presence. On the contrary, one of the key emphases in the account of the 'Dionysian' falls on the rhythm of wild cruelty that runs through the world as such, through all of Being. This is why what follows Silenus's reference to birth is so important: 'nicht zu *sein, nichts* zu sein' ('not to *be*, to be *nothing*'). The key words are 'sein' and 'nichts', and, although spoken to an individual interlocutor, their import is general. They concern a collective entity in terms of a notion of Being, the obscure notion of not-being ('nicht zu sein') as being-nothing ('nichts zu sein'). This is not the vehicle of a moral criticism of mankind. It is not about the awfulness of humans, but about the awfulness of their condition, their entrapment in an ontology of endless and unendurable suffering. The 'best' is not what is best for a world *without* them, but what is best *for* them, were it not by definition too late.[34]

This is the primal 'wisdom' (Nietzsche's word) to be absorbed rather than refused, a necessary condition of its sublimation in the affirming 'Yes'. The Yes says 'no' to the No, not by rejecting it, but by incorporating it. That task he claimed to have been the great task assumed by Greek culture, and especially Greek tragedy,[35] up to the point where the ancient wisdom was forgotten, lost and displaced by 'Socratic optimism'. Nietzsche, however, is not – despite occasional musings roughly to the contrary – himself an ancient Greek. He is a modern seeking to reconnect with the ancient, a very different thing, and his recounting of the Silenus story is but one among many modern appeals to it. Silenus's jeremiad (along with Job's) travelled down through the ages to times and places well beyond those of the ancient world. As a post-antiquity corpus, it is something of a lexical and grammatical medley, with initially a strong imprint of Christian thinking. In the modern period, it begins with Calderón, who plumps for the perfect infinitive and links the whole notion to birth as the commission of a 'crime': 'Pues el delito mayor del hombre es haber nacido' ('For man's greatest crime is to have been born'). Schopenhauer (one of Nietzsche's early teachers until Nietzsche turned against him) quotes the Calderón apothegm more than once in *The World as Will and Idea*, glossing it in Christian terms as the 'Erbsünde' ('original sin') and the 'fault' or 'guilt' of 'Being' ('Schuld des Seins'). Nietzsche also quotes it in *Human, All Too Human*, although in the context of a savage attack on 'the insufferable superlative Christianity of Calderon', while giving the quotation itself short shrift, in the interestingly formulated guise of 'the craziest paradox that can be'.[36] Not the least of its interest consists in how this description might stand to the Silenus speech in *The Birth of Tragedy*. If indeed – to anticipate – there *is* a paradox at the heart of wishing never to have been born, there is not even the slightest hint of that in Silenus's 'nicht geboren zu sein'.

In the twentieth century, Samuel Beckett will allude to a version of the Schopenhauer source in his early essay on Proust ('the original sin, and the eternal sin of him and all his 'soci malorum', the sin of having been born'), while carrying it over into his fictional and dramatic work in a manner both serious and comic. In the early novel, *Murphy*, Mr Neary 'curses, first the day he was born, and then – in a bold flashback – the night he was conceived', a capacious view echoed by Mr Tyler in the radio play, *All That Fall*, with an inventively precise switch of timing for the first stage of the whole business ('the wet Saturday afternoon' of his conception). In rough overlap, if a trifle belatedly in more senses than one, there are the 'thoughts' of Emil Cioran, who drifts onto the scene of Parisian existentialism, self-confessedly spends his life in a state of unrelieved 'boredom', dabbles in Nietzsche from time to time while just about managing a yawning imitation of Silenus. There is a jaunty first shot at this in *A Short History of Decay*: 'Not to be born is undoubtedly the best plan of all. Unfortunately, it is within no-one's reach' (who, one might want to ask, is to be the agent behind this 'plan'?). In the major statement of the theme, the jaunty gives way to the languid, the tediously enervating 'inconvenience' of having been born (Cioran once said that 'inconvenient' was his favourite adjective).[37] *De l'inconvénient d'être né* informs us that 'we have lost, being born, as much as we shall lose dying. Everything'. Set against that are the counterfactual pleasures of the 'idea' that, had it not been for the 'ill fortune of being born', we could have remained encapsulated in a 'state of pure possibility', enjoying the 'freedom, happiness and space' that are 'the terms' of the pre-natal condition. It has to remain something of a mystery as to how this blissful possibilitarian state can exist, let alone be sustained, in light of Cioran's version of flip-back to the moment of conception, with sperm cast in the role of arch-criminal ('sperm is the bandit in its pure form'). Surely, if life in the womb is the 'best', then sperm has to qualify as a noble citizen rather than as an outlaw (unless the thought is that bandits produce better babies, or rather embryos). If ever there were occasion for countering certain adaptations of the Silenus counterfactual with its opposite (the altruist 'wonderful life' counterfactual of the angel, Clarence, in the Frank Capra film), this is surely it.

It has been wryly noted that it took some time for Cioran to get round to letting us know of his having been inconvenienced as of day one; he was 62 when *De l'inconvénient d'être né* was published. But with this sort of thing, we are nevertheless brought, if horizontally, to the cusp of the antinatalist nihilism of the philosopher David Benatar and the extraordinary spectacle of colliding premises and sequiturs in statements such as 'given that there are no real advantages over never existing for those who are brought into existence, it is hard to see how the significant risk of serious harm could be justified'.[38] It is also hard, very hard, to know how this might stand to the ancient 'wisdom' Nietzsche associated with the satyr. If there is to be any reference back to Silenus, it will resemble wilful parody, in the mutilating form of a utilitarian cost–benefit analysis weighing the terms of a trade-off: 'On my view there is no net benefit to coming into existence and thus coming into existence is never worth its costs.'[39] How you calibrate the comparative costs of being and non-being, or more exactly of being and not-ever-having-been, would seem to call for an unusual form of the spreadsheet or the book-keeping ledger; non-being may well be painless, but how one can know that isn't clear, and in any case, if indeed painless, it is not painless for *you* (in this scenario 'you' do not exist; if there is no pain it's because there is no you). In the world of the trade-off, cash, however, is king, and the law of tort and contract never far away. Nor is the case that has been hovering in the wings.

# IV

This is the case – free-standingly philosophical but also involving legal deliberations – that is the subject of Williams's paper, 'Resenting one's own existence'. We have already seen how 'if only' counterfactual regret can spawn grievance, leading in turn to demands for compensation that are sometimes sought through litigation, for example the three cases cited in the previous chapter: grievance at having won (not lost) the lottery, at not having secured a First at Oxford (allegedly on the grounds of deficient teaching), or at having spent most of a life behind bars as a consequence of wrongful conviction. This new case, however, runs deeper; it concerns a life rendered intolerable by virtue of a defect acquired prior to birth, where the only 'choices' or alternatives are between life with the defect or no life, expressed as the preference not to have been born. In order to pursue the relevant questions that arise as philosophical questions, and in particular as questions to do with 'personal identity', Williams has to put up some working assumptions. These by no means exhaust, or indeed even get close to, his fuller view of what it is to have an 'identity', but they serve their purpose in connection with the issues immediately to hand. There is, first, the restriction of 'identity' to the relation with 'possibilities', and from there the distinction between possibilities that are consistent with the integrity of the self and those which could be properties only of some other person. This in turn comes out as the distinction referred to earlier between the '*life story of a different individual*' and the '*different life story of the same individual*. Williams illustrates the differences by means of two 'birth' stories about 'Robert': in one, he is counterfactually born in France instead of Britain, and as a consequence we have 'an alternative possible life-history of the person Robert'. In the other, Robert is counterfactually 'the son of his mother's first fiancé', but this is not 'genuinely a thought about Robert, but about someone else, with a different father, who might have existed instead of Robert'.[40]

In other words, for these purposes, the grounds of identity derive from biological origins, and specifically parentage, as the unique union of two gametes (the zygote); any constitutive difference at the level of the zygote[41] – effected by, say, some form of genetic engineering – would mean 'a different human being would have been formed and born'. These assumptions inform, if with different outcomes, two overlapping but importantly distinguishable categories: 'wrongful identity' and 'wrongful life'. Both lead into a philosophical quagmire and a legal minefield. In respect of the latter, there are enormous variations across national jurisdictions and constitutions (in some – for example, Germany – the concept of 'wrongful life' is constitutionally inadmissible). Within a given jurisdiction, there is often endless to-and-fro between district courts and supreme courts, with cases as legal footballs often kicked into the long grass. The issues deliberated also vary greatly, depending on the precise circumstances. Where there is conceptual controversy in framing and interpreting law, the issues typically include (this is a short list): difficulties in assessing compensation claims that involve comparing existent and non-existent states; in discriminating between the impaired and non-impaired life, how to avoid classifying the former as 'inferior' (memories of euthanasia programmes lurk); the problem of linking grievance solely to the fact of birth after, more or less, the manner of Job, and the related question as to whether 'life' itself can be construed as a source of 'injury'; whether the plaintiff can be said to have had legal standing as a person if he or she did not exist at the time of the injury; whether the legal rights of the mother override those of the foetus, against the background of the long-standing view in some but not all jurisdictions that the foetus is not a separate 'entity' but a part of the mother.

The principal philosophical question associated with wrongful life claims is the following: under the biological definition of identity as the union of two gametes, what range of alternatives ('possibilities') is coherently imaginable for the offspring, and more specifically whether that can include the counterfactual preference not to have been born without that wish being self-defeating. For the most part, the courts ruled that it could not, or at least insisted that any admissible liability claim be of restricted reference, of a kind that expressly bracketed the deeper genealogical-existential questions raised by the philosophical argument. Williams, however, while fully alert to the fact that there is no transparently clear way through the paradoxical traps, adopted a different tack. The difference of opinion is partly due to different concerns. Legal deliberation was fundamentally about the validity of compensation claims and thus the question of how to estimate the 'value' of a life, where value meant cash payouts. The difficulty of how to make a comparative estimation that involves a non-existent state or person as one of the terms of the comparison is obvious. On the other hand, the philosophical claim that, as a person born with a serious defect, it is incoherent to wish never to have been born – on the argument that this involves appeal to a state (of non-existence) to which you have no access – cut little ice with Williams. He invoked a different and larger principle of 'value', one in which your life has no value for you and is thus worthless (how that might stand to a demand for financial compensation is moot). It is perfectly coherent, he suggested, to wish not to have been born when this is translated as the view that your life is not worth living, a view that can be entirely 'constructed from inside the actual life'.

To say that your life is not worth living, of course, makes perfectly coherent sense, for example, in relation to a decision to end that life.[42] But whether the same holds in relation to that life's beginning, in the form of wishing there had been no beginning, is another matter and less obviously paradox-free. There is an argument to be had as to whether, on this axis, Williams's propositional translation moves in the wrong direction, and perhaps should in fact be reversed: instead of a life not worth living as the translation of preferring not to have been born, it is the other way round. The reversal can readily bring one to see wishing not to have been born as more a rhetorically heightened representation of the felt worthlessness of a life, a way of saying that one's suffering is unbearable. While this makes compelling emotional sense (angel Clarence's counterfactual plea on behalf of being born in *It's a Wonderful Life* clearly has less grip when applied to the case of someone suffering from an unbearable and irremediable genetic defect), it does not necessarily dispose of the logical paradox whereby you counterfactually wish for something which undermines the very conditions of you being able to wish for anything.[43] One might also want to query the other support of the translation bridge, the expression which gives the piece its title: 'resenting one's own existence'. It is not clear that 'existence' can plausibly be an object of resentment. The collocationary field for 'resent' will include feeling aggrieved, bitter or indignant. It implies harbouring a grudge for a wrong done and the registering of a complaint. When, in Nietzsche's terms, it becomes *ressentiment*, it will also be linked to demands for 'justice'. Existence cannot qualify here; existence as such has no agency in respect of which a resentful claim can be lodged. It is one reason why the courts have declined to recognize 'life' or 'birth' as a legally admissible source of alleged 'injury'. Existence is a state, not an act with effects and consequences. This may help shed further light on what perhaps Nietzsche was trying to say about 'birth' with the expression 'nicht geboren zu sein'.

However, the full implications of the 'wrongful life' problem are so complex that it is safe to say that the jury is still out, philosophically as well as legally. There is, however, the other question (the one with which that of 'wrongful life' is sometimes confused): that of 'wrongful identity'. Where there has been 'prenatal damage', the person whose life has been affected by that damage is likely to wish they had had another life rather than no life, namely, one without the damage. On the assumptions laid out by Williams, this is not an option. Where ineluctably – because zygotically – constrained, there are only two options (either a life with defect or no life); there is no possibility of adding a third option in which you could have been born in better shape and with better prospects. The desire for this option is continuous with some of the examples discussed earlier in this chapter, but now in the more drastic form of the counterfactual wish to have been genetically 'someone else' while holding, for the most part unreflectingly, to the belief that inside that option you would nevertheless have remained 'you'.[44] It being by definition too late for any then available intervention *in utero*, you may conclude that you would have preferred not to have been born at all. And since there is no time-travel rewind back to the point where you are aborted in the womb or not conceived, you may also demand compensation and go to law to secure it. Williams calls this 'counter-identical grievance', and rightly qualifies it as incoherent (it is incoherent for you to run an argument about the life you might have had if that life would not have been yours).

It is a type of case that has acquired increasing ethical urgency given advances in the technology of genetic engineering, heralding the prospect of designer babies and the nightmare world of children suing parents for not having availed themselves of the technology to equip them for optimal life outcomes (smarter, better looks, 'right' gender, etc.), or of electorates pressing the expectation of universal provision of these facilities by states and governments.[45] Another way of expressing this might be to say that the plaintiff is implicitly objecting to the parents he has, that 'wrongful identity' is a consequence of having had the 'wrong parents'. We might here briefly consider a contrast by returning to ancient Greece, and the invoking of the idea of 'wrong parents' in the Oedipus story. Oedipus feels many things at what has befallen him, horror, shame, guilt, but also indignation, anger and resentment. In *Oedipus at Colonus*, he rails against his sons, against Creon and his fellow Thebans in general for the way he has been treated. In his exchanges with the Chorus, he also rails against an unjust 'fate': 'I tell you, then, I have endured foulest injustice; I have endured wrong undeserved; God knows nothing was of my choosing.' One thing already identified at the terrible moment of discovery in *Oedipus Tyrannus* as 'wrong', and certainly not of his choosing, is his parents: 'I who have been born from whom I ought not.'

We might want to call this a special case of a 'wrongful life' claim, specific to Greek tragedy. They are, of course, the 'wrong' parents because of what he has unwittingly done to and with them, because he has slain one and had sex with the other, though this in turn is a consequence of fulfilling the 'curse' inflicted by the gods on an entire family line and issued when, in his own words, Oedipus 'was still unborn ... Unborn? Nay, unbegotten, unconceived.' But there is no counterfactual in play here, in the sense of wishing he had had other parents, or no parents at all. There is a time-limited sense in which he wants to believe his 'real' parents were Polybus and Merope, but that's not about counterfactually wanting something to have been the case that he knows wasn't; it's about wanting something believed to be true to be actually true because, if true, he also believes he escapes the prediction of the Oracle. However, were it true, he could escape the prediction not by being Oedipus with different parents, but by being someone other than Oedipus, perhaps with the same name but in a different story. Oedipus might therefore reasonably wish he had never been born, in that way avoiding having the 'wrong' parents by having none. In *Oedipus at Colonus*, the Chorus echoes Silenus, presumably with Oedipus in particular in mind, while stating as a general law: the 'best' is 'not to be born' and the 'second best' is 'to return quickly to whence you came'. Oedipus does indeed soon walk to his death. There is also the wish expressed in *Oedipus Tyrannus*, that, as per the instructions of his true parents, he had been left as a baby to die on the mountainside.

That is, of course, a wholly coherent form of counterfactual regret,[46] but the wish for his life to have ceased once born is not the same as taxing either 'fate' or parents with having allowed him to be born in the first place.[47] As for anything that involves notions of legal claim, we can only assume that the Athenian law courts would have been baffled by suits brought against parents in respect of 'birth with less than optimal genetic composition' (as David Heyd puts it).[48]

While it is hard to say whether it comes as light relief, this modern nightmare of biological might-have-beens has on occasion been anticipated by black farce. Take the story of the redheaded teenager who didn't wish to be one (a redhead, that is), and who sued his parents for what his lawyer described as the 'incredibly conservative' sums of $1.3 million as compensation for his 'pain and suffering' along with a claim for $800,000 for 'loss of enjoyment of life'. In a statement to the press, the plaintiff described his life as 'a torture' because 'people keep calling me Carrot-top, Strawberry, Shortcake or Ginger Freak, and all of that is my parents' fault. They knew they were offering me a life of misery, and they selfishly decided to have children anyways.' The case was wrongly described as one of 'wrongful life'. It is more intelligibly classified in the category of 'wrongful identity', or more exactly as an extravagantly willful confusion of one with the other. The relevant choice here is not between a life with red hair or no life, but between a life with red hair and one without red hair. The young teenager simply wanted a more agreeable life, but the guise in which he imagined that (no red hair) would have entailed an alternative zygotic endowment, one that did not entail the transmission of an inherited trait; the ensuing life might have been altogether more pleasant, but it wouldn't have been his. The parents, unsurprisingly, took a different view (all the terms of which, in their third-person reported form, are contestable but that question belongs in an entirely different philosophical place): 'God gave him red hair, not them ... he should "be happy to be alive"'. One crisp comment on the case more or less sums it up:

> The biggest problem that kid has is his brain. He should be thankful his parents had sex in the first place. I ended up bald early in life but surely can't imagine suing my folks over it. I think I'd take the ginger hair over NO HAIR. If that brat doesn't like it, shave your damn head. Also, if this is what our country has become, where the hell does it all stop? Sue you parents for blue or brown eyes when you think green is better?

It will doubtless come as good news that this tale is fake news, printed by an online media source, *The World News Media Report*, with the aim of attracting 'clicks', a pure fiction, with consolations for being such that it is nevertheless hard to put one's finger on. But it serves as a fitting allegory for the fatuity that can lie beneath the surface noise, and as a guide to what, with astonishing imperturbability, Robert Nozick several decades ago contemplated as the creation of a 'genetic supermarket', and the more perturbed David Heyd called 'supermarket access to genetic menus'. This, we might say, is the dystopian terminus of a human journey of the counterfactual, from regret through repentance to resentment, and from there into a zone at once hugely complex, hugely fraught and hugely confused, mainly because deep emotions, material interests, and, in a peculiarly resonant sense, matters of life and death are involved. These are the outer badlands of the relation between 'identity' and the 'what if', populated by shadowy counterparts of you that are either someone else with a life that is not yours, or no-one at all by virtue of never having existed.

Where, then, might this leave us in respect of the self's 'possibilities'? In *Problems of the Self*, Williams remarks that 'identity is its identifications'. This is an interesting but flexible equation, its flexibility deriving from the multiple descriptive uses of the term 'identifications' (it can refer to acquired group allegiances, assigned social roles, and less determinately controlled imaginative projections). For Williams's purposes, it appears to mean primarily the concrete, embodied projects which you assume and which constitute and define a self in and through the practice of living. It would be one way of describing the 'core' in the running dispute with the Cartesian model of the core as the 'featureless' self of a disembodied centre of consciousness (less flatteringly, what Williams calls the 'unregenerate Cartesian relic').[49] This anti-Cartesian view of the core assorts well with certain types, the strong decision makers who approach the turning point with resolve as the sole path possible because for them, for what it is to *be* them, it represents the only game in town. Gauguin seems to come out well on this score. So too, and perhaps above all, do certain ancient Greeks; Eteocles (in Aeschylus) and Ajax (in Sophocles), for example, the lives and deaths of both shaped in part by a decision-making power that does not permit of deflection. A further term for this focused determination in Williams's account is 'inner necessity'.[50] The latter is a complex notion (in an interview in the last year of his life, Williams singled it out as more or less summarizing what philosophy for him had fundamentally been about).[51] In the Greek case, in contrast to notions of 'external necessity' (whether as natural forces or as the role of the supernatural and the agency of the gods), 'inner necessity' denotes an ethic of decision and action rooted in *ethos*, a term for 'character' and a synonym for the set of motivational dispositions that form a 'core' of self. Eteocles decides when he does (to go into battle) because this is what, being him, he must do. Ajax, shamed by the dishonouring moment of madness inflicted on him by Athene, commits suicide because there is, for him, simply no other option consistent with his sense of who he is. For Ajax, there is only one way, namely 'where my way must go', and the 'must' of that way is built from the imperatives of an 'inner necessity'.[52]

For Williams, these cases are not just examples of a historical culture, they are also exemplary, for us as well as for the ancient Greeks. While rejecting the nostalgic idealizations of eighteenth-century and Romantic philhellenism, there is, he claims, much we can learn from them.[53] However, quite what and how much we can take from that past into what for us it means to have a self and live a life is far from straightforwardly obvious, and in Williams's case may involve a degree of wishful preference, perhaps animated by Nietzschean enthusiasms.[54] It was Nietzsche, after all, who said that 'we want to go back' (to ancient Greece) and also, in a fit of wanton intellectual recklessness, that 'day by day we are becoming more Greek'. The honour codes of an aristocratic warrior culture (Ajax's 'the noble man should either live finely or die finely') may be in some ways admirable, but the historians rightly tell us to beware of their 'nobility'.[55] It is certainly far from clear what these exemplars might have usefully to say to a modern culture of 'self' burdened (or blessed) by a very high degree of reflexive self-consciousness. In connection with Ajax's moment of 'madness', Williams interestingly reanimates the moribund expression 'not his usual self', with a view to alienating the expression into a sense of its sheer strangeness. For Ajax, it is not merely 'unusual', it is unrecognizable as well as shaming, absolutely not his 'self' at all. Then consider that other warrior decision-maker who is also visited by delirious hallucination, Macbeth. It is doubtful that in this latter case we can so confidently distinguish between 'usual' and 'unusual' selves. Macbeth is, precisely, a man radically divided, that is to say, divided all the way down into the 'core', a division caught in the reflective deliberations that are typical of that early modern invention, the soliloquy. Or take the Shakespearean prince of the soliloquy, who spends most of the play paralysed at the crossroads of decision, Hamlet, the quintessentially 'modern' figure not because he thinks too much, but, as Nietzsche says (in *The Birth Of Tragedy*), because he thinks too well. Among so many other things, Hamlet's version of thinking too well is what contextually exposes Polonius's 'to thine own self be true' as vacuous platitude. The question, precisely, is what, for a person who – to invoke another idiomatic curiosity – is always 'in two minds', thine own true self *is* and where to find it.

Our 'identifications' have historical settings that mould and mark the 'identities' made in them. Other than in certain kinds of philosophical thought experiment, 'personal' identity cannot be hived off from those settings. If being true to yourself is what comes naturally to Ajax, it is something that comes far less naturally to those who come after, partly as an effect of introspective perplexity (the self as its own object of inspection), and partly as the consequence of different understandings of what it is to make a 'choice' arising from the different range and kinds of choices that a historically formed society makes available, whether unrestrictedly to all its members or restrictedly to but some. What Williams calls the 'liberal' order of modernity entails (for better or for worse; this is not about judgements of 'superiority') a different relation to the 'possible' and its imaginings. In *Problems of the Self*, Williams is, of course, right to caution against the obvious traps of imaginative identifications, citing a rejoinder of Leibniz's ('when he said to one who expressed the wish that he were King of China, that all he wanted was that he should cease to exist and that there should be a King in China').[56]

Here we are back with the self-defeating paradoxes of the counterfactual wish to be 'someone else' by ceasing to exist as 'you'. It is easier, Williams maintains, to sustain first-personal counterfactuals than third-personal ones ('"I might have been …" is a form of thought that holds up much longer than "he might have been …"'), but the end of the line is the loss of what it is to have a self ('if we press this hard enough, we readily get the idea that it is not necessary to being *me* that I should have any of the individuating properties that I do have').[57] In order to run the counterfactual, I have to posit myself as a disembodied and portable essence of a Cartesian sort ('an "I" without body, past or character'). 'Character' echoes *ethos*, the great driving force of the ancient Greek hero. But, since questions of personal identity are inseparable from questions to do with what Foucault termed the 'historical subject', there is only so far we can run with this emphasis on 'character' and its ancient pedigree as *ethos*.[58] Place that emphasis alongside, for example, the *Mögklichkeitmenschen* of Robert

Musil, and a vast historical chasm between ancient and modern immediately opens up.

On the bridge across that chasm we may encounter one further twist. Alongside the wish never to have been born or the wish to die soon, there is the wish to live forever. Where Cioran associated birth with 'inconvenience', in 'The Makropulos Case', Williams associates the prospect of immortality with unrelieved 'tedium'.[59] Life forever would indeed be a life not worth living. The projects (or what here Williams calls our 'categorical desires' as distinct from the merely fleeting 'conditional' ones) that define our sense of who we are belong to our finite engagement in the world, and death is part of their meaning. Were our life immortal, these desires would eventually exhaust themselves by way of their satiation; whence the dismal outlook of unrelieved tedium that would await us as immortals, Nietzsche's 'recurrence' as the unending condition of motivationless apathy. Such a life would be insupportable ('an eternal life would be unliveable'). Its sole counterfactual would be a reprise of Silenus coupled perhaps with the frightening thought that closes *The Genealogy of Morals*: the will to nothingness filling the void when there is nothing left to will (*lieber will noch der Mensch das Nichts wollen als nicht wollen*).[60] We should therefore count ourselves 'lucky in having the chance to die'. The philosopher, Samuel Scheffler, has, however, drawn a perverse implication from this argument, so perverse indeed as to send Williams towards company he doubtless would never have wanted to keep. Scheffler's point is this:

> Categorical desires give us reasons to live, and they support such engagement. But when we are engaged, and so succeed in leading the kinds of lives we want, then the way we succeed is by losing ourselves in absorbing activities. When categorical desire dies, as it must do eventually if we have sufficient constancy of character to define selves worth wanting to sustain in the first place, then we will be left with ourselves, and we ourselves are, terminally, boring. The real problem is that one's reasons to live are, in a sense, reasons *not to live as oneself*. It is I who wants to live, but I want to live by losing myself – *by not being me* (my emphasis).[61]

This turns the whole business of the 'self' on its head. The reason eternal life would be irredeemably boring is because *we* would be irredeemably boring, doubtless to other immortals, but above all to ourselves. Immortality would bore us because we would be 'left to ourselves' forever. My desire to be me thus becomes inseparable from not being 'left to myself', from losing myself exactly where I find myself, in the 'absorbing activities' driven by categorical desire. 'Losing myself' belongs with those other odd commonplaces that are re-energized when placed in a new context ('not one's usual self', 'in two minds', 'not in one's right mind' and 'left to oneself'). Here the expression 'losing myself' is especially curious, inextricably bound to my being me 'by not being me'. These paradoxes of identity, being and living are music to the ears of the 'people of possibility'.

# 7 ON THE RUN WITH FERNANDO PESSOA

*Each of us is several, is many, is a profusion of selves. So that the self who disdains his surroundings is not the same as the self who suffers or takes joy in them. In the vast colony of our being there are many species of people who think and feel in different ways.*

**FERNANDO PESSOA**

Musil's 'people of possibility' is one of the more peculiar expressions in the modernist lexicon, and sounds even stranger if in translation we retain the form of the original compound noun ('Possibilitypeople'); images of futuristic aliens swim mistily into view, or alternatively an ad man's dream tag for the capture of the millennials' life-style market. What Musil himself meant by the expression, especially in respect of his principal character, Ulrich, is subject to much debate, crucially whether or not it furnishes one of the many objects of his brand of elusive 'irony'. In some accounts, it is more or less synonymous with the type that gives the novel its title, where the 'man without qualities' is joined with the 'possibilitarian' as enervated drifters in a twilight world disconnected from what is conventionally understood as reality (the latter compared to 'a bad play' they are intent on avoiding). A man without qualities, however, would seem by definition to be indistinguishable from a version of what philosophers call the 'featureless self', whereas the possibilitarian would seem to be made of more creative stuff, and if 'without qualities', only so in the sense in which the great nineteenth-century novelist of 'possibility', Stendhal, could say of the 'soul', that it has 'only states and never qualities'.[1] Considered from this point of view, Musil's people of possibility would seem to be more the antonym of the man without qualities, not vacuous man in a world that no longer offers genuine 'experience' (a 'world of qualities without a man, of experiences without the person who experiences them'), but 'potential man' performing in another play where the script consists of 'the unwritten poem of his existence' that 'confronts man as recorded fact, as reality, as character'.[2] This, we are told, is what it is to live in the 'subjunctive mood', or more exactly in a space between the indicative and the subjunctive, athwart the empirical press of *realis* and the modal intimations of *irrealis*.

> If there is a sense of reality, and no-one will doubt that it has its justifications for existing, then there must also be something we can call a sense of possibility. Whoever has it does not say, for instance: Here this or that has happened, will happen, must happen; but he invents: Here this or that might, could, or ought to happen. If he is told that something is the way it is, he will think: Well, it could probably just as well be otherwise. So the sense of possibility could be defined outright as the ability to conceive of everything there might be just as well, and to attach no more importance to what is than to what is not.[3]

This is probably the most widely cited passage of *The Man without Qualities*. But whether it deserves its reputation as a kind of Possibilitarian Manifesto is very much an open question. Unless a target of irony, portions of it cannot be taken seriously, at least not if we are also to take seriously the implied balancing act of the (indicative) 'sense of reality' and the (subjunctive) 'sense of possibility'. If there can be no 'doubt' that the sense of reality 'has its justifications for existing', then what to do with the bizarre thought to the effect that everything that is or has been 'could probably just as well be otherwise'. Just as well? That seems merely cavalier, and emphatically not what counterfactuals are supposed to be about; 'just as well' belongs in La La Land, and no amount of trumpeting on its behalf will rescue it from indefinite detention in the prison-house of nonsense. Much of the difficulty here derives from generic confusions, and most notably the tendency, encouraged by the mode of writing Musil called 'Essayism', to parse the reflections on 'possibility' and the 'subjunctive' as ersatz philosophy. 'Essayism' was meant to have a Montaignian ring to it (the 'essay' as experimental, provisional, above all tuned to uncertainty), but all too often the discourse operates in ways that irresistibly attract a more formal association with the sequential steps of 'philosophical' exposition. Despite the efforts of philosopher Jacques Bouveresse to remove Musil from the grip of the philosophers (apart, of course, from his own), the tendency persists, and sometimes in remarkably exotic forms.[4] One such is the improbable pairing of Musil with (of all people) Bernard Williams, as partners in the cause of 'anti-Kantianism'.[5]

This possibilitarian conjunction is not merely exotic; it makes no useful sense at all. Williams was indeed a resolute anti-Kantian, but in his case the value of the 'subjunctive mood' and the counterfactuals it sustains is essentially negative, played off against the resolute, goal-oriented Gauguinesque type, emphatically in and of the project-driven world; there is nothing here of the split and divided Hamlet type whom Harold Bloom singled out as the true literary ancestor of Musil's hero.[6] And when Williams gets anywhere near ideas of 'multiple selves', he is quick to mobilize philosophical argument in order to deny them any status in relation to deep-level questions of 'identity'. In, for example, his discussion of the textbook Sally Beauchamp case, he discusses the case as a story of 'dissociations' that speak of fluctuating 'moods' and different manifestations of 'personality', but concludes the discussion, with what feels like a sense of relief at finding safe harbour for the theory of the unitary individual, by citing what Beauchamp herself is reported as having said of these multiple dissociative experiences: 'After all, it is always myself.'[7] Being always oneself, whatever – and however extreme – the surface fluctuations, has great appeal in connection with a philosophy of the self, aiming for a coherent defence of the idea of an abiding 'core'. It is, as we saw in the previous chapter, the basis of the important distinction between the 'life story of a different individual' and the 'different life story of the same individual', and thus a bulwark against the traps of outer-limit counterfactuals that entail imagining oneself as either someone else or no-one at all. But, as we also saw, this too has its own limits, made clear in the paradox highlighted by Scheffler, where in order to be strongly oneself one has to 'lose' oneself.

These complications may be a reason for finally passing the baton from philosophy to literature (an exemplary place of self-losing), not, it should be stressed, with a view to 'settling' anything, but more as a switch of perspective predicated on there being more things in heaven and earth, etc. They may also be a reason for also passing it to another writer, Musil's contemporary (with whom indeed he is often compared or juxtaposed), but who, notwithstanding certain dabblings, is less constrained by the 'essayistic' mode, and whose central preoccupation was, persistently, with how to be oneself by losing oneself: namely, that 'rumour of something', as Octavio Paz put it, bearing the name Fernando Pessoa.[8] Paz also noted (along with many others) the perfect irony that, in Portuguese, 'Pessoa' means 'person'.[9] While the semantic coincidence of common noun and proper name has become something of a tired critical trope, the irony can still resonate when seen in relation to a poem such as 'I'm a Runaway' (one of the poems appearing under the name 'Fernando Pessoa'). In it we encounter a split first-person, divided between the roles of fugitive and hunter. On the one hand, the 'I' is on the run from 'myself', from, we might want to say, a 'usual' self, constructed as a sort of gaol by an unspecified 'they':

> 'I'm a runaway.
> When I was born
> They shut me up
> Inside myself.
> Ah, but I ran away.'

On the other hand, the 'I' is also a pursuer, on the look-out for its accusative 'me' as a delinquent escapee who knows how to hide:

> 'My soul is on
> The lookout for me
> But I lie low.'[10]

Pessoa has many places in which to lie low: 'the shortcuts and roads in the faraway woods/where I hypothesized my being' (in one of the two 'Lisbon revisited' poems); behind the door in the 'factless autobiography', *The Book of Disquiet* ('I hide behind the door, so that Reality won't see me when he enters'); or, also in *The Book of Disquiet*, at the 'roadside inn where I have to stay until the coach from the abyss pulls up'.[11] Some of the abyssal talk can smack of a nihilism acquired on the cheap. 'I am a Runaway' opens with an image of the self locked away at birth, and from there it is but a step to a passing flirtation with the Silenus story of the 'best' consisting in not being born at all. This motif was indeed incorporated as a line into the poem, 'Time's Passage', though, on second thoughts, the line was later deleted.[12] The favourite place for lying low is not the nihilistic hostelry, but the 'no place' between places, where one cannot be found because there is no determinate location either side of a boundary of which it could be said 'I am here' or 'he is there': 'I am the space between'; 'I am the interval between what I am and what I am not'; 'I am the bridge between what I don't have and what I don't want', these are but three examples of the ubiquitous variations on the theme of 'between-ness' in the Pessoan corpus, several of them scribbles on scraps of paper among the many thousands found after Pessoa's death in the famous trunk, the dishevelled posthumous collection that is itself a reflection of the fractured and dispersed nature of the Pessoan writing self. The most striking of these expressions (from *The Book of Disquiet*) is the inventively economical, 'I inter-am', the preposition 'entre' in the original Portuguese itself an 'inter' term, meaning at once 'between' (two) and 'among' (many).[13] In 'I'm a Runaway', the business of being 'no-one at all' means primarily not being 'pinned to myself', implying a preference for the several over the one. And in *The Book of Disquiet* the 'inter' modalities of the circulating 'I' includes as their 'author' one Bernardo Soares, who in turn has a predecessor in composing the early drafts, one Vicente Guedes.[14]

Which brings us to what is universally seen as the very heart of the Pessoan 'inter-am', the adoption, or rather the creation, of the heteronyms. The circumstantial story of the heteronymic adventure in Pessoa has been told and re-told over and over, and in some quarters has understandably engendered a degree of weary impatience. There is, however, nothing quite like it. Starting in childhood with the invention of the Chevalier de Pas, Pessoa accumulated over seventy heteronyms, some of them also posthumously discovered. Early ones include what look like small Pessoan allegories (Alexander Search, C.R. Anon, Thomas Crosse). There is also the mischief-making category of 'heteronymic possibilities', in a taxonomy that also includes 'pre-heteronyms' and 'semi-heteronyms', a rich lode of counterfactual 'possibility' if ever there were one. The most important of the full-fledged heteronyms consists of the trio of poets, Alberto Caeiro, Alvaro de Campos and Ricardo Reis (the prose writer, Soares, as a mere 'semi-heteronym', is excluded from the elite group).[15] The trio is occasionally joined for purposes of discussion or correspondence by 'Fernando Pessoa', the orthonymic origin becoming itself one of the heteronymic group. Thus, if being on the run with Fernando Pessoa is being on the run from him, it is also fleeing in the company of what, provisionally, we could call his aliases, until we are disconcertingly told that one of the aliases is someone called 'Fernando Pessoa'. And if we think of this as merely a game, and more particularly a game of masks, we do well to turn to Pessoa's account (in a 1935 letter to the young poet, Adolfo Casais Monteiro) of what, aptly and momentously, has been called 'the day of the heteronyms'.[16]

One day, on the verge of giving up – March 8th 1914 – I approached a high chest of drawers and began to write something down on a piece of paper, while standing, as I like to do, whenever possible. And so, taken over by some strange, indescribable kind of trance, I wrote 30 something poems in one stretch. That was the most triumphant day of my life and I will never experience another like it. I began with the title *The Keeper of the Flocks*. And what followed was the birth of someone within me, whom I immediately named Alberto Caeiro. Please excuse the absurdity of the expression: my master had, then and there, appeared within me ... I immediately took up another sheet of paper and wrote ... the six poems that make up 'Oblique Rain' by Fernando Pessoa ... It marked the return from Fernando Pessoa–Alberto Caeiro to Fernando Pessoa alone. Or better still, it was Fernando Pessoa's inexistence as Alberto Caeiro. With Caeiro's appearance, I set out immediately – intuitively and unconsciously – to find him some disciples. I wrenched the latent Ricardo Reis from his false paganism. I found him a name and adjusted him to himself ... And then suddenly from an opposite source, another individual surged up impetuously. In a flash, without interruption or revision, the 'Triumphal Ode' of Alvaro de Campos sprang forth – the ode now known by that title and the man by that name. I created therefore an inexistent coterie. I ... gauged influences, discovered influences, discovered friendships, and heard, within myself, discussions and disagreements over criteria. In all this, the creator of everything and everyone mattered the least, I think. It seemed as if everything had taken place independently of me. And this is still the way things still work. If someday I am able to publish Ricardo Reis's discussion with Alvaro de Campos on aesthetics, you will see just how different they are and that I am of no importance in the whole business.[17]

This must count as one of the more extraordinary examples of the 'Day-in-the-Life-of' genre, a demonstration of the death (and birth) of the author(s) on an epic scale. Various interpretive frames can be placed around this tale of latencies and irruptions. It can be seen as simply a conceit for an extended exercise in literary ventriloquy, Pessoa adopting 'disguises' in order to try out different styles and voices. Or we can see it as recounting an experience of radical 'personality' dissociation, part of the Doppelgänger tradition and its often hysterical, terror-struck experiences of the doubled self. There is, however, nothing of terror in

Pessoa's letter, and relatedly nothing of the psychotic splinterings of self we find in the Beauchamp case.[18] It makes far more sense to construe it as a process of willed dispossession, linked to a radical form of 'negative capability' in the tradition of Nerval's 'je suis l'autre' and Rimbaud's 'je est un autre', a clearing out of self in accordance with Soares's view that 'to live is to be other'. How we are to think these heteronymic others in relation to Pessoa 'himself', as at once part of him and yet independent of him, is precisely where the yawning aporia opens. It is given an especially delicious inflection by the statement 'only Alvaro de Campos knew me personally' (rarely has an adverb spoken so eloquently). The 'only' moreover captures a sense of regret over a collective might-have-been. Pessoa never stopped thinking about a grand heteronymic gathering for a 'family discussion' at which differences and commonalties would be aired (though quite how the kinship system was structured remains a question one doubts any anthropologist would want to get near).

Suppose, in an increasingly desperate attempt to cope, we revert to the philosophical framework and apply to the use of the heteronym the modal logic of proper names along with a version of the Kripkean model of the 'rigid designator', which has names refer to a same 'identity' across all relevant possible worlds ('Mark Twain' as always 'Samuel Clemens', and not, say, Abraham Lincoln). With the strange case of Pessoa, it is not clear that this will yield anything at all. We are dealing here with what has been called an experience of 'extreme depersonalization' and 'an adventure in extra- and inter-subjective plurality unprecedented in literature'.[19] The rigid designator will hold only if we convert the heteronyms to pseudonyms, but this would be to fly in the face of Pessoa's own counter-insistence: 'A pseudonymic work is, except for the name with which it signed, the work of an author writing as himself; a heteronymic work is by an author writing outside his own personality; it is the work of a complete individuality made up by him.'[20] And to the elementary point that everything by Caeiro, de Campos and Reis is, of course, written by Pessoa, he has another answer: written, yes, but only as someone writing under 'dictation':

> Each of the more enduring personalities, lived by the author within himself, was given an expressive nature and made the author of one or more books whose ideas, emotions, and literary art have no relationship to the real author ... Neither this work nor those to follow have anything to do with the man who writes them. He doesn't agree or

disagree with what's in them. He writes as if he were being dictated to. And as if the person dictating were a friend (and for that reason could freely ask him to write down what he dictates), the writer finds the dictation interesting, perhaps just out of friendship. The human author of these books has no personality of his own. Whenever he feels a personality well up inside, he quickly realizes that this new being, though similar, is distinct from him – an intellectual son, perhaps, with inherited characteristics, but also with differences that make him someone else.[21]

That still leaves intact the common-sense objection to the endless recycling of the heteronymic story and the somewhat dyspeptic view of it as a mere 'distraction' (jaundiced wits are fond of saying that the four great modern Portuguese poets are Fernando Pessoa, while one ingenious suggestion has been to re-baptize the heteronyms as simply 'titles' for the work that appears under the names).[22] After all, Pessoa *is* the author of the works, he *is* the person behind the personae, the 'identity' behind all of the 'voices'. But this misses the whole point of the heteronyms, which is to saturate the 'is' with a self-othering activity of erasure and inscription. As Eduardo Coelho insisted, there is no orthonymic presence at the 'centre of the heteronymic circle' because this particular circle is one without a centre.[23] To be sure, there is a 'master' poet, but his name is not Fernando Pessoa. It is the heteronymic Alberto Caeiro, of whose dramatic 'birth' we are told in the letter to Monteiro, appearing in the Pessoan poetic firmament as the 'Shepherd' of the poet-flock, notwithstanding the fact that he 'writes bad Portuguese'. He is not alone in this regard. Alvaro de Campos also makes mistakes, in particular mixing up – of all things – the nominative and accusative forms of first person pronouns. 'It's all the fault of the pronouns,' cries out one of the narrators of Samuel Beckett's *The Unnamable* in a moment of complete self-loss. This makes a suitable companion for Campos' faults *with* them, especially in alerting us to the broader context of Pessoan heteronymy, namely, the important fact that it involves not only proper names, but also the interplay of name and pronoun, and hence the drama of the 'shifter' (the first-person pronoun that signifies only in the existential moment of its utterance). The 'I' marks the spot occupied by a speaking self but as a spot quickly deserted, if not on the run then constantly on the move, in the shifting web of relations woven round the other form of the first-person pronoun, the singular 'I' as the plural 'we'. There and gone, lost and found, and lost again, 'forever alien to myself, and with no central core inside me', the singular 'I' is decanted into a plural otherness.[24] The best description of this process I have encountered is as the circulation of a 'multiplicity of unconsciouses' within a single embodied form.[25]

Other than in some 'continental' variants,[26] this is not the natural territory of philosophies of the self. Modals are nevertheless very much part of the territorial marking, including those bearing on the conditional and counterfactual existences of Pessoa himself. John Hollander observed that if Pessoa had never existed, Borges would have to have invented him, while Alvaro de Campos has his own counterfactual about his heteronymic companion: 'Fernando Pessoa would be a pagan if he weren't a cat's cradle of snarled up yarn inside.'[27] The presence of modal terms is especially pronounced in *The Book of Disquiet*, the factless autobiography that lives and breathes various forms of the counterfactual, the majority of them the pining kind, infused with the bittersweet flavours of *saudosismo*, as in the following description from one of the most quoted passages of *The Book of Disquiet*: 'the longing for impossible things, precisely because they are impossible; nostalgia for what never was; the desire for what could have been; regret over not being someone else. All these half-tones of the soul's consciousness create in us a painful landscape, an eternal sunset of what we are.' This is vintage 'modal' Pessoa, where the emphasis on the 'impossible', and in particular the wish to have been 'someone else', seem to reset and then fall into the traps of the fantasized link between identity and counterfactuals discussed in the previous chapter, notwithstanding the fact that the beautifully composed half-tones of the soul's consciousness make for more seductive reading than Woody Allen's autobiographical musings on the same theme.

Seduction, however, is not the same as persuasion, and, reduced to a set of propositions, few are likely to be persuaded that, with Bernardo Soares as the 'author' of these affecting words, Fernando Pessoa has found a way of being at once himself and someone else, or being himself *as* someone else. On the other hand, there can be little doubt that, at the very least, Pessoa's deep identification with the heteronym threatens those more anchored conceptions of selfhood based on the integrating force of a deep and driven *ethos* within. 'To create, I've destroyed myself; I've so externalized myself on the inside that I don't exist on the inside except externally.' Since this is Bernardo Soares again, where, in terms of the inside/outside relation, is Fernando Pessoa? That question really does scramble the deck of cards. In most contexts, the first clause of Soares's remark would be little more than a hyped reprise of the theme of the sacrificial martyrdom of the artist. But the second clause makes it much more than that, the relevant idea the precise opposite of the one that informs the Gauguin example, who in creating creates himself, becomes or realizes what it is to be 'Gauguin'. Trying to chart the inside/outside movements of Pessoan heteronymy is like finding oneself in a hall of mirrors and not knowing whose reflection belongs with whom. Pessoa-Campos' own mirror poem ('Lisbon revisited') speaks in its opening line of 'the magical mirror where I saw myself identical', but that is prefaced (and the magic broken) by line-initial 'Shattered', the shards as a discontinuous mosaic of the fragmented self ('in each fateful fragment I descry only a piece of myself').[28]

This may also bring to mind that other fan of both the heteronym and the mirror, Duchamp (rather than Beauchamp), especially the 'Five Way Portrait of Marcel Duchamp', five 'identical' photographic images of Duchamp seated at a table with implied mirrors on the walls (possibly a 'hinge' mirror). The (notional) 'master' image, the 'real' Duchamp, is seen from the back looking at what appear to be reflections, two in front and two in respectively left and right profile, a perfectly plausible naturalistic explanation except that the more one looks the more the explanation collapses (an effect of what Duchamp called the 'renvoi mirrorique'). In the same family, there is Magritte's cannily titled *Reproduction interdite*. It has a young man looking at what appears to be himself, identical in every single respect except for the one which makes it impossible for the figure in the mirror to be a reflection of the man looking at the mirror: just like the latter, the former is also seen from the back, an exact replica in that sense. But this, of course, is the very thing that undoes the replica; whomever the reflection is a reflection of, it can't be of the man we see looking into the mirror (where he would be turned towards the viewer). One further reason for mentioning the Magritte painting is the curious fact that it adorns the front cover of Bernard Williams's *Problems of the Self*. We might want to ask how this image stands to the conception of the self the arguments of the book it graces set forth.

It nevertheless remains the case that, in both the poetry and the prose, the larger part of Pessoa's modal mood music is composed from the plangent notes of *saudosismo*. At the Pessoan crossroads of possibility, the wistful does seem to predominate, especially in *The Book of Disquiet*, projecting back to the forks in the road with a 'yearning at times for the one he didn't choose', and visited by the 'longing for whom I might have been'. The heteronyms can also be interpreted as representing aspects of these desired might-have-beens, albeit not without ambivalence: as Paz puts it, they are 'what Pessoa could and would have liked to be: in another deeper sense, what he did *not* want to be: a personality'.[29] For Pessoa what in fact matters most in respect of the heteronymic 'circle', as both writers' collective and figure without a centre, is not so much the wishing to be something or someone else, as its exploration, from the position described in *The Book of Disquiet* as 'someone seeking at random, not knowing what object he's looking for, nor where it was hidden'. This exploratory endeavour is not solely nostalgic, the compulsive turning to a past of lost possibility that makes of the 'person' in the name Pessoa a 'missing person' in the sense of both 'lost' (absent without leave, on the run) and 'regretted' (inside the metanoiac structure of the 'missed opportunity'). There is something else too, to do with an imbrication of past and future that takes us back to an earlier moment of this book, the Faulknerian epigraph of Chapter 3 ('The past is never dead. It's not even past.'). There is an echo of this thought in a text called 'Interior Ecolalia': 'It is hard to tell if it is our past that is our future, or if it is our future which is our past.'[30]

Faulkner's notion of the past played out as never-ending transmission to a present and a future belongs in his version of the tragic curse, where the counterfactual is but one of the jokes of 'fate' or what delusively we hold onto as the last resort of desperation (the 'might-have-been which is the single rock we cling to above the maelstrom of unbearable reality'). This is not where we find Pessoa. We might, however, catch, if from far off, an echo of Walter Benjamin's way with history and anachronism, his allegorical weaving of the utopian counterfactual knot that ties past and future together. It would, of course, be foolish to think of Pessoa as a 'utopian' writer, apart perhaps from a (forced?) parallel of the repeated stress on the theme of 'nowhere' with the 'no place' that was the meaning of the name 'Utopia' in Thomas More's founding contribution to the genre.[31] 'Build no Utopia, Lydia, for the time/You fancy yet to be' is the admonition with which a poem by Ricardo Reis begins. Pessoa was not remotely interested in the utopian as holistic blueprint for the perfect society or as grand narrative of collective emancipation. Nor was his adoption of the heteronym intended as a recipe for the ecstatic communion of the many as the 'one'. It was the key that opens a door to a geography of the heterotopian. Where, if anywhere, utopia and heterotopia converge has been much discussed.[32] But wherever it is they are deemed to meet, it is a junction inhabited by counterfactuals, most actively by those which question settled orders of 'identity' ('the snot of subjectivity', as *The Book of Disquiet* has it).[33] It is where Pessoa's explorations could be said to find a degree of common cause with utopian Ernst Bloch's talk of the 'process of latency of a still unfinished world', his famous assertion 'Man is not solid', and his eminently Pessoan remark 'I am, but I do not possess myself'.[34]

Bloch's qualification of the utterance 'I am' with the disclaimer of self-possession is a challenge to the tradition that runs back to Locke's ideas of personhood, property and 'self-ownership', a tradition echoed in modern times by the philosopher-exorcist of the Cartesian ghost in the machine, Gilbert Ryle, poring over the relation between the statement 'I am a person' and what is understood as 'belonging to one person' (and further buttressed by musings on the puzzle of the Sally Beauchamp phenomenon of many selves in one body).[35] The heteronymic life of the 'Pessoa-person' plays havoc with this relation of personhood and belonging, whether understood causally (what makes me hang together) or proprietorially (how what is mine is what makes me). The statement 'I am' is everywhere in the Pessoan corpus, the overwhelming majority of instances, however, set in a context of dispossession and negation. This can take the form of an imaginary obliteration. We recall how Campos dallied briefly with Silenus, his own contribution to the never-be-born theme smuggled into the poem 'Time's Passage' as a line that was subsequently deleted. Was this perhaps because of a preference for the image of the 'abortion that survived' in *The Book of Disquiet* and the idea of a self not fully delivered, a kind of hit-and-miss, like the person not quite born in some of Beckett's writings. At the same time, and also in *The Book of Disquiet*, 'deletion' (along with 'negation') endures as a more general strategy of writing.

> Sometimes the best way to see an object is to delete it, because it subsists in a way I can't quite explain, consisting of the substance of its negation and deletion; this is what I do with vast areas of my real-life being.

Something that subsists as the substance of its negation, a residue or extract preserved from a past for a future, is an intriguing thought, and doubly so in relation to what, unusually for Pessoa, is called 'real-life being'. In what does this 'substance' consist? Is this one of the forms of what it is to be the abortion that survives? And is what survives connected to what is perhaps *The Book of Disquiet*'s most enigmatic sentence: 'What in me dies when I am?' It is, naturally, a question, and its drift can be interpreted in many ways. I read it as obliquely evoking a mode of being replete with counterfactual implication, the subsisting 'substance' in part a compound of the might-have-beens of a lost (and erased) past. On the other hand, the 'I am' is not just the crypt where the deletions lie buried; it is also the ante-chamber where a combination of residue and potential waits to be born, forever posthumous.

# Postscript

A short postscript to posthumous Pessoa might speculate that it was but a matter of time before he was transported (on at least two occasions) to Virtual Reality, the land where Algoritmi rules, Silicon Valley displaces Delphi with the 'mathematical oracle', the search-engine yields a glimpse of 'the mind of God', dreams abound of 'building an artificial island in the middle of the sea, not hosted by any nation-state' (perhaps to be called Utopia, after that other sixteenth-century island), and where, of course, 'selves' multiply at the drop of a hat or the speed of a snapshot.[36] The Pessoan trips – one a technically sophisticated editing game, the other a well-intentioned but unhappy analogy – belong, of course, in a contemporary mass migration to VR that also includes, under the general heading of 'playing with the past', the practice of counterfactual history (Ferguson's rebranding of the latter as 'virtual history' proving a front-runner candidate for digital mediation).[37] One of Pessoa's sojourns also involves 'playing', this time with literary text, specifically the 'programmatic virtualization' of *The Book of Disquiet*, the recently accomplished project of the *LodD Digital Archive*, one of whose aims, according to its prospectus, is 'to enable readers to generate new virtual forms of the work, assuming the roles of editor and/or author'. The programming constructs *inter alia* a counterfactual 'network of potential authorial intentions' that includes the vertiginous process whereby 'the heteronym edits himself as an author'.[38]

The literary shapings and re-shapings that result from this programmed manipulation of the 'dynamics of textual and bibliographical variation' are described as 'radial configurations', reminiscent of the expression 'radiant textuality' coined by Jerome McGann for these kinds of digitally governed operations with textual potential.[39] Especially where there is a significant corpus of 'variants', there is a very great deal we can learn from these methods about the underlying generative logic of literary works, as a system of crossroads structures where choices actually made are just one set from a range of possibilities consistent with the underlying logic.[40] The work of few modern writers would seem to lend itself more readily to these experiments than Pessoa's, and most notably the scrappy life of so much of *The Book of Disquiet*, thrown more or less randomly into the trunk like bits of a jigsaw puzzle or the pieces of a cut and paste document as a cornucopia of vagaries for subsequent editing and publication. But if the digital sphere seems a fertile place for the afterlives of an oeuvre drenched in contingencies and counterfactuals, there are other less appealing aspects of the crossing to VR. One analogy in particular has Pessoa's writings not just going digital, but *as* the digital, his 'imaginative space' as 'like the internet', and like it as a space 'where people can express themselves through a variety of personalities'.[41] Across the bridge of this analogical 'like', it is then but a step to the 'likes' of the online universe, and into the digital hall of mirrors in which the narcissistic Selfie seeks its reflected others, or, as some in the blogosphere put it, its 'counterfactual identities'.[42]

Imagine, for example, an encounter with HoneyCC. She has a 'like' of her own ('she likes to say that she scarcely remembers the last time someone called her by her given name, Lin Chuchu').[43] The online name is, naturally, culled from a movie, but is as nothing compared to the 'identity' range provided by her selfie apps and filters. After all, 'a single picture can say only so much', but so much more if you 'photo-edit' it, although if you're not in the artistic mood, there is an iPhone function that will do automatic 'upgrades' for you.[44] The main app is called Meitu (no prizes for guessing what this means in Chinese), accompanied by a suite of subsidiaries (for example, BeautyPlus, BeautyCam and SelfieCity). They have over a billion users. The advertised purpose of circulating doctored pics is 'to make the world a more beautiful place'. For this aesthetic utopia, the design model for 'more beautiful', when not a bodily – usually female – model, is a celebrity (the ideal face is 'Internet-celebrity face'). As Jiayang Fan (from whose piece I derive all the details mentioned here) wryly notes, this 'has almost literally transformed the face of China'. As she also observes, the whole business is haunted by two well-founded fears. The first is the cost (both physical and financial) of pursuing the elusive will-o'-the-wisp of perfection (after numerous 'procedures', Li Yan still feels as if 'she were a rough draft in the process of revision'). Second, there is the fear of homogenization, whereby everyone ends up looking the same (clear-skinned, large-eyed, not to mention facial adjustments requiring literal cracking of bone structures). So a 'filter' that permits of 'personality' variation is an added option with a menu of choices ('boho', 'mystique' and so on). There is also a dash of the Zuckerbergian brand of the utopian ('giving everyone in the world the power to share'): 'if you are going to share it with your friends', then – as 'a matter of ordinary courtesy' you 'should have the decency to Meitu your face'.

Thus we have the advanced heterotopian formula for the utopian marketing of the dystopia of the heterogeneous digitized self, as, in the words of Gillian Terzis, 'bodiless, elastic and multiple',[45] precisely, Possibilitypeople as men (and women) without qualities. It does not, of course, end well, at least not for Abner ('a name he'd chosen because it sounded "seductively exotic"'). Abner is at a promotion party for Meitu's 'ecosystem of beauty' (the expression is the company's). The party is spread around a 'kidney-shaped pool' in which no-one swims, most of the guests are too busy taking selfies and live-streaming videos. Abner, while 'trying on various glow-in-the-dark accessories that Meitu had provided, taking a selfie with each new look', is in fact a worried young man: 'I still don't know why my video from this morning hasn't gone viral.' It needs repeating that going on the run with Fernando Pessoa and his heteronymic companions does not settle any of the philosophical issues bound up with the question of the self as singular or plural; indeed they could be construed by the sceptic as going on the run *from* them, although the riposte to that – the one sketched here – is that at the very least they shed light on what remains unsettled in the philosophical analysis itself, and possibly unresolvable by it. But, apart from those considerations, one unambiguously clear reason for going back to the early twentieth century to find Pessoa's self-evacuating 'I am' is cultural rather than philosophical: to 'lie low' in relation to the horror story of the app-generated virtualities and commodified counterfactual identities of the technologized early twenty-first century.

# NOTES

## Introduction The Conjectural Breeze of Time

1   Michael Wood, *The Road to Delphi*, London, 2005, p. 66.
2   See Thomas Baldwin, 'The Might Be Nothing', *Analysis*, vol. 56, no. 4, Oct. 1996, pp. 231–8. See also Graham Priest, *Towards Non-Being*, Oxford, 2016.
3   See Eila Mell, *Casting Might-Have-Beens: A Film-by-Film Directory of Actors Considered for Roles Given to Others*, North Carolina, 2005.
4   Such are the sensitivities involved in this regard, that a true paranoia can suddenly erupt, expressed in the fear that the consequence of taking counterfactuals seriously will be to 'overwhelm our perception of what really happened in the past' (Richard Evans, '"What if" is a waste of time', *Guardian*, 13 March 2014). 'Whose "perception"?' is the only response that readily comes to mind in the face of that epic anxiety; as for the adverb 'really', one hopes it would take a lot less than a counterfactual or two to sink that. In *Altered Pasts: Counterfactuals in History* (London, 2014), Evans takes a very different view, 'really' despatched in favour of the even trickier 'essentially' (I discuss this briefly in Chapter 2).
5   It is also part of the price for any reader of this book, given my own pennyworth of polemical input here and there (though the latter is entirely reserved for those trading in the same currency).
6   Bernard Williams, *Shame and Necessity*, Berkeley, CA, 1994, p. 151.
7   Alfred Bloom, *The Linguistic Shaping of Thought: A Study on the Impact of Language in China and the West*, New York, 1981. Bloom's study has spawned a substantial literature, much of it from Chinese scholars and for the most part critical of Bloom's approach. See Wu-Kuang-ming, 'Counterfactuals, Universals, and Chinese Thinking: *A Review of The Linguistic Shaping of Thought: A Study in the Impact of Language on Thinking in China and the West*', *Philosophy East and West*, 37(1) (Jan. 1987): 84–94. In his landmark book, *The Ideals of Inquiry* (Oxford, 2016, p. 117), Geoffrey Lloyd argues that there are in fact modes of linguistic expression (based on particles rather than tenses and moods) which carry counterfactuals. In these constructions there is also a prefatory caveat to mark the speculative nature of the

counterfactual, but (translated as 'assuming that x is false, if x then y') this allows more room for acknowledging the hypothetical than the more categorical restriction cited by Bloom ('x is not the case, but if x, then y').

**8** A particularly intriguing research test was a game based on the invention of counterfactual stories, one of which figures a Greek philosopher and how, if he had been able to write in Chinese, he would have handled counterfactual conditionals. The outcome is as above, though it remains unclear whether a counterfactual of this kind genuinely serves any useful purpose.

**9** The anthropological classic is Alfred Gell's, *The Anthropology of Time*, London, 1992.

**10** Fernand Braudel identified 'the ability to choose' as 'the chief privilege of capitalism'. This was mainly a point about proliferating centres of power in capitalist societies, but also about new forms of social complexity and speed of change. Counterfactuals, as part of the psychology of the experienced life worlds, are more likely to thrive in such settings (*The Perspective of the World*, Paris, 1984, p. 622).

**11** Reinhart Koselleck, *Futures Past. On the Semantics of Historical Time*, New York, 2004. Bernard Williams broaches the question of the kinds of society that do not seem to have a sense of 'alternatives' to their own (typically hierarchical) forms of organization. With some exceptions (small communities cut off from contact with a wider world), that does not necessarily mean they lack knowledge of the existence elsewhere of other kinds of social organization. It is more that, notwithstanding that knowledge, they do not envisage alternatives for themselves as a consequence of seeing their own social order as 'necessary'. This usually involves a legitimation myth, as, for example, in religious conceptions of a divinely ordained order of things. We shall glimpse something of the turbulence of Europe in the sixteenth and seventeenth centuries when in certain strands of theology to think counterfactually was to skirt blasphemy (*Ethics and the Limits of Philosophy*, London, 1985, pp. 164–5).

**12** Régis Debray, 'Civilization, a Grammar', *New Left Review*, September–October 2017, p. 107.

**13** Johannes Fabian, *Time and the Other*, New York, 2014.

**14** Counterfactual thinking as such is politically neutral. Both Right and Left deploy counterfactuals, but on different terms and for opposed ends, the former usually to ratify the status quo by means of 'downward' counterfactuals stipulating the alternative as worse, the latter usually to challenge the status quo by means of 'upward' counterfactuals that offer the alternative as better (often associated with the 'utopian' imagination).

**15** Catherine Gallagher, 'What Would Napoleon Do? Historical, Fictional and Counterfactual Characters', *New Literary History*, vol. 42, no. 2, Spring 2011, pp. 315–39.

**16** Richard J. Evans, 'Preface', *Altered Pasts* (London, 2014). The choice of 'seemed' theoretically leaves the door open to an awareness of how appearances, assuming they exist at all, may prove deceptive. But the door is soon slammed shut.

**17** Evans, *Altered Pasts*, p. 129. Evans also quotes Aviezer Tucker as if citing Gospel: 'What are historiographical counterfactuals good for, beyond an entertaining exercise of our imaginative faculties' (*Altered Pasts*, p. 35).

**18** Thomas Pavel, *Fictional Worlds*, Harvard, Cambridge, MA, 1989.

**19** The folding of a counterfactual into a counterfactual is elevated from a mere narrator's musing to a fully-fledged counter narrative in Philip K. Dick's *The Man in the High Castle* (London, 2015). The main plot rests on the counterfactual of the Axis powers having won World War 2; the nested plot is a widely read 'alternate-history' novel, written by Hawthorne Abendsen in which the Allies win the war, thus conforming to historical fact, but where counter-to-fact history again takes over, in the form of a rivalry between America and Britain, the outcome of which (and thus the ending of the novel) remains unstated, though there is a hint that Britain emerges the winner. We may call this modernist *mise en abyme* put to work in the genre.

**20** It seems to make sense in the terms of Lewisian possible-worlds semantics, according to which a possible world can have its own adjacent possible worlds, existing alongside each other in the same fashion as the counterfactuals at the beginning of Roth's novel. However, it's not clear what cognitive or epistemic access we can have, other than in fiction, to a 'world' in which a counterfactual President Lindbergh is counterfactually imaginable as not President. There is a potentially infinite regress here, as one possible world door opens onto another, and so on indefinitely into logical outer space. This matters because Lewis's theory was also committed to a form of ontological realism (these worlds actually exist). There is also the issue of 'identity': at what point in the proliferation of possible worlds for Lindbergh does the proper name cease to refer to the 'Lindbergh' in question. The relation of name, person and identity in possible-worlds theory is extensively discussed by Saul Kripke in *Naming and Necessity*, Harvard, Cambridge, MA, 1980.

**21** Richard Ned Lebow uses the example of Roth's novel as a means of 'revisiting the binary of fact and fiction' in terms very different from Evans's concern over threats to proper 'borders': 'the binary between fact and fiction is to a great extent artificial and can creatively and usefully be bridged for analytical as well as artistic purposes' (*Forbidden Fruit: Counterfactuals and International Relations*, Princeton, NJ, 2010, pp. 51–2). There is, of course, also a debate to be had as to just how secure the ecumenical bridge is, but that is not one of the themes of this book.

22 Geoffrey Hawthorn, *Plausible Worlds: Possibility and Understanding in History and the Social Sciences*, Cambridge, 1991 (on back cover).

23 Nelson Goodman, 'The Problem of Counterfactual Conditionals', *The Journal of Philosophy*, vol. XLIV, no. 5, 1947, p. 113.

24 In his practical teaching of how to make a good speech, Isocrates was a dab hand at exploiting counterfactuals, but mainly in the 'epideictic' mode, as forms of rhetorical showmanship. Perhaps the greatest counterfactual of them all in the history of oratory is not *in* but *about* speech, namely the speeches written by Cicero that were never delivered but, so he tells us, would have been if political circumstances had permitted.

25 Alan Megill, 'The New Counterfactualists', in Donald A. Yerxa (ed.), *Recent Themes in Historical Thinking. Historians in Conversation*, Columbia, SC, 2008, p. 101.

26 We have to distinguish here the actor's and the historian's perspective. The historian, armed with a body of evidence, might reasonably say of Napoleon on the battlefield, that he could have done such-and-such, that this was a genuine option. It does not however follow automatically that this option was seen by Napoleon himself as an option, either *in situ* as a 'might-be' or retrospectively as a 'might-have-been'. A record of the options entertained but discarded by actors when facing an indeterminate future may be explicitly registered in the historical archive, along with the reasons why they were both considered and discarded. But, if not, they can be only the constructions of the historian, guesswork as to what was consciously considered at the time or descriptions of circumstantially available possibilities but not necessarily considered or even perceived by the relevant actors.

27 Until that point (when a perceived possible future becomes a non-realized future past), the projections are, of course, future-oriented only, outside the realm of both 'fact' and 'counterfact'. They are embryos of possibility that abort. See Catherine Gallagher, *Telling It Like It Wasn't*, Chicago, 2018, p. 99.

28 Fernand Braudel, *The Mediterranean and the Mediterranean World in the Age of Philip II*, vol. 2, New York, 1977, p. 18. There is, conversely, a sense in which *longue durée*, or at least longer duration, is more the friend than the enemy of the counterfactual: the cases, both collective and individual, where alternative options might have come into view had the enterprises of the historical actors had even more time. It is sometimes suggested, for example, that the Almoravid empire would probably have established a thriving urban 'culture' if it had had more time to consolidate.

29 Fernand Braudel, *On History*, Chicago, 1982, p. 10.

30 See Quentin Deluermoz and Pierre Singaravélou, *Pour une Histoire des Possibles. Analyses contrefactuelles et futurs non advenus*, Paris, 2016, p. 108.

31 In the Rabelais example, a key that opens the door to that world could be Bonaventure des Périer's *Cymbalum mundi*, and the furore around its

publication unleashed by the charge of atheism. It was not so much that atheism was 'unthinkable' as that it was disallowed.

32 Hawthorn uses the principle of 'imaginative extension' in relation to the decision-making of the public authorities around the Black Death in the form of back importations of what was both thought and tried in later periods, accompanied by the question as to whether there was in principle any major conceptual or practical impediment to operating in the same way. In a very different vein, Jay Lampert has sketched a way of thinking about the relation between decision-making and the 'future' as not just defined by the categories of pre-given 'options', in favour of the principle of options that are created in the process of decision-making itself, in the context of the idea of 'a future that has not yet become determinate' (*The Many Futures of a Decision*, London, 2018, p.98). This way of construing the option, the decision and the future provides even richer potential scenarios for retrospective counterfactuals.

33 The 'hindcast' is a device for the testing of mathematical models, into which is fed information of past weather patterns, the models then run to see if it delivers results consistent with what we know.

34 They may simply be invisible, to both historical actors and the later inquiring historian. What, however, follows is not necessarily that alternatives didn't exist but that we can say nothing about them (though, for the investigator, to all practical intents and purposes that comes to the same thing). Short of that dead end, there is the murky zone of residual traces whose 'meaning' is not self-declaring and which call upon the arts of the historian as detective working with 'clues' invoked by Collingwood. As special and complex objects of inquiry, counterfactuals routinely require the use of these arts.

35 Insurrections and revolutions are especially fertile contexts for counterfactuals: Lenin's question 'what is to be done' at some point invariably joins with the question of what could have been done. 'Filled with might-have-beens and missed opportunities' is how Stephen Smith has characterized the Russian revolution. Neal Ascherson has described the historiography of insurrection and civil war in 1930s Spain as adorned with 'a dazzling fringe of what ifs'. They are also fulcrum episodes when *longue durée* history (of centralizing state formation in the case of France, for example) and 'event' history meet in a moment of crisis and emergency. Lenin again: 'there are decades where nothing happens, and there are weeks when decades happen.'

36 Niall Ferguson (ed.), *Virtual History: Alternatives and Counterfactuals*, London, 1998, p. 17.

37 Hawthorn, *Plausible Worlds*, p. 58.

38 Nelson Goodman puts it thus: 'a counterfactual by its nature can never be subjected to any direct empirical test by realizing its antecedent' ("The Problem of Counterfactual Conditionals', *The Journal of Philosophy*, vol. 44,

no. 5 (27 February 1947), p. 114). That being so, the same must hold for what is deemed to follow from the *protasis* in the *apodosis*.

39  Consider the blurb on the back cover of Ferguson's *Virtual History*. It self-describes as 'a revolutionary book in which leading historians explore what *would have* happened if nine momentous events had turned out differently' (my emphasis). It must be gratifying to be in possession of such apodotic certainty. The 'would have' claims are certainly incompatible with what Ferguson rightly says in his introductory chapter: 'The most historians can do is to make tentative statements about causation with reference to plausible counterfactuals, constructed on the basis of judgements about probability' (p. 89). No plausible judgement of this type can attain hundred per cent probability, but that is exactly what (unqualified) 'would have' claims entail.

40  Stephen Mumford and Rani Lill Anjum, *Causation: A Very Short Introduction*, Oxford, 2013.

41  The full glory of this is captured by the equation: 'A is an INUS condition of a result P if and only if, for some X and for some Y, (AX or Y) is a necessary and sufficient condition of P, but A is not a sufficient condition of P, and X is not a sufficient condition of P.'

42  In these terms Ferguson is right: the issue was never whether railways be built but where (*Virtual History*, p. 18).

43  For a discussion, see Dorothy Edgington's fine paper, 'Counterfactuals and the Benefit of Hindsight', in P. Dowe and P. Noørdhof (eds), *Cause and Chance: Causation in an Indeterministic World*, London, 2004, pp. 12–27.

44  Keith DeRose, 'Lewis on "Might" and "Would" Counterfactuals', *Canadian Journal of Philosophy*, vol. 24, no. 3, Sep. 1994, pp. 413–18.

45  Evans, *Altered Pasts*, p. 177. Historians are often notoriously lax in this regard, visible in the slapdash ease with which they can switch, often within the same paragraph, from 'would have' to 'might have' without so much as a split second awareness of the fact that these are not the same. Someone who is exemplary as a counter to this is Geoffrey Hawthorn. At the heart of his study of historical cases stands a claim, whose centrality is marked by its status as a kind of refrain, repeated with slight variations throughout his book: 'Possibilities, under explanation increase as well as decrease.' The decreasing curve is what describes standard explanatory endeavours, as elimination, on the basis of the best evidence, of competitors until one gets to a winner or set of winners (in philosophy of science it's sometimes called 'inference to the best explanation'). The increasing curve, on the other hand, tracks the shadow-world of the winning candidates by outlining the 'loser' alternatives that hover like ghosts over the enterprise of explanation. In Hawthorn's text they consistently appear under the banner of the 'might-have-been'. On the other hand, the modal that appears most frequently is 'could have', consistent with Hawthorn's concern with the 'doable' in the exercise of practical reason. This leaves 'should have' counterfactual

assessments of what was and was not 'right' to do. When not questions of practical reason, they are generally moral and religious questions. These make a limited appearance in Chapter 5, in the discussion of the relation between *metanoia* and 'repentance'.

46  See Catherine Gallagher's discussion of the two paradigms of 'probability' as an 'Afterword', in Victoria Wohl (ed.), *Probabilities, Hypotheticals and Counterfactuals in Ancient Greek Thought*, Cambridge, 1996, pp. 251–3. In Plato's *Phaedrus*, Socrates summarizes the relevant ancient conception in terms of a view he attributes to Tisias: 'Does he not define probability to be that which the many think?' Socrates has little patience with this unless probability is 'engendered in the minds of the many by the likeness of the truth'.

47  Daniel S. Milo and Alain Bourreau (eds), *Pour une histoire expérimentale*, Paris, 1991.

48  Edgington, 'Counterfactuals and the Benefit of Hindsight', p. 12.

49  Edgington, 'Counterfactuals and the Benefit of Hindsight', p. 26.

50  See the immensely engaging book by Stephen Greenblatt, *The Rise and Fall of Adam and Eve* (New York, 2017, p. 16):

> The Bible story suggests that something happened to the species shortly after it was authored by God. Humanity did not have to turn out to be the way it is now; it could all have been different. The image of the man and woman in the perfect garden suggests a tension between things as they are and things as they might have been. It conveys a longing to be other than what we have become.

This is the theme of counterfactual 'regret' (see Chapter 5) writ as large as it can possibly get.

51  Boer Deng, 'Machine Ethics: The Robot's Dilemma', *Nature*, 1 July 2015. One of these is illustrated by the trolley problem, in which you imagine a runaway railway trolley is about to kill five innocent people who are on the tracks. You can save them only if you pull a lever that diverts the train onto another track, where it will hit and kill an innocent bystander. What do you do? In another set-up, the only way to stop the trolley is to push the bystander onto the tracks. People often answer that it is all right to stop the trolley by hitting the lever, but viscerally reject the idea of pushing the bystander. The basic intuition, known to philosophers as the doctrine of double effect, is that deliberately inflicting harm is wrong, even if it leads to good. However, inflicting harm might be acceptable if it is not deliberate, but simply a consequence of doing good – as when the bystander simply happens to be on the tracks.

52  Ryota Kanai, 'We Need Conscious Robots: How Introspection and Imagination Make Robots Better', *Nautilus*, 27 April 2017.

53  My thanks to Patti Smith and her book *Woolgathering* (Hanuman, New York, 1992).

54  Courtesy of my good friend Stanley Corngold.

# 1 A Naile, A Nose and a Traitor

1 Establishing a plausible counterfactual to the effect that, if the nail had not been missing, Richard would not have lost his kingdom requires a 'thick' contextual description which would have to specify *all* the relevant conditions, which, when gathered, will most likely lead to the opposite conclusion: the missing nail makes no difference. Wesley C. Salmon discusses the proverb in 'Causation', in Richard M. Gale (ed.), *The Blackwell Guide to Metaphysics*, Oxford, 2002, p. 27.

2 Conrad Russell, 'The Catholic Wind', in John Merriman (ed.), *For Want of a Horse. Choice and Chance in History*, Lexington, KY, 1985. The argument in summary form is that if in November, 1688, instead of the 'Protestant wind' which enabled William of Orange's fleet to evade interception, the wind had favoured James II's naval forces, what would have ensued was a Catholic England under absolutist monarchy. The wind is a natural world equivalent of the quivering butterfly wings in chaos theory, though to get its full glory we would have to track back from wind to the sources of the wind and the sources of the sources ... Conrad Russell relates the tale with gusto as if it were historical fact, a mode which instantly declares its status as spoof.

3 Ferguson invokes chaos theory as a model for counterfactual (or 'virtual') history, while leaving unproven how this could possibly work other than in the most radically speculative of guises. He claims that 'virtual history is a necessary antidote to determinism' ('Virtual History: Towards a "Chaotic" Theory of the Past', *Virtual History*, p. 89), but, when properly weighed, 'necessary' is the one adjective that really does sit awkwardly in a professed anti-deterministic position, as for that matter does chaos theory itself, which, as Ferguson himself notes, is a determinism (of causal explanation) that incorporates the 'unpredictable'. In science and mathematics, the theory provides less an 'antidote' to determinism than a re-description of it. The fact that an outcome in the natural world is unpredictable doesn't mean it is not governed by law-bound processes that ensure its occurrence, but only that, given the dynamically interactive character of the processes, it can't be reliably foreseen. Ferguson's theoretical case looks like a bet on two horses (Determinism and Unpredictability) where, if the winning horse is also to be called 'Antidote', there can't be a winner and thus a payout. The point about counterfactuals in science is that they are counterfactuals for science; that is entirely different from using them as an analogue or model for human history. Ferguson himself notes 'history does not proceed as science does' (p. 90); if that is so, then much of what he argues by analogy simply falls apart. Naturally, I do not here intend the metaphorical gloss of the 'nail' proverb in the terms of chaos theory as anything other than metaphor; it has no scientific standing whatsoever.

4 Leibniz combines both possibilitarian and necessitarian positions. He allows for an infinity of possible worlds (in the counterfactually stocked mind of

God), but posits any given world as a holistic system of necessarily interconnected and interdependent parts such that the slightest alteration entails alteration to and of the whole; given worlds, including this one, are counterfactual-free by the very fact of their existence. As for Einstein's 'God does not play dice', there has long been debate as to whether this means that, in creating the universe, God can freely choose from a menu of possibilities about which physical laws are to govern it, or whether he is 'constrained by mathematical truth' (as Richard Dworkin has it in *Religion without God*, London, 2002). There is also the story of the great Einsteinian counterfactual. In his biography of Einstein (*Subtle is the Lord: The Science and the Life of Albert Einstein*, New York, 2005), Abraham Pais tells the story of Einstein handing a student a cable informing him that the bending of light by the sun was in agreement with his general relativistic prediction. When the student asked what he would have said if there had been no confirmation of his theory, Einstein is said to have replied (in German): 'Then I would have to pity the dear Lord. The theory is correct anyway.' Stephen Hawking was resolutely of the view that God (if he exists) not only plays dice, but hides them (in black holes).

5   For a detailed account of the key place after Leibniz and Leibnizianism in the history of counterfactualism, see Gallagher, *Telling It Like It Wasn't*, pp. 17–23. See also Michael Hooker (ed.), *Leibniz: Critical and Interpretive Essays*, Minnesota University Press, 1982.

6   Martin Rees, 'From Mars to the Multiverse', *European Review*, vol. 26, February 2018, p. 13.

7   Stephen Gould, *Wonderful Life: The Burgess Shale and the Nature of History*, New York, 1989, p. 48. See Ian Hesketh, 'Counterfactuals and History: Contingency and Convergence in Histories of Science and Life', *Studies in History and Philosophy of Biological and Biomedical Sciences*, August 2017, pp. 41–8.

8   See, for example, the question raised by Mark Linville: suppose bees had been endowed with minds like ours and a capacity for moral reasoning, would the processes of apian 'natural selection' have allowed for 'siblicide and infanticide' as morally acceptable? 'The Moral Argument', in William Lane Craig and J. P. Moreland (eds), *The Blackwell Companion to Natural Theology*, Oxford, 2009, p. 19.

9   Ian Morris, *Why the West Rules – For Now*, London, 2010, pp. 3–11.

10  Niall Ferguson, *Kissinger: 1923–1968: The Idealist*, London, 2015, p. vi.

11  *New York Times*, 20 June 2016. Trump has a particular fondness for this version of the 'upward' counterfactual. He returned to it in connection with the Marjory Stoneman Douglas High School shootings in February 2018: 'If the coach had a firearm in his locker when he ran at this guy – that coach was very brave, saved a lot of lives, I suspect. But if he had a firearm, he wouldn't have had to run, he would have shot him, and that would have been the end of it.' The fuller rhapsody was as follows: 'If the Florida gunman thought that other people would be shooting bullets back at him, he wouldn't have gone there,'

adding: 'A teacher would have shot the hell out of him before he ever knew what happened.' But perhaps the prize for the top Trumpian counterfactual so far is his reaction to the Woodward exposé: 'The Woodward book is a scam. I don't talk the way I am quoted. If I did I would not have been elected president'.

12  *Telegraph*, 9 June 2016.
13  'Introduction', in Andrew Roberts (ed.), *What Might Have Been. Imaginary History by Twelve Leading Historians*', London, 2004, p. 1. Roberts's contribution to Ferguson's collection ('Hitler's England. What if Germany had invaded Britain in May 1940') relies on statements prefaced by the likes of 'it is not inconceivable that' and 'it is not impossible to imagine'. Indeed lots of things are not *impossible* to imagine (including half-decent contributions to counterfactual history). As for Thompson himself, despite his intemperateness, he was hardly a classical determinist and wrote, in *The Making of the English Working Class*, about Britain being 'within an ace' of revolution in 1831, 'which, once commenced', might have prefigured 1848 or the Paris Commune (London, 1968, pp. 898–9).
14  The tale is retold with a poker-face as if incontrovertibly true by John Merriman ('Introduction', *For Want of a Horse*, p. x).
15  Shirley Williams (née Catlin) auditioned for the part but was allegedly pipped at the post by Elizabeth Taylor. Other sources however claim that she didn't get past the first round.
16  David Lewis, *Counterfactuals*, London, 1986, pp. 32–3.
17  Donald Trump has, of course, greatly extended what can now be said about directors of the FBI, given his thoughtful characterization (before two high-ranking Russians!) of the director he fired as a 'nut case'.
18  The analytical representation of this looks as follows: the nearest P-world (a Russian-born Hoover) is a Q-world (a communist Hoover); but the nearest Q-world is an R-world (an American traitor). Under these conditional assumptions, it is very hard to see how a P-world could also be an R-world, without booking a ticket to logic's version of extra-planetary space.
19  Lebow, *Forbidden Fruit: Counterfactuals and International Relations*, p. 54. One of the listed 'criteria' is 'Clarity'; that would seem to a sine qua non of *any* argument.
20  Alan Meghill, 'The New Counterfactualists', *Historically Speaking*, vol. 5, no. 4, p. 102. One of the insuperable problems associated with attempts to control variables by means of the *ceteris paribus* clause is the phenomenon of the feedback loop. Aviezer Tucker opines as follows: 'every counterfactual has a *ceteris paribus* clause: the historian assumes that the historical reality remained constant, except for the examined factors' (cit. Evans, *Altered Pasts*, p. 164). If that *is* the assumption, it comes at a huge exclusionary cost. The 'factors' to be 'examined' have to include guesstimates of the new elements that would enter the historical field as a consequence of feedback loops triggered by the substituted antecedent.

21 Adam Smith, *The Theory of Moral Sentiments*, Cambridge, 2002, pp. 157–8.
22 One might want to suggest here that Lewis's philosophically conservative (or 'parsimonious') views on counterfactual 'distance' can attract an ideological dimension. Both Ernst Bloch and Paul Ricoeur stressed the value of 'distance' in imaging things otherwise, the kind of 'distance' that enables a critical deconstruction of the given (see Ronald Paulsen, 'The Counterfactual Imagination', in R. Swedberg (ed.), *Theorizing in Social Science*, Stanford, 2014, p. 172).
23 Philip Tetlock and Aaron Belkin, *Counterfactual Thought Experiments in World Politics: Logical, Methodological and Psychological Perspectives*, Princeton, NJ, 1996, p. 24.
24 Blaise Pascal, *Pensées* (Philippe Sellier (ed.)), Paris, 2000, pp. 50–1.
25 Jacques Attali, citing the 'butterfly' example, invites us to take seriously the thought that Pascal here anticipates modern chaos theory (*Pascal, ou le génie français*, Paris, 2000, p. 473). The invitation is acceptable only under conditions of considerable anachronistic strain.
26 Lebow dismisses it as 'objectionable' on the grounds of its being 'arbitrary and contrived'; it fails to satisfy the first of his 'criteria', namely 'realism' (*Forbidden Fruit*, p. 54). The objection misses Pascal's point and purpose entirely. Where historians typically deride, philosophers more interestingly come out to play, most inventively in relation to possible-worlds analysis. Examples include: 'if Cleopatra's asp had been human, it would have been a mammal', or 'if Cleopatra's asp had been human, it would have been immaterial', examples, that is, in which the 'inconceivable' yields the 'meaningless' (see Peter van Inwagen, 'Laws and Counterfactuals', *Noûs*, vol. 13, no. 4, Nov. 1979, pp. 439–53).
27 An attempt to take it seriously as a historical counterfactual is J. P. Bury's 'Cleopatra's Nose', *Selected Essays*, Cambridge. 1930. Bury posits it as the outcome of the 'contingent' confluence of two independent causal chains; one is biological, the nose as the product of heredity; the other is political, the strand of Roman history which brings Anthony to Egypt. Bury concludes that unlikely 'contingencies' of this kind were far more common in earlier periods than in modern histories increasingly shaped by science and hence at once more controlled and more predictable. Others, of course, would argue that it is in modern societies of 'choice' and 'risk' that the incalculable is more prominent.
28 'For her beauty, as we are told, was not in itself incomparable', Plutarch, 'Mark Anthony', *Makers of Rome*, London, 1987, p. 294.
29 See Richard Scholar, *The Je-Ne-Sais-Quoi in Early Modern Europe: Encounters with a Certain Something*, Oxford 2005.
30 Jacques Lacan, *Écrits: A Selection* (trans. and ed. Michael Sheridan), London, 2001, pp. 135–6.

31 See Gallagher: 'His famous counterfactual was designed to challenge, not exalt, our ability to find divine reasons in history', *Telling It Like It Wasn't*, p. 24. John Lyons sees the Cleopatra fragment as illustrating Pascal's view of the sheer unintelligibility of history (to human reason), graspable only as the play of pure chance (*The Phantom of Chance: From Fortune to Randomness in Seventeenth-Century Literature*, Edinburgh, 2012, pp. 20, 67–8).

32 The allusion to Pascal's use of the Cleopatra counterfactual as 'strange' in the first of the *Lettres sur l'hérésie imaginaire* was subsequently excised. But Nicole's text also presents (and retains) a conception of history driven by 'les moindres bagatelles' that is a mirror-image of Pascal's (in Blaise Pascal, *Les Provinciales* (Jean Steinmann (ed.)), Paris, 1962, vol. II, pp. 180–1).

33 See Chapter 3.

# 2 Just the facts, ma'am: Fact and Counterfact

1 The best-known ancient source is Aristotle's doctrine of *entelechia*, developed notably in the *Physics* and the *Metaphysics*.

2 This, of course, is an intellectual minefield, most notably the explosions that can erupt when the epistemology of the 'factual' is historicized in a manner triggering what can look like an irreconcilable conflict between 'realists' and 'constructionists'. A case in point was the reaction in some quarters to Mary Poovey's account of the emergence of the 'modern fact', or more exactly of the modern regime of 'fact', as a creation of the scientific revolution and the 'counting' operations of a capitalist market economy, with its origins in double-entry bookkeeping and the prestige accorded to numbers (the developments that, in Poovey's words, 'helped confer cultural authority on numbers'), *A History of the Modern Fact: Problems of Knowledge in the Sciences of Wealth and Society*, Chicago, 1998, p. 54. Although it nowhere explicitly argues for a version of epistemic relativism, Poovey's historical account was seen as vulnerable to the charge of confusing an explanation of the growing importance attached to the 'factual' in the production of knowledge with a formal epistemology of the nature of 'facts' as such. For a trenchant, but also contestable, critique along these lines, see the review by Margaret C. Jacob, 'Factoring Mary Poovey's, *A History of the Modern Fact*', *History and Theory*, vol. 40, no. 2, May 2001, pp. 280–9.

3 Here is Arron Banks, one of the principal sponsors of Brexit, on the nature of the referendum campaign: 'It was taking an American-style media approach,' said Banks. 'What they said early on was "facts don't work" and that's it. The Remain campaign featured fact, fact, fact, fact, fact. It just doesn't work. You have got to connect with people emotionally. It's the Trump success,' *Guardian*, 29 June 2016.

4   See Barbara Cassin (ed.), *A Dictionary of Untranslatables* (trans. and ed. Emily Apter, Jacques Lezra and Michael Wood), Princeton, NJ, 2014, pp. 113–17.

5   On the complex history of the notion of the 'matter of fact' as a central category for modern scientific and secular thought, see Simon Schaffer, 'Making Certain', *Social Studies of Science*, vol. 14, no. 1, Feb. 1984, pp. 137–52.

6   For a helpful overview, see the entry for 'Fact' in the online version of the *Stanford Encyclopedia of Philosophy*.

7   The argument is that all statements of the form 'it is a fact that' are timeless in the way that true propositions are true for all time even when they refer to contingent events and states. This alliance of the factual and the true is not, of course, to be confused with the invention of the category of the 'true fact'. See, for example, the report that Florida's Department of Environmental Protection blocked the use by its employees of the words 'climate change', after Florida's governor insisted that they did not express a 'true fact'. This is the ideal partner for Conway's 'alternative facts'.

8   'As Clemenceau famously said at Versailles to a German who had wondered what future historians would say about all this, "They won't say that Belgium invaded Germany"', Bernard Williams, *Truth and Truthfulness*, Princeton, NJ, 2002, p. 243.

9   The relation of archive and internet has changed our own relation to the former, and not just in quantitative terms. One outcome is an effect of 'compressing historical time; what seems distant becomes close', a consequence of which is that the 'archive isn't merely available to us; it actively pursues us' (William Davies, 'Reasons for Corbyn', *London Review of Books*, 13 July 2017). It can also lose as well as store. In the shift from microfilm to digitization vast amounts of print information has been lost forever.

10  See Jacques Derrida, *Archive Fever*, Chicago, 1996.

11  Perhaps the most famous example of the forged document in Western history is the *Donation of Constantine*, which for many hundreds of years was taken to be authentic. Evidence of history being written by winners was the placing in the UK National Archives of false documents establishing that Himmler did not commit suicide but was murdered by British Special Operations. A party favourite is the exercise in brazen fakery by the fifteenth-century Crowlands monks, the *Historia Crowlandensis*, accepted as genuine for 500 years as the basis for substantial but entirely fraudulent land claims. Some claims of forgery are, of course, simply deranged or themselves forgeries. Some are simply awesome: for an unforgettable mix of wild paranoia and incomparable learning, one can do little better than Jean Hardouin (his dementedly tenacious 'researches' yielded 'Hardouinismus'). Himself a notable scholar and librarian, in 1693 he published *Theory of Universal Forgery*, whose main purpose was to trash virtually the entire

corpus of classical texts as a confection by a band of demonic thirteenth-century monks as part of a plot to discredit Christianity and make pagans of us all. While plainly demented, it is also amazingly scholarly at the level of detecting errors and unreliable details.

**12** See also the librarian, Rebecca Lossin, on 'paper-hatred' and 'tomecide', and the 'digital library' as a contradiction in terms. 'Against the Universal Library', *New Left Review*, 107, September–October 2017.

**13** Richard Evans, *In Defence of History*, London, 2000, p. 17.

**14** The expression 'what actually happened' is standard historian-speak, often on the part of practitioners brandishing the seriousness of what they do in explicit contrast to the idle pastimes of counterfacualists. Strictly speaking, however, it is loose usage. In Lewis's 'possible-worlds' philosophy 'actual' is an indexical term unbreakably tied to a present as something that means and refers only in the moment of its utterance. The relevant idea is reflected non-technically in French usage; the term 'actuel' is used in relation to present states of affairs only (*actualités* as 'current affairs'). To speak of something in the past as something that 'actuellement' happened is, in French, a nonsense. Koselleck makes another but important point, in the form of what he calls an 'epistemological remark', about the linking of historical 'fact' to 'actuality': 'the facticity of events *ex post* is never identical with a totality of past circumstances thought of as formerly real. Every event historically established and presented lives on the fiction of actuality; reality itself is past and gone,' (*Futures Past*, p. 111). On the other hand, there remains an important philosophical context for the use of 'actual', namely in relation to 'potential', in the tradition that runs back to Aristotle's doctrine of entelechy. This is also a context in which the 'actual' can be coherently used in relation to the 'counterfactual' as one of the forms of our sense of 'potential' or 'possibility'.

**15** This is the view famously expressed by George Santayana, albeit pressed into the service of a full-on scepticism that also impugns the moral credentials of history's story-tellers (they are all liars): 'History is a pack of lies about events that never happened told by people who were never there.'

**16** Max Hastings, 'Diary', *London Review of Books*, 10 September 2015.

**17** Edward Ingram, 'Is the Dark Light Enough', *Recent Themes in Historical Thinking*, Columbia, SC, 2008, p. 86.

**18** The historian of mediaeval manuscripts, Christopher de Hamel, said of the question whether the psalter in the Parker Library alleged to have belonged to Thomas à Becket actually did so: 'Whether it really belonged to Becket – well, I wasn't there' (while going on to add 'But I bet it did'). More generally, he has characterized 'all history' (by which he means the historical record) as a 'dodgy dossier' (Alison Flood, 'Thomas Becket's personal book of psalms found in Cambridge library', *Guardian*, 1 October 2016). The whole question of what it is to 'know' the past is, of course, highly sensitive, and for good reason. Sceptical critique can come out sounding threateningly solipsistic, or worse, put to disreputable use (as in Holocaust denial). Perhaps therefore the question should be reframed as a question about what, here, 'knowing' means.

19  Cited in Rosemary Hill, 'Herbert and Herbertinas', *London Review of Books*, 20 October 2016.
20  Deluermoz and Singaravélou, *Pour une histoire des possibles*, pp. 154–5.
21  Daniel Milo, 'Pour une histoire expérimentale', *Annales. Économies, Sociétés, Civilisations*, vol. 45, no. 3, 1990, pp. 12–15.
22  See Edward Becker, *The Themes of Quine's Philosophy: Meaning, Reference and Knowledge*, Cambridge, 2012, p. 222.
23  This is a subject of fierce debate. Durkheim's aim was not to furnish a positivist ontology for the social sciences. His interests were more taxonomic than ontological, social life grasped as a collection of 'facts' and 'things' ordered like 'specimens' in a museum.
24  The philosopher-guru of modern Conservative Man, Michael Oakeshott, described him thus: 'He eyes the situation in terms of its propensity to disrupt the familiarity of the features of his world' ('On Being Conservative', *Rationalism in Politics and Other Essays*, London, 1962, p. 434.). While this seems to have been intended as a compliment (exemplar of the virtues of 'rational prudence'), there's more than a hint of irony as well.
25  See Mikkel Lahtinen, *Politics and Philosophy. Niccolò Machiavelli and Louis Althusser's Aleatory Materialism*, Leiden, 2009.
26  See 'Introduction', pp. 19–22. On the *fait accompli*, see also Simon Schaffer, 'The Accomplishment of Facts at the End of the Enlightenment', in Cheryce von Xylander and Alfred Nordmann (eds), *Vollendete Tatsachen*, Bielefeld, 2019. Schaffer cites Theodor Adorno's beautifully incisive description of how the 'disenchanting' force of the regime of 'fact' that emerged during the Enlightenment was turned against itself to become an ideological tool for the systematic exclusion of the sense of the 'alternative' (which presumably includes the counterfactual alternative):

> The processes of enlightenment have destroyed magical and supernatural ideas by confrontation with empirical reality, that which exists. All this has tended to invest the factual itself with that very halo against which the idea of fact was originally coined. That something exists is taken as a proof that it is stronger than that which does not exist, and that therefore it is better. The *fait accompli* technique exploits this disposition.
> *The Psychological Technique of Martin Luther Thomas' Radio Addresses*, Stanford, 2000, pp. 44–5

27  Pierre Bourdieu and Loïc Wacquant, *Réponses: Pour une anthropologie réflexive*, Paris, 1992, p. 143.

28  Paulsen affirms the value of counterfactuals as a space where defamiliarization and imagination work together in challenging the accumulated and imposed weight of 'power': 'to be able to observe power at all, one must imagine how those subject to power would behave differently if it were not for the exercise of power.' Paulsen also proposes this as a basis for discriminating 'instrumental' and 'utopian' counterfactuals. The former project solutions that leave power structures intact, while the latter project solutions that challenge those structures ('The Counterfactual Imagination', p. 16).

29  Alfred North Whitehead, *The Aims of Education and Other Essays*, New York, 1967, p. 93.

# 3  Flying Blind: *Angelus Novus* and *Allegory of Prudence*

1  In the Capra film the angel, Clarence, persuades the suicidal George to look on the brighter side by means of a logically dizzying counterfactual centred on the awful consequences for biological loved ones of George never having been born. I pick up on the historical and conceptual complexities of the never-having-been-born counterfactual in Chapter 6.

2  It has been remarked that the cult of angels in the contemporary US is for the most part akin to treating them as 'pets'.

3  In his *Three Books of Occult Philosophy*, Cornelius Agrippa devised the 'angelic script' (sometimes known as the 'celestial alphabet') for the purpose of communication with the angels. In *The Lives of Angels*, Swedenborg informatively reports (as distinct from merely asserting) that angels speak, on the eminently reasonable grounds of having himself travelled often to the spirit world to converse with them, at length, congenially and even merrily. The angels in fact live rather like us, though at a higher level of spiritual development. They inhabit houses, work, and have an active community life. There is angel marriage, though on the delicate question of sexual congress Swedenborg manages to be at once fulsome and obscure: angels have sex inside monogamy; it involves the pleasures and gratifications of the flesh, but is also spiritual, chaste and childless.

4  The question of whether or not angelic thinking includes the counterfactual is connected to the place occupied by angels in the temporal order. Since for Aquinas angels are non-material, they cannot occupy either space or time after the manner of material things. As divine emanations, their metaphysical place in time is that of all time.

5  It seems, however, that the claim is restricted to 'might have' counterfactuals; 'would-haves' are beyond even divine reach. There is the related counterfactual concerning the status of God's promises: what would be their

status if heaven and earth were to cease to exist? Citing Jeremiah, Jesus asserts that they endure nevertheless, on the grounds that, whatever happens to heaven and earth, God's words do not pass away. Elizabeth Anscombe amusingly narrates her bafflement when as a teenager she came across the conundrum of the divine relation to counterfactual conditionals:

> As a result of my teen-age conversion to the Catholic Church – itself the fruit of reading done from twelve to fifteen – I read a work called *Natural Theology* by a nineteenth-century Jesuit. I read it with great appetite and found it all convincing except for two things. One was the doctrine of *scientia media*, according to which God knew what anybody would have done if, for example, he hadn't died when he did. This was a part of theodicy, and was also the form in which the problem of counterfactual conditionals was discussed. I found I could not believe this doctrine: it appeared to me that there was not, quite generally, any such thing as what would have happened if what did happen had not happened, and that in particular there was no such thing, generally speaking, as what someone would have done if . . . and certainly that there was no such thing as how someone would have spent his life if he had not died a child. I did not know at the time that the matter was one of fierce dispute between the Jesuits and the Dominicans, who took rather my own line about it. So when I was being instructed a couple of years later by a Dominican at Oxford, Fr Richard Kehoe, and he asked me if I had any difficulties, I told him that I couldn't see how that stuff could be true. He was obviously amused and told me that 1 certainly didn't have to believe it, though I only learned the historical fact I have mentioned rather later.
> 'Introduction', *Collected Papers*, vol. 2, Oxford, 1981

6   In 1920 the party was renamed the National Socialist party and Hitler himself was gaining prominence as a public speaker; on the other hand in 1920, it was still just one among many right-wing parties. The association with Hitler may have come later, in the 1930s when Klee was harassed by the Gestapo and removed from his teaching appointment at the Düsseldorf Academy. There are also the angel drawings in the last years of his life, with the inscrutable titles such as *Angels still ugly* and *Angel as yet untrained in walking*.

7   Walter Benjamin, *Theses on the Philosophy of History*, *Illuminations*, London, 1992, p. 249.

8   Jürgen Glaesemer describes it thus:

> He painted thin Japan paper with black oil paint, and when the paint was sufficiently dry, he placed a sheet like a tracing paper under the drawing and traced the contours of the drawing through with a metal needle. As a result the paper below showed not only the outline of the drawing in a new way, but also the deliberately distributed patches and structures of the oil paint made by the rubbing or the placing of the hand during the tracing process. His first drawings made in this way were left uncoloured,

but he afterwards used many drawings of this type as the basis for watercolours (in *Paul Klee: Handzeichnungen I*, Bern, 1973, p. 260).

9   This observation is not, of course, intended as a counterfactual. A minimum condition of possibility for it qualifying would be Benjamin making it to age 93 (born in 1892, and the film out in 1985). The point would not be worth making were it not that Benjamin himself, as autobiographical subject, has become the site of a veritable industry of post-mortem counterfactual speculation. Perhaps the most exotic product in this line is David Kishik's *The Manhattan Project*, in which Benjamin doesn't take his life in Port Bou and instead fakes a death, gets across the Atlantic to New York where, under an assumed name (Carl Roseman), he avoids all contact with his exiled Frankfurt School colleagues and instead devotes most of the rest of his life to compiling a version of the *Passagenwerk* for twentieth-century New York (with Hannah Arendt standing in for Karl Marx). It's charming nonsense, from virtually every conceivable point of view. Carl Roseman 'dies' from a fall in 1987, thus allowing for a period of two years in which he could have seen 'Back to the Future'.

10  Helga Geyer-Ryan calls it the place where we find 'release material for an alternative, counterfactual history' ('Counterfactual artefacts: Walter Benjamin's philosophy of history', in Edward Timms and Peter Collier (eds), *Visions and Blueprints. Avant-garde Culture and Radical Politics in Early Twentieth-Century* Europe, Manchester, 1988, p. 76). On the politics of the counterfactual in Benjamin as the 'imagining of a history that might have been if justice had prevailed instead of "the victors"', see Crystal Bartolovich, 'History after the End of History: Critical Counterfactualism and Revolution', *New Formations*, no. 59, Autumn 2006.

11  For Reinhart Koselleck the virtue of studying losers' history lies in its special power to generate causal understanding of the past, a power arising from the need of the loser to reflect on why things did not turn out as intended, expected or hoped for (as distinct from the less taxing assumption of the winners that historical outcomes were foreordained). Counterfactual thinking is intrinsic to this enterprise, as it is also to winners' history. In connection with the latter, see Catherine Gallagher on America and the two wars that were 'won', the Civil War and World War 2 (in *Telling It Like It Wasn't*).

12  *Theses on the Philosophy of History*, p. 246. Much is missed if the implied connection between Benjamin's Angel of History and his use of the Heliotropic metaphor is not made. China Miéville sees the angel as having become 'a cliché of radical pessimism', which indeed it has when seen in isolation from the imagery of the 'secret heliotropism' ('Introduction', Thomas More, *Utopia*, London, 2016, p. 8).

13  Nietzsche, *Untimely Meditations*, Cambridge, 1999, p. 61.

**14** The perennial ambiguity of all utopian thinking is captured in Ursula K. Le Guin's formulation: 'Every utopia contains a dystopia, every dystopia contains a utopia.' More's Utopia is the creation of a violent warrior king, Utopus, who conquers and enslaves an indigenous population as the means of its creation (Thomas More, *Utopia*, 'Introduction' by China Miéville, Essays by Ursula K. Le Guin, London, 2016).

**15** *The Savage Mind*, London, 1966, p. 11.

**16** Christopher Lehrich, *The Language of Demons and Angels: Cornelius Agrippa's Occult Philosophia*, Leiden, 2003, p. 216.

**17** Marcel Hénaff, *Claude Lévi-Strauss and the Making of Structural Anthropology*, Minneapolis, 1998, p. 109.

**18** 'Enthusiastic partisans of the idea of progress are in danger of failing to recognize – because they set so little store by them – the immense riches accumulated by the human race on either side of the narrow furrow on which they kept their eyes fixed,' *Tristes Tropiques*, London, 1992, p. 393.

**19** Lévi-Strauss, *From Honey to Ashes*, London, 1973, p. 475. Elsewhere the claim is more elaborately formulated:

> the ethnologist's goal is to grasp, beyond the conscious and always shifting images which we hold, the complete range of unconscious possibilities. These are not unlimited, and the relationships of compatibility or incompatibility which each maintains with all the others provide a logical framework for historical developments which, while perhaps unpredictable, are never arbitrary.
> *Structural Anthropology*, New York, 1963, p. 23

For an exemplary introduction to this aspect of Lévi-Strauss's thought, see Christopher Johnson, 'All Played Out? Lévi-Strauss's Philosophy of History', *New Left Review*, January–February 2013, p. 79. Johnson also highlights 'Lévi-Strauss's explicitly Leibnizian vocabulary'.

**20** Lévi-Strauss, *Tristes tropiques*, p. 393.

**21** See Suzanne Hobson, *Angels of Modernism: Religion, Culture, Aesthetics, 1910–1960*, London, 2011.

**22** *The Origins of German Tragic Drama*, London, 1977, pp. 233–5.

**23** Lévi-Strauss wrote favourably of Claude Makowski's *Albrecht Dürer, Le Songe du Docteur et de la Sorcière*. See also Donat de Chapeaurouge, *Paul Klee und der christliche Himmel*, Stuttgart, 1990; and Sanja Bahun, *Modernism and Melancholia: Writing as Countermourning*, Oxford, 2013.

**24** The wolf paired with the old man signifies the sinking of the past into oblivion (the rapacious wolf devouring memory); the lion paired with the mature man signifies the intelligent occupation of the present moment; the dog paired with the young man signifies eager anticipation of the future.

(Erwin Panofsky, 'Titian's *Allegory of Prudence*. A Postscript', *Meaning and the Visual Arts*, London, 1993, p. 184).

25  To say that Titian's painting is 'about time', of course, potentially opens a very large can of worms. I do not here engage with the deep questions of philosophical aesthetics that since Lessing have been brought to bear on the relation between time and the visual arts. Here, I mean by 'time' only what in Titian's painting signifies what is meant by one of its titles (*Allegory of Time Governed by Prudence*). On the deeper issues, see Mikel Dufrenne, *The Phenomenology of Aesthetic Experience*, Evanston, IL, 1989.

26  Panofsky, 'History of Art as a Humanistic Discipline', *Meaning in the Visual Arts*, p. 45.

27  Hawthorn, *Plausible Worlds*, pp. 123–56.

28  T. J. Clark, *Picasso and truth*, Princeton, 2013, p. 88. The argument turns on the sense in some modernist paintings of 'lost pasts' and a nostalgic but non-sentimental turning towards them as repositories of a pictorial language of humanly inhabited and inhabitable space.

29  Panofsky, *Renaissance and Renascences*, Uppsala, 1969, p. 29.

30  On Burdach, see Asher D. Biemann, *Inventing New Beginnings. On the Idea of Renaissance in Modern Judaism*, Stanford, 2009.

31  In the other sense of 'present' (as the opposite of 'absent' rather than of 'past' or 'future'), Titian was often understood as the Renaissance painter for whom the shadow-world of semi-absence was more of a signature than the bright clarity of the fully present. In the seventeenth century, Philippe de Champaigne drew attention (in his discourse on Titian's *Christ Carried to the Tomb*) to the manner in which Titian placed Christ's face in shadow. He meant this as praise in opposition to other Academy members who decried it, on the grounds that brightness, the fully-lit, was required by the painting's subject. The argument proposed here carries the shadow motif over into the domain of the temporal, the past conditional as the shadow companion of the past and future tenses.

32  If there is something in the Titian painting to this effect (what I have called the 'crossroads look'), there is also something in the Klee image. The Angel can be seen as figuring a crossroads, its two pummelled wings as forks in the road, or it can be seen as stranded at a crossroads by the storm that blows it into the future. In terms of his formal interests, Klee was much preoccupied by the crossroads (as evidenced by the watercolour, 'House at crossroads', and Klee's accompanying comments in the *Notebooks*). Benjamin too was drawn to the crossroads motif, pre-eminently in connection with the disturbing figure that he called the 'Destructive Character', who 'because he sees ways everywhere, he always stands at a crossroads. No moment can know what the next will bring' (*Selected Writings, 1931–1934* (Michael W. Jennings (ed.), Cambridge, MA, 1999, p. 542).

# 4 Crossroads: Three Tales, Three Gamblers

1  See the 'Catholic Wind' example mentioned in Chapter 1.
2  Cited by Fernand Braudel, *A History of Civilisations*, New York, 1994, p. 5.
3  My personal favourite is in Tower Hamlets, East London: Hamlets Way (alas, without the possessive apostrophe).
4  For where this can lead us, at least those of us who can take it, in the sphere of historical linguistics and comparative philology, see Victor H. Mair:

> The archaic pronunciation of Tao sounded approximately like *drog* or *dorg*. This links it to the Proto-Indo-European root *drogh* (to run along) and Indo-European *dhorg* (way, movement). Related words in a few modern Indo-European languages are Russian *doroga* (way, road), Polish *droga* (way, road), Czech *dráha* (way, track), Serbo-Croatian *draga* (path through a valley), and Norwegian dialect *drog* (trail of animals; valley) ... The nearest Sanskrit (Old Indian) cognates to Tao (*drog*) are *dhrajas* (course, motion) and *dhraj* (course). The most closely related English words are "track" and "trek", while "trail" and "tract" are derived from other cognate Indo-European roots. Following the Way, then, is like going on a cosmic trek. Even more unexpected than the panoply of Indo-European cognates for Tao (*drog*) is the Hebrew root *d-r-g* for the same word and Arabic *t-r-q*, which yields words meaning "track, path, way, way of doing things" and is important in Islamic philosophical discourse.'
>
> *Tao Te Ching: The Classic Book of Integrity and the Way,*
> NewYork, 1990, p. 132

5  Herbert Fingarette, *Confucius – the Secular as Sacred*, New York, 1972, p. 20.
6  According to Heidegger, the crossroads image also lies at the origin of philosophy, Parmenides's foundational distinction between the 'paths of inquiry', the one that leads to error and the one that leads to true knowledge of what is (*Parmenides*, Bloomington, IN, 1992, p. 66). A hugely controversial issue in the interpretation of Parmenides's logic concerns the role of modals (key to the logic and grammar of counterfactuals).
7  For the details, see Theodor Mommsen, 'Petrarch and the Story of Hercules', *Journal of the Warburg and Courtauld Institutes*, vol. 16, nos 3/4, 1953, pp. 178–92.
8  My colleague, the mathematician Martin Hyland, has furnished me with this priceless gloss:

> Interesting point of terminology: that is two intersecting lines. From the point of intersection there appear four distinct line segments. But the lines are conceptually primary. How does one justify a claim like that? It is a matter of feeling: you have to think hard about what makes a

beautiful development of geometry. That kind of thinking is not popular these days.

Private letter

9   Walt Whitman, 'Song of the Open Road', *Complete Poetry and Prose*, New York, 1982, pp. 297–307.

10   Yves Bonnefoy, *Arrière-pays*, London, 2012, p. 25.

11   In his study of the logic of decision-making, Jay Lampert distinguishes analytically between 'forks' and 'branchings' as converses rather than synonyms, a salutary warning against cavalier uses of metaphor (*The Many Futures of a Decision*, p. 197). For my purposes, however, they belong together as ways of representing scenarios based on the 'crossroads' motif.

12   Wood, *The Road to Delphi*, p. 73.

13   R. Drew-Griffith, 'Oedipus Pharmakos? Alleged Scapegoating in Sophocles', *Oedipus the King*' *Phoenix*, vol. 47, no. 2 (Summer 1993), p. 113.

14   See the map in Jeremy McInerney's, *The Folds of Parnassos; Land and Ethnicity in Ancient Phocis*, University of Texas Press, 1999. McInerney's map has only the south-west fork to Ambrossus. However, it is clear from a French contour map that at the junction there was also a clear way running north-east to Daulis.

15   Given what the maps tell us, there is in fact a far wilder version of the options available to Oedipus from the Delphi starting point. Using McInerney's map in conjunction with the French contour map, we can, within a restricted compass, plot the following. From Delphi there are in fact two roads that head into Phocis territory, one going to the Phocis crossroads, the other to the Korykian Cave. Here there is a junction at which the road bifurcates, one fork continuing north to Tithorea and from there on to Pedleis, the other south to Daulis; at Tithorea there is another road that cuts back down via Patronis also to Daulis. As for the road out of Delphi that Oedipus actually takes, this goes via the towns of Anemorei and Aiolidai, after which there is the Schiste Odos fork to Ambrossus which continues to Phlygonion and then Stiris, at which there is a turn-off to Medeon, etc. What Wood calls his own exercise in 'cartographical pedantry' (*The Road to Delphi*, p. 72) is such but in a minor key compared to this constellation. This fuller, topographical description would yield eleven towns where Oedipus could have stopped and stayed, eight junctions (if it's crossroads you're interested in), and no fewer than four ways to Daulis. The madness of this way of 'mapping' counterfactual alternatives lies, of course, in its inevitable extension to virtually the entire road network of ancient Greece. If ever there were a compelling reason to remember that Sophocles's play is a literary fiction, whose shape is to be respected and (again citing Wood) 'not be drawn into fabulous speculations about plays he didn't write', this is it. More broadly, taking these multiple itineraries seriously could readily be taken as a demented attempt not just to effect a gratuitous re-writing of *Oedipus Tyrannus*, but to undermine the very basis of ancient Greek tragedy. A more accurate and less drastic construal

might see topographical mania as rather a tool in re-thinking that basis, with a view to opening it up to the force of the counterfactual, whatever it is that 'Destiny' appears to have in mind. It may be that one of the functions of the literary fiction is to repress exposure to the idea of an alternative from the pressure of a terrified will to order. Conversely, there is the view expressed by Jean Anouilh in connection with his adaptation of Sophocles's, *Antigone*, that any counterfactual opening to the contingent or accidental is a betrayal of the sense of the tragic, and a move out of tragedy into melodrama. This view is discussed by Rowan Williams in his recent book, *The Tragic Imagination*, Oxford, 2016, pp. 67–70. There is a perfectly reasonable counter-view, namely that the melodrama in fact lies in a hyped-up 'absolutizing' of tragedy, the thrill of Irremediable Awfulness. There is one further complication worth mentioning. The roads of Ancient Greece were so-called rut roads, built for the passage of vehicles (chariots, wagons). This has implications for Laius's options at the crossroads. Whatever he can do, he cannot turn off or round in order to get out of Oedipus's way. But Oedipus kills him anyway. If you want to push hard on the structure of tragedy, this would a good place to begin.

**16** Jeffrey Rusten, 'Oedipus and Triviality', *Classical Philology*, vol. 91, no. 2, 1996, p. 98.

**17** The mediaeval *Histoire ancienne jusqu'à César*, a collection of stories of antiquity compiled for Roger IV, châtelain of Lille, has Oedipus travel to the outskirts of Daulis for the eminently mediaeval reason of witnessing some jousts. It is here that, in a melée ending in a generalized brawl, he meets and kills Laius. Robbe-Grillet's *nouveau roman* 'inversion' of the Oedipus story in *Les Gommes* 'detects' a (clunky) anagram in Laius/Daulis; make of that what you will. Some scholarly accounts have Laius travelling to Delphi from Daulis, but these are simply examples of a mistake.

**18** Michel Foucault, *On the Government of the Living: Lectures at the Collège de France 1979–1980*, London, 2014, p. 3.

**19** I have used both the translations, respectively, by H. D. F. Kitto (Oxford, 1962) and E. F. Watling (London, 1947).

**20** 'In Thebes, City of Light, from the Pythian House of Gold/The gracious voice of heaven is heard.' It was also seen (for example by Lucretius in *De Rerum Natura*) as an 'originary' city, going back even further in time than Troy.

**21** There is also the question of how in the first place Oedipus gets from Corinth to Delphi (of which we are told nothing). The quickest would be by boat across the Gulf of Corinth. If by road he would have to go via Thebes, which, though much slower, could be a short-cut in one possible dimension: killing his father and bedding his mother before even making it to the oracle forecasting that he will do what he has already done.

**22** In Aeschylus's *The Libation Bearers* Orestes and Pylades go to the palace, pretending they are strangers from Daulis, to inform Clytemnestra that Orestes is dead. We thus have a further inversion: Daulis as part of a ruse connected to the son killing the mother to avenge a murdered father.

23 Jean-Pierre Vernant and Pierre Vidal-Nacquet, *Myth and Tragedy in Ancient Greece*, New York, 1998, p. 44. Bernard Williams discusses this in terms of the immensely complex relation (of both similarity and radical difference) between 'them' and 'us'.

24 In Pasolini's film version, at a succession of crossroads Oedipus plays a gambling game, spinning his body around blindfold roughly in the way that a roulette table might. Naturally, it always lands on the equivalent of black (the arrow pointing to the road to Thebes). See Wood, *The Road to Delphi*, p. 86. Vernant describes the moment of decision in ancient tragedy as 'a kind of wager – on the future, on fate, and on oneself, ultimately a wager on the gods for whose support one hopes' (*Myth and Tragedy*, p. 44).

25 See Wood, *Road to Delphi*, p. 98.

26 See Chapter 1.

27 Bernard Williams, *Shame and Necessity*, pp. 142–8.

28 Bernard Williams, *Shame and Necessity*, p. 151.

29 Bernard Williams, *Shame and Necessity*, p. 143.

30 The time of Sophocles has itself also been described as a crossroads moment (the 'crossroads of religion and reason' when the 'gods go down'). In *Shame and Necessity*, Williams also allows for major variations: in Euripides we find an 'abandoning ... of a shaping necessity' in favour of the 'uncertainties of an unnerving chance' (p. 148). In Thucydides we have 'a powerful sense ... of the uncontrollable impact of chance' (p. 150). There are clearly degrees of 'bewilderment', some of them relative to genres and generic dispositions (tragedy, for instance, is – as Aristotle insisted – not the same as history).

31 That is to say, of uncertain reference rather than equivocal meaning. In Oedipus's case, oracular vagueness turns not on what the terms 'father' and 'mother' mean but to whom they refer.

32 The *locus classicus* is Herodotus. The oracles discussed in the *Histories* have been described by one commentator, John Marincola, as 'reminders of what might have been' ('Introduction', Herodotus. *The Histories*, London, 2003, p. xxv). This is especially true of oracles that combine prediction with the function of warning.

33 It is also a moveable feast; in the surviving Aeschylus fragment of *Laius* the crossroads is elsewhere, at Potniae. Those who maintain that the crossroads is redundant need to contend with Vernant's claim to its symbolic centrality as to tragedy, as the genre which places individuals 'at the crossroads of a choice' (*Myth and Tragedy*, p. 44).

34 Stephen Halliwell, 'Where Three Roads Meet: A Neglected Detail in the *Oedipus Tyrannus*', *The Journal of Hellenic Studies*, vol. 106, 1986, p. 188.

35 Mark Gloubermann, *The Raven, the Dove, and the Owl of Minerva: The Creation of Humankind in Athens and Jerusalem*, Toronto, 2012, p. 260. The Sphinx has three body parts (the head of a woman, the wings of an eagle and the tail of a lion); its riddle turns on the three stages of man's 'walking' life, one

of which is three-legged; Teiresias thrice accuses Oedipus of being the son of Laius; and so it goes on. The key number three is, of course, made of two parents and one child, echoed by Oedipus with his two daughters, described as 'three joined in sorrow' in *Oedipus at Colonus*. For Foucault, on the other hand, the magic number is two, invoked with reference to the structure of the tragedy as a mechanism for the delivery of 'truth'. In these terms it is 'a play of halves', where the disclosure of one half of the truth is then complemented by the other half, the latter in turn sometimes sub-divisible into two halves of its own (*On the Government of the Living*, pp. 25–32).

36 A curious, and drastic, potential consequence of having Oedipus take the Daulis road is that, unless things turn out exactly the same anyway, Oedipus not only defeats the prophecy (at least in part: no Thebes, no Jocasta), but also walks out of the play. It is not clear what one might do with that thought. It amounts to saying that there *is* no play. Or if there is one in which the prophecy is to be fulfilled, the machinery will have to be unrecognizably different. My thanks to Stephen Whitford for this observation.

37 'Crossroads' is Nicholas Mann's translation ('Petrarch at the Crossroads', a paper given at the University of Warwick, 1992). The actual metaphor in the letter itself is more exactly rendered as being caught between two rocks.

38 Jacob Burckhardt, *The Civilisation of the Renaissance in Italy*, London, 1944, p. 179. Burckhardt's great admirer, Nietzsche, spoke of 'the banner of the Enlightenment, the banner with the three names: Petrarch, Erasmus, Voltaire', *Human, All Too Human*, Lincoln, NE, 1984, p. 32.

39 The predilection has its limits, as if the counterfactual that informs one of the *Canzoniere*: 'The steps would be less lonely/of my exhausted feet/over the fields and hills/my eyes not so wet always/is she burned who is like a block of ice/but leaves no drop of me/that is not fire and flame' (*The Essential Petrarch* (ed. and trans. Peter Hainsworth)), Indianapolis, 2010, p. 44).

40 Gur Zak has suggested that the Petrarchan notion of the 'care of the mind' has an echo in Foucault's account of 'care of the self' as one of the great Hellenistic virtues (*Petrarch's Humanism and The Care of the Self*, Cambridge, 2010, p. 83).

41 The translation used here is Peter Hainsworth's (*The Essential Petrarch*, pp. 220–6).

42 Hans Blumenberg, *The Legitimacy of the Modern Age*, Cambridge, MA, 1983, p. 341.

43 A. C. Grayling has appositely remarked that one of the curious features of the Vice/Virtue story is that, given his other incarnations, the person least qualified to embody Virtue was Hercules himself (*The Choice of Hercules: Pleasure, Duty and the Good Life in the 21st Century*, London, 2007).

44 The Pythagorean ypsilon he perhaps took from Lactantius's use of it to stage the binary form of the Christian moral drama. In Book 3 of the *Secretum*, Franciscus speaks of 'the theory of the so-called Pythagorean letter' as

'not an empty one', applying it moreover to the moral drama of his own life: 'I was following the straight path upward, and I arrived at the fork an unassuming, self-controlled person. I was told to take the right path, but – shall I call myself rash or simply headstrong – I turned off to the left ... I have been astray since that moment on a crooked, sordid path' (*The Essential Petrarch*, pp. 170–1). I draw heavily here on Nicholas Mann's 'Petrarch at the Crossroads'. Mann in turn relies extensively, as we all must, on Panofsky and Mommsen.

45 'For the young writer Petrarch, Dante seems to have been more like a threatening father than an inspiration' (Hainsworth, 'Introduction', *The Essential Petrarch*, p. xi).

46 There was also a quotient of pure snobbery in this: Dante's vernacular was poetry for the plebs, Petrarch's work was for the educated.

47 There is also a mountain peak scene in Dante, at the summit of Mt Falterona from where he has a sweeping view to the Adriatic and the Mediterranean.

48 In 'I'vo pensando', Petrarch also self-describes: 'by indecision I've always turned to ashes the best part of my life's brief thread.' On Carracci, see Christopher Braider's brilliant account of the place of his Hercules painting in the Renaissance tradition and its more general significance for the early modern period: 'Carracci suspends him in a solution of anxious introspection at a moment when not only his decision, but his own heroic identity hang in the balance.' Braider further adds that the painting stages 'an agony of indecision' and 'a sense of historical time that marks a radical departure: a world in which the future has become literally incalculable because its form is no longer determined by the exemplary, mythological and allegorical past' (*Baroque Self-Invention and Historical Truth: Hercules at the Crossroads*, London, 2004, pp. 125, 132).

49 Mann, 'Petrarch at the Crossroads', p. 6.

50 Matthew Politsky, *Mimesis*, London, 2006, p. 63.

51 In the first of the *Eclogues* and the 'Preface' to *Africa*, Petrarch conflates Apollo and Christ.

52 Most famously, Zeus, Hades and Poseidon playing dice to decide on respective shares of the Universe. God may not play dice, but the gods certainly did; how different might things have been if Poseidon, rolling the dice with the oceans as the stake, had lost?

53 It was not for nothing that the motto adopted for the Jesuit 'Constitution' was *perinde ac cadaver* ('as if a dead body').

54 Ignatius dictated the autobiography to Father Louis Gonzalez. Reference here is to the version edited by J. F. X. O'Conor, SJ, New York, 1900.

55 'While studying in Barcelona, he wished to practice his former penances. Accordingly, making a hole in the soles of his shoes, he tore them, little by little, until nothing but the upper portion was left' (p. 77). In extremis, the

thirst for penance drives him on one occasion to contemplate the ultimate sin (for which, of course, ironically no penance would be possible: suicide (p. 44)).

56  The crossroads scene in the *Autobiography* has been eloquently discussed by Alain Boureau. He also makes the interesting point about the methodological value of the 'anecdote' for the study of 'schemas of action, constraint and decision' (*L'Histoire expérimentale*, p. 202). This emphasis on the 'anecdotal' is, of course, part of the point of the three stories told here.

57  It is unlikely that at this stage he was familiar with the views of the thirteenth-century Catalan thinker, Ramon Llull, on the question of the Immaculate Conception (in *The Disputation between the Hermit and Ramon*).

58  This was famously the ruling of Saint Louis in the case of the Jew who queries the virgin birth.

59  Fr Mitch Pacwa, *How to Listen when God is Speaking*, Frederik, MD, 2011. Catherine Gallagher has made the telling naturalistic point (in private correspondence) that horses do not normally deviate from high roads unless directed to do so. If God is believed to have a hand in what Ignatius's horse does, the belief would look stronger if the horse, against natural odds, had taken the low road. There's a counterfactual for you!

60  In the *Spiritual Exercises*, Ignatius treads warily, writing that 'We ought not, habitually, speak much of Predestination'. Given the huge religious and political convulsions of the sixteenth century over this very question, it may come as no surprise that Ignatius chooses discretion. Some might, of course, see it as a hedging of bets (London, 1923, p. 45).

61  In fact, Ignatius was, on the whole, well-disposed to the Dominican order (see John W. O'Malley, *The First Jesuits*, Cambridge, MA, 1995, p. 248).

62  Desiderius Erasmus, *Adages*, vol. 2, *Collected Works of Erasmus*, Toronto, 1982, p. 190.

63  Oedipus belongs in a tragic story over which he has no control, even as he acts and appears to 'choose'. Ignatius and Petrarch narrate their own story within the more 'modern' genre of autobiographical and confessional writing and can thus be described as the makers of their own perplexities, even as they invoke 'providentialist' resolutions or part-resolutions of the dilemmas to which the perplexities give rise.

# 5 Looking Back: From Metanoia to Buyer's Regret

1  Yanis Yaroufakis confirms the 'bath' story (versus the rival 'shower' version), but makes no mention of the Piaf song, and seems to imply that Lamont was hostile to membership of the ERM all along (*And the Weak Suffer What*

*They Must? Europe, Austerity and the Threat to Global Stability*, London, 2016, p. 129). I leave on one side here Mr Sinatra's 'My Way', which also sings of 'Regrets' but in the luxuriously sanguine terms of 'I've had a few, but too few to mention'.

2   There are, of course, numerous affective and moral relations to the counterfactual. As Gallagher shows in her wide-ranging history of counterfactual thought, most counterfactuals fall into the 'downward' rather than 'upward' class, that is, they work on the assumption that the posited alternatives would probably have been worse. Some of these are merely absurd, fodder for satire (Pangloss's infuriating optimism in Voltaire's *Candide* is the most famous example). Otherwise, 'downward' counterfactuals are typically about scenarios evoked in connection with the avoidance or mitigation of disaster, or, more modestly, on behalf of the reassurances of stability and 'normality'. Without endorsing Kafka's view that whatever road you take you will regret it, I nevertheless still maintain (the point is, of course, debatable) that the most interesting of the affective dimensions of counterfactual thinking is regret and its various ethical cognates. There is also regret's powerful neighbour, what Gallagher calls 'the rhetoric of counterfactual recrimination' (*Telling It Like It Wasn't*, p. 200). This is the more aggressive form of the 'if-only', fuelled by blame rather than regret.

3   The classic viewpoint here is, of course, that of the 'midlife crisis'. For an engaging philosophical account, see Kieran Setiya: 'There are distinctive problems that arise from the temporality of midlife, from our multiple orientations to the past and the future, from our relation to unrealized possibilities or counterfactuals' (*Midlife, a Philosophical Guide*, Princeton, NJ, 2017, p. 26).

4   Setiya provides a highly nuanced account of different kinds of 'regret', as well as a sophisticated account of kinds of unrealized desires and projects that do not coherently qualify as proper objects of regret (where the only meaningful attitude is to 'regret regret'). Appropriate objects include those that straightforwardly turn on 'mistakes' and 'failures', the sense that we would have done better if we had taken a different road. This is one context for interpretations of *metanoia*. At the other extreme, however, are the roads not taken by virtue of decisions and choices that involve 'incommensurable' goods. Possibilities lost in these crossroads scenarios should rather be embraced as tokens of the 'richness of human life' (if only for those endowed with the privilege of having such dilemmas), but on the understanding that 'irreparable loss' is crucial to the richness. The loss must not be confused with a 'defect in the outcome one is living' (*Midlife, a Philosophical Guide*, pp. 60–1, 70).

5   Friedrich Nietzsche, *Human, All Too Human*, Cambridge, 1996, p. 323.

6   Caroline Humphrey, 'Regret as a Political Intervention. An Essay in the Historical Anthropology of the Early Mongols', *Past and Present*, no 186, February 2005, pp. 3–45.

7   The most elaborate 'if only' in Greek tragedy is the great rolling lamentation of the Nurse at the beginning of Euripides' *Medea*. It is clearly not intended as a counterfactual in the sense of the Nurse actually entertaining a belief that things might and could have turned out differently. The cumulative 'ifs' are a rhetorical device to intensify an expression of grief. More generally, we might also want to highlight here the profound difference between 'regret' and 'mourning'. Jane Haynes does so in the following terms: 'I have discovered that mourning is a privilege. When there are not enough memories of joy and engagement, nor of sorrows shared and soothed, grief may become replaced by lonely regret, or a melancholy for what might have been' (*If I chance to Talk a little Wild*, London, 2018, pp. 148–9).

8   As has often been pointed out, in the ancient world changing one's mind after the event, even where the focus is purely practical, is often viewed critically; the relevant thought is that you should have got it right in the first place (see Laurel Fulkerson, *No Regrets. Remorse in Classical Antiquity*, Oxford, 2013, p. 6).

9   Here is Andromache in the *Trojan Women*: 'Bitter are these regrets, unhappy mother, bitter these woes to bear; our city ruined, and sorrow evermore to sorrow added, through the will of angry heaven.' 'Regret' here translates *pothos*, the longing for a homeland that now lies in ruins. The 'woes' and the 'sorrow' are both renderings of *algea*. As essentially ceremonial lamentation, there is however no counterfactual here; the outcomes are determined by 'the will of angry heaven'. For a discussion of the relation between *pothos* and 'regret' in ancient Greece, see Fulkerson, p. 35.

10  Herodotus's purpose, of course, is propagandistic as well as analytical: to throw into sharp relief the crucial role of Athens in saving and securing the entire Hellenic world at a time of hostility to Athens. The counterfactual here is an admonition, and in so far as it engages the theme of 'regret', it is by saying: 'if Athens hadn't resisted in this way, you would rue it.' This is close to the spirit of 'counterfactual recrimination' (targeted at those questioning the wisdom of Athenian actions).

11  This image of Thucydides is misleading. For a rich account of the types and forms of the counterfactual in his *History of the Peloponnesian War*, see Robert Tordoff, 'Counterfactual History and Thucydides', *Probabilities, Hypotheticals and Counterfactuals in Ancient Greek Thought*, pp. 101–21. Tordoff shows that in fact Thucydides often uses counterfactuals, crucially of the 'downward' kind also favoured by Herodotus, as reminders of what we (Athenians) must not forget, namely how the Peloponnesian War could have turned out, namely worse.

12  Thucydides, *The War of the Peloponnesians and the Athenians*, Cambridge, 2013, pp. 182–3.

13  Conversely, the 'turning of the soul' towards the light in *Republic* VIII is often associated with *metanoia*. That association will enjoy a rich afterlife in both religious and secular moral thought.

14  In the *Secret History*, the ruler Chingiss is depicted as speaking publicly and, it would seem, sincerely of 'making mistakes' and 'changing his mind' (Humphrey, 'Regret as a Political Intervention', p. 8).

15  For the faithful there is a disturbing paradox in the form of the notionally 'upward' counterfactual: if Judas hadn't betrayed Jesus, he might not have been crucified; but if no crucifixion, then no resurrection, and no redemption. Whence the paradox of good tidings as bad ones, and the upward as the downward.

16  Ausonius, *Epigrams*, London, 2001, p. 97.

17  In Chapter 43 of *Leviathan*, Hobbes discusses the religious aspect of 'repentance' as the road to 'salvation', foregrounding the problem of 'feigned repentance' ('no man is able to discern the truth of another man's repentance further than by external marks taken from his words and actions'). In the earlier *Human Nature, or the Fundamental Elements of Policie*, he discusses metanoiac 'change of mind' from the point of view of practical reason, in relation to the ability to convert disconsolate regret over what has not worked into joyful anticipation of better outcomes in the future. Michel Foucault also wrote of 'political metanoia' in terms of 'conversion', whose principal context in modern conditions is 'revolution' and the revolutionary actor. See Armen Avenessian and Anke Henning, *Metanoia, A Speculative Ontology of Language: Thinking and the Brain*, London, 2014, p. 171.

18  See Jean Duverny, *Le registre d'inquisition de Jacques Fournier*, Paris, 1978.

19  See Jens Zimmermann (ed.), *Re-Envisioning Christian Humanism: Education and the Restoration of Humanity*, Oxford, 2016.

20  Martin Luther, *Luther's Works* (eds Jaroslav Pelikan and Helmut T. Lehman), Philadelphia, 1963, vol. 48, pp. 66–7.

21  All references are to 'On Repenting', in Michel de Montaigne, *The Complete Essays*, London, 1991.

22  If, plausibly, we want to conclude from this that Montaigne is the enemy of the counterfactual, we might be checked by two other moments in the *Essais* where, at least formally, there is explicit recourse to counterfactual argument, one in relation to his personal history, the other in connection with a wider sixteenth-century European history. The first is from the last *essai*, 'On Experience' where he remarks on how he would have been suited to the role of royal consigliere had he been asked. However, this is more a rhetorical figure designed to accentuate his own worth than a true counterfactual involving a genuinely possible option available to Montaigne. It is a could-have-been (in the sense of, in Montaigne's estimation, satisfying certain conditions of possibility), but not a might-have-been of his actual life trajectory. The second case is from 'On coaches' where Montaigne speculates on how different (better) the outcomes would have been if the European colonization of the New World had been instead undertaken by ancient Greece or Rome. This too, however, cannot be intended as a true

historical counterfactual. It is more a heuristic device for an evaluative comparison of civilizations. My thanks here to Richard Scholar.

23 Pascal, *Oeuvres complètes*, Paris, 1963, p. 270.
24 References are to La Rochefoucauld, *Oeuvres complètes*, (Pléiade), Paris, 1964.
25 See Michael Moriarty, *Disguised Vices. Theories of Virtue in Early Modern French Thought*, Oxford, 2011, p. 254.
26 Moriarty, *Disguised Vices*, p. 353.
27 The one exception is sexual attraction (see *Maximes*, p. 70).
28 As ever, the Trump presidency provides an exception. Here is his first press spokesman on the allegation that Trump has been under surveillance by British intelligence: When asked if he regretted repeating the allegation, he said: 'I don't think we regret anything.' 'Think' is a nice touch, while 'we' is a real jewel. For a discussion of the place of 'regret' in modern politics, see Jeffrey K. Olick, *The Politics of Regret: On Collective Memory and Historical Responsibility*, New York, 2007.
29 'On a combattu la volonté des Juifs de vivre dans une communauté qui ne respectait pas toutes les règles de la république française.'
30 The writer, Michael Cohen, notionally brings to the question of regret the egalitarian enthusiasms of the historical activist: 'I have a socialist approach to my regrets: they're all equal' (*Guardian*, 15 July 2017). 'Equal', of course, means equally inconsequential, and therefore unlikely to detain him. Lucky chap, up there with Frank Sinatra.
31 Rachel Smallman and Neal J. Roese, 'Counterfactual Thinking Facilitates Behavioural Intentions, *Journal of Experimental Social Psychology*, July 2008, pp. 845–52. See also Neal J. Roese and James M. Olson (eds), *What Might Have Been: The Social Psychology of Counterfactual Thinking*, New York, 2014. 'Management' is the *mot juste*, now inextricably bound up with manipulation for commercial and political ends.
32 Some recent neurological research on mice suggests the possibility of erasing from humans certain categories of fear memories (though mercifully not the 'adaptive' sort 'necessary for our daily lives'). This might in due course extend also to regrets, thus opening, for YOLO fans, onto the prospect of the eternal sunshine of the spotless mind.
33 Counterfactuals are especially prominent in both game-theoretical modelling of 'rational choice' economics, and 'behavioural' economics based on 'nudge' theory.
34 Richard A. Posner, *The Problems of Jurisprudence*, Harvard, Cambridge, MA, 1990, p. 204.
35 The presiding judge ruled against the plaintiff on the following grounds:

> Whilst it cannot be said that some aspect of a person's education – inadequately delivered – can never be the cause of that person's failure to

achieve some otherwise attainable objective, the hurdles in establishing a claim for compensation based upon that inadequate delivery are great and often insurmountable. In this case, I have not been satisfied that the delivery of one particular feature of the claimant's undergraduate degree course was inadequate or, in any event, that it had the consequences claimed for it.

In contrast, there is the court case in the United States involving First Amendment rights to freedom of speech. The plaintiff, joined by the Knight First Amendment Institute at Columbia University, sued in respect of Donald Trump blocking access of those he dislikes to his Twitter account.

> The Knight Institute has joined the case as a plaintiff ... asserting that the viewpoint-based exclusion of the individual plaintiffs from this forum prevents the Knight Institute and other forum participants from hearing the speech that the individual plaintiffs would have engaged in had they not been blocked.
>
> *Guardian*, 6 March 2018

# 6 On Not, Never or Forever Being Me

1. 'Paul represents in his person ... the paradoxes not only of Jewish identity, but ... of all identity as such' is how Daniel Boyarin puts it, in his splendid study, *A Radical Jew: Paul and the Politics of Identity* (Berkeley, 1997, p. 3). But what hangs by the expression 'in his person'? Does the disjunct between the values and projects of Saul and those of converted Paul run all the way down to a ground level of being, such that the singular expression 'his person' begs a question of 'identity' that can then be managed only by parking it in the realm of 'paradox'? The bubble of paradox can, of course, simply collapse if we go by the evidence suggesting that Saul/Paul didn't actually involve a name change, but that he had both from the word go by virtue of his father having the status of Roman citizen.

2. Bernard Williams, 'Resenting One's Own Existence', in *Making Sense of Humanity*, Cambridge, 1995, p. 224.

3. Bernard Williams, 'Moral Luck', in *Moral Luck*, Cambridge, 1981, p. 34.

4. R. Jay Wallace formulates the point as follows: 'If the things had been otherwise in the past, then the point of view from which we look back on them would also have been different' (*The View from Here: On Affirmation, Attachment and the Limits of Regret*, Oxford, 2013, p. 62).

5. Wallace secures continuity of self where 'the alternative standpoint of retrospective assessment that the counterfactual possibility would have brought into existence would have preserved the values and attachments that characterize one's actual standpoint' (*The View from Here*, p. 62). That, however, is a huge ask, at least in respect of any creatively fluid life; it is not

at all certain that it could plausibly be made to fit an Erasmus who either does or doesn't write *In Praise of Folly*. In particular, it is difficult to see how, in the counterfactual scenario where Erasmus *doesn't* write *In Praise of Folly*, he could be said to be an Erasmus with the same 'values and attachments' as those of the Erasmus who wrote it.

6   Williams, 'Moral Luck', in *Moral Luck*, Cambridge, 1981, pp. 20–39.
7   I say 'allegedly' since that aesthetic judgement is not universally shared.
8   Adam Gopnik, 'Van Gogh's Ear. The Christmas Eve that Changed Modern Art', *The New Yorker*, 4 January 2010, p. 52.
9   Meir Dan-Cohen, 'Luck and Identity', *Theoretical Inquiries in Law*, vol. 9, no. 1, 2008, p. 13.
10  Or what, in relation to Greek tragedy, Williams terms the principle of 'inner necessity', discussed later in this chapter.
11  Access to and freedom to act on what *kairos* brings to a life are not equally distributed to all, whether because of the force of habit, limitations imposed by natural impairment, legal constraint (the age of adulthood), or social inequality. A history of counterfactual regret would also need to take into account its differential social mapping.
12  It is perhaps no accident that Williams was drawn to both. The scenarios sketched by Williams presuppose possession of agency and choice that are not found in the circumstances of most lives.
13  Adam Gopnik, 'Van Gogh's Ear. The Christmas Eve that Changed Modern Art', p. 54.
14  As part of this conceptual space, there is also the hugely complicating case of 'identity theft', of the type where one builds a whole life around the misappropriation. Whose life is 'Don Draper's' in the series *Mad Men*, and how do we, along with him, deal with the counterfactual of the alternative life that would have been lived as 'Dick Whitman'?
15  Nietzsche, *Thus Spake Zarathustra*, Cambridge, 2006, p. 55.
16  How to translate Übermensch into English is a somewhat fraught matter. 'Superman' resonates in all the wrong ways. 'Overman' sounds simply silly.
17  Friedrich Neitzsche *The Will to Power*, New York, 1968, pp. 35–6.
18  Nehamas provides one of the most lucid clarifications of the obscurities of the doctrine ('This Life – Your Eternal Life', *Nietzsche. Life as Literature*, Harvard, Cambridge, MA, 1985, pp. 140–69).
19  'The eternal recurrence is not a theory of the world, but a view of the self,' Nehamas, *Nietzsche. Life as Literature*, p. 150.
20  *The Gay Science*, Cambridge, 2001, p. 150.
21  *Ecce Homo*, Cambridge, 2005, p. 99.
22  Nietzsche, *Thus Spake Zarathustra*, p. 263.
23  Nehamas, *Nietzsche. Life as Literature*, p. 164.

24 Nehamas hesitates over the role of counterfactuals in this kind of argument. He sketches a contrast with the example of fiction and 'literary characters', on the claim that the latter do not support counterfactual alternatives. But, as he himself acknowledges (p. 165), that is debatable. One might indeed claim, more assertively, that the what-if/as-if logic of fiction renders it especially open to the imagining of alternative storylines and alternative outcomes.

25 '*If*, in all that you wish to do, you begin by asking yourself: Am I certain that I would wish to do this an infinite number of times? This should be for you the most solid centre of gravity ... My doctrine says, the task is to live your life in such a way that you must wish to live it again – for you will anyway! *If* striving gives you the highest feeling, then strive! *If* rest gives you the highest feeling, then rest! *If* fitting in, following and obeying give you the highest feeling, then obey!' *Notebook*, 1881, cited in Luc Ferry, *What is the Good Life?*, Chicago, 2005, p. 95.

26 See Paul S. Loeb on Nietzsche's use of 'heuristic thought experiments involving counterfactuals', 'Will to Power and Panpsychism', Manuel Dries and P. J. E. Kail (eds), *Nietzsche on Mind and Nature*, Oxford, 2015, p. 79. See also Maudmarie Clark, *Nietzsche on Ethics and Politics*, Oxford, 2015, p. 86.

27 Nehamas acknowledges the murky status of the counterfactual and its refusal. He tries to square the circle by maintaining that Nietzsche's move is to make the self resemble a 'literary character' where no counterfactuals changes are admissible without a generalized collapse of the entire fictional scaffolding. This too is highly debatable.

28 Carl Jung, *Nietzsche's Zarathustra*: *Notes of the Seminar Given in 1934–1939*, Princeton, NJ, 1988.

29 Nietzsche, *The Birth of Tragedy*, Cambridge, 1999, p. 39.

30 Nietzsche, *The Birth of Tragedy*, pp. 22–3.

31 Nietzsche's German reads: 'Das Allerbeste ist für dich gänzlich unerreichbar: nicht geboren zu sein, nicht zu sein, nichts zu sein. Das Zweitbeste aber ist für dich – bald zu sterben.'

32 Strictly speaking, 'nicht geboren zu werden' for 'not to be born' and 'nicht geboren worden zu sein' for 'not to have been born'.

33 The closest we might get to that is with the remark of Beckett's Molloy in the eponymous novel, that the pre-natal time was 'the only endurable, just endurable, period of my enormous history'. It can, of course, be said third-personally, as in the advice of a medical specialist ('it would be best for him/her not to be born'), but that concerns only future outcomes and has no counterfactual component.

34 In the Hebrew Bible, Job echoes Silenus, while upping the ante on the terms of the 'second best' (which is not just to die quickly but immediately, in the post-natal moment: 'Why did I not perish at birth and die as I came from the womb?').

35 The relevant moment echoing Silenus, in the famous lamentation of the Chorus in *Oedipus at Colonus*, is customarily translated as 'not to be born'. The grammar of ancient Greek is, of course, utterly different, in the terms of which a debate about the difference between the present and the perfect infinitives in the passive mode would be unintelligible.

36 Nietzsche, *Human, All Too Human*, p. 98.

37 Cioran considered several candidates for his title, including 'aberration', 'misfortune', 'mistake' and 'inopportuness'. 'Inconvenience' took the prize, presumably because it evoked a certain nonchalance, a form of existentialist dandyism, the other terms could not capture.

38 David Benatar, *Better Never to Have Been: The Harm of Coming into Existence*, Oxford, 2008, p. 92.

39 Benatar, *Better Never to Have Been*, p. 13.

40 Williams, 'Resenting One's Own Existence', p. 224.

41 Williams calls it the 'Zygotic Principle' and the cases under consideration are those that involve a 'strongly genetic defect, with which the character of the genome is unalterably expressed as the defect' ('Resenting One's Own Existence', p. 227). The Zygotic Principle is clearly an anchoring ground principle for what is to be construed as having an 'identity' (basically we are what a DNA test would establish). It is also a key constraint on the range of counterfactual speculation in respect of life-histories, delimiting the point beyond which such speculation would become meaningless by virtue of imagining the person as 'someone else'. However, there is also merit in retaining something of the flexible uses of the term 'identity' and the fluid boundaries between the related concepts of 'self', 'personhood' and 'individuality', an approach closer, for example, to Kwame Anthony Appiah's *The Lies that Bind: Rethinking Identity* (London, 2018). This 'looser' approach is important for the drift of the next and concluding chapter. Gallagher pertinently asks how the zygotic principle could be applied to collective historical entities; the answer, of course, is that it can't (*Telling It Like It Wasn't*, p. 12).

42 There is here nevertheless, from one point of view (Augustine's, for example), an element of the gamble on the unknowable: 'The reason I am unwilling to die', writes Augustine in *De Libero Arbitrio*, 'is not because I would rather be unhappy than not be at all, but a fear that after death I may be still more unhappy'.

43 Williams, citing Sophocles, gets close to this thought when he writes of any given person that 'while he can think egoistically of what it would for him to live longer or less long, he cannot think egoistically of what it would be for him not to have existed at all'. He casts this in terms of the limits, for these purposes, of 'possible worlds' thought experiments, barring as simply inadmissible, because unintelligible, 'my reflection on a world in which I never occur at all' ('The Makropulos Case: Reflections on the Tedium of Immortality', *Problems of the Self*, Cambridge, p. 87).

**44** N. Zohar asks a question in the title of an influential paper on genetic therapy ('Prospects for "Genetic Therapy". Can a Person Benefit from Being Altered?', *Bioethics*, 5, 1991). The question as such begs the question (as to whether the person 'altered' is still that person).

**45** Williams mentions it, while referring us to the extended account by David Heyd ('Are "wrongful life" claims philosophically valid?', *Israel Law Review*, 1986). This is a landmark intervention. The technology has, of course, since moved on. We now have the beginnings of 'gene editing' which alters DNA forever, which in turn means that any 'mistakes' made cannot be corrected.

**46** But even this is debatable. Michael Wood remarks astutely: 'For Oedipus himself his rescue is who he is' (*The Road to Delphi*, p. 94). Being saved by the shepherd is a necessary condition of the fulfilment of the oracle, and Oedipus is nothing if not the destiny reserved for him. An Oedipus who doesn't murder his father and sleep with his mother would have to be some other Oedipus who just happens to have a swollen foot.

**47** One complication here is the determination of Laius and Jocasta not to have children as a consequence of Laius's consultation of the Oracle, and his subsequent failure to abide by that decision as a result of surrender to drunken lust. In that highly pertinent sense, we can say that Oedipus has the 'wrong' parents and represent the alternative of none at all as the more desirable option. But that too raises philosophical questions as regards coherence.

**48** David Heyd, 'From Wrongful Life to Wrongful Identity: A (Controversial) Solution of a Hard Case', *Jahrbuch für Recht und Ethik/Annual Review of Law and Ethics*, vol. 9, 2001, p. 175.

**49** Bernard Williams, 'Strawson on Individuals', *Problems of the Self*, p. 125.

**50** This is the counterpart to what, as we saw in Chapter 4, Williams calls the 'sense of pre-arranged necessity', and its relation to the experience of 'modal bewilderment' in Greek tragedy.

**51** 'The Quest for Truth', *Guardian*, 30 November 2002.

**52** *Shame and Necessity*, pp. 130–45. In connection with the moment of madness, Williams interestingly reanimates, for philosophical purposes, the moribund expression 'not his usual self', alienating the expression into a sense of its sheer strangeness. For Ajax it is not merely 'unusual', it is unrecognizable.

**53** 'Our ethical situation is not theirs, because the modern world isn't the ancient world. But there is more in common, ethically, than we think, and we actually mislead ourselves when we suppose otherwise' ('Interview with Bernard Williams', *Cogito*, vol. 8, no. 1, 1998, p. 8). Just *how* 'much more' is a question on which there is likely to be substantial divergence. Lebow pushes even harder on the claim that, where the sense of 'identity' is concerned, the gap between ancients and moderns is not great (Richard Ned Lebow, *The Politics and Ethics of Identity*, Cambridge, 2012, pp. 273–4).

54  Mark Jenkins suggests that, in his admiration for the Greek hero, Williams was guilty not only of idealization, but also of anachronism, back-importing to the ancient world essentially modern notions of 'authenticity' (*Bernard Williams*, London, 2006, p. 176).

55  Peter Green's account is ruthlessly unflattering: 'a stubborn adherence to, and preference for, the type of rule that was vanishing: that of local royal aristocracies obsessed with blood and lineage, hunting, horsemanship, and the peculiar sense of honour contingent on successful warfare and the code of the warrior' ('Class War', *London Review of Books*, 20 April, 2017).

56  Williams, 'Imagination and the Self', *Problems of the Self*, pp. 42–3.

57  Williams, 'Imagination and the Self', p. 41.

58  Foucault, of course, had a very different view of the 'modern' historical subject, institutionally and politically constrained by the incarcerating ideologies and practices of modern 'reason'.

59  'The Makropulos Case' is a reference to the opera by Janacek based on a play by Karel Capek.

60  Nietzsche, *The Genealogy of Morals*, New York, 1956, p. 299. In 'The Makropulos Case', Williams cites the chorus in *Oedipus at Colonus* on the best as never being born (p. 87).

61  Samuel Scheffler, *Death and the Afterlife*, Oxford, 2016, p. xxxiii.

# 7 On the Run with Fernando Pessoa

1  Stendhal, *The Private Diaries of Stendhal* (Robert Sage (ed.)), London, 1955, p. 69.

2  Robert Musil, *The Man without Qualities*, London, 2017, pp. 158, 270.

3  Musil, *The Man without Qualities*, pp. 10–11.

4  Jacques Bouveresse, *Robert Musil, l'homme probable, le hasard, la moyenne, et l'escargot de l'histoire*, Paris, 2013.

5  Kevin Mulligan, 'Moral Emotions', in David Sander and Klaus R. Scherer (eds), *The Oxford Companion to Emotion and the Affective Sciences*, Oxford, 2009, p. 4. *The Man without Qualities* contains a trenchant view of philosophers: 'Philosophers are violent and aggressive persons who, having no army at their disposal, bring the world into subjection to themselves by locking it up in a system' (p. 272).

6  Harold Bloom, *Novelists and Novels*, Philadelphia, 2005, p. 259. In connection with Gauguin, to recapitulate, the relevant counterfactual is what would have become of Gauguin if he had not taken the decision to abandon his family for a life in Tahiti. Was that decision not a necessary condition of Gauguin being 'Gauguin'?

**7** Williams, 'Personal Identity and Individuation', *Problems of the Self*, pp. 15–18. The classic study of the Beauchamp case is by Morton Prince, *The Dissociation of a Personality*, New York, 1906.

**8** Octavio Paz, 'Introduction', in *A Centenary Pessoa*, Manchester, 1995, p. 20. Forms of both the 'essayistic' and the 'philosophical' are naturally to be found in the collection of Pessoa texts gathered in Nuno Ribeiro (ed.), *Philosophical Essays. A Critical Edition*, New York, 2012. Pessoa's interest in philosophy was genuine (he attended philosophy seminars at the University of Lisbon). However, despite the efforts of several commentators (Alain Badiou, Simon Critchley, John Gray, for example) to take 'philosophical' Pessoa seriously, most of the material is thin gruel. Nicole Balso has echoed others in aligning Pessoa with Heidegger, only then to break the link by insisting, sensibly, on their 'separation' (*Pessoa, Le Passeur Métaphysique*, Paris, 2006). R. F. J. Seddon puts it thus: 'Perhaps it is doubtful that multiplicity is philosophically desirable, and no less doubtful that for non-Pessoas it is philosophically possible'. Seddon further adds: 'I don't, in the end, particularly advocate taking Pessoa's life and work as a methodological guide for doing philosophy. Yet there may nevertheless be something interesting and even useful for philosophers to discover in Pessoa and the heteronyms, if we see in his employment of a literary imagination a particularly striking illumination of an imaginative element in philosophical practice' ('Fernando Pessoa as Philosopher', Durham, 2010, p. 10). We might want to link these distinctions to the question of counterfactuals and 'genre', in the broad sense of generic dispositions, those which are hospitable to counterfactuals and those which are not.

**9** Paz, 'Introduction', in *A Centenary Pessoa*, p. 4.

**10** References are to *The Poems of Fernando Pessoa*, translated and edited by Edwin Honig and Susan M. Brown, San Francisco, 1986.

**11** References to *The Book of Disquiet* are to the version edited and translated by Richard Zenith, London, 2001.

**12** 'However that might be, it was better not to have been born'. It is no surprise to find Cioran sniffing around this, perhaps also tempted by versions of Pessoan *tedio*, the 'boredom that's bored even of itself', ('Lisbon revisited'). See Dagmara Kraus, 'On Pessoa's Involvement with the Birth Theme in Cioran's *De l'inconvénient d'être né*', *Pessoa Plural: A Journal of Fernando Pessoa Studies*, vol. 7, Spring 2015.

**13** Richard Appignanesi, 'Fernando Pessoa: Missing Person', in Juliet Steyn (ed.), *Other than Identity. The Subject, Politics and Art*, Manchester, 1999, p. 50.

**14** For details, see the new edition of *The Book of Disquiet*, translated and edited by Jeronimo Pizarro (New York, 2017). The first published extract ('In the Forest of Estrangement', in the magazine *A Àguia*), was signed 'Fernando Pessoa'.

**15** In the famous letter to Monteiro, Pessoa describes Soares as a 'semi-heteronym' and 'not so much different from myself as he is a distortion of my personality' ('The Genesis of My Heteronyms', *Always Astonished. Selected*

*Prose* (ed. and trans. Edwin Honig), San Francisco, 1988, p. 12).

16  Nicole Balso, 'La journée des hétéronymes', *Pessoa: Le Passeur Métaphysique*, pp. 7ff. See also Manuel Dos Santos Jorge, *Etre pluriel: Les hétéronymes*, Paris 2005.

17  Fernando Pessoa, 'The Genesis of My Heteronyms', pp. 9–10.

18  When challenged on this question, Pessoa's response was simultaneously to agree and disagree. While he wrote of the 'pyschiatric part' and 'the aspect of hysteria that exists within me' (*Always Astonished*, p. 7), he also hedged his bets: 'That such an attribute in a writer could be said to be a form of hysteria, or a so-called dissociation of personality, the author of these books does not contest, nor does he support it' ('The Genesis of My Heteronyms', pp. 7, 13). In the Ricardo Reis poem 'Recalling who I was, I see somebody else', there is an echo of the Doppelgänger scene of memory, misrecognition and recognition in Schubert's *Schwanengesang*.

19  Appignanesi, 'Other than Identity.' p. 45.

20  L. C. Taylor, 'Life and Times', *A Centenary Pessoa*, pp. 133–4.

21  'Presenting the Heteronyms', *Always Astonished*, p. 13. Elsewhere he described his relation to the heteronymic others as that of a 'literary executor': 'Today I have no personality: I've divided all my humanness among the various authors whom I've served as literary executor' (*Selected Prose*, p. 262). This mix of similarity and difference, sameness and otherness, 'offspring' of the self and birth of 'someone else' spectacularly disrupts the categories and overflows the boundaries of philosophical argument of the kind exemplified by Bernard Williams's remarks on birth, self and identity.

22  This was a suggestion from Mario de Sacramento (in Joanna Courteau, 'Orthonymous Poetry', *The Man Who Never Was* (George Monteiro (ed.)), Providence, RI, 1982, p. 94).

23  Nicole Balso, 'La journée des hétéronymes', *Pessoa, Le Passeur Métaphysique*, p. 37. One of the poems composed in the epiphanic experience of 1914, 'Oblique Rain', reflects the moment 'Fernando Pessoa' re-emerges on the other side of the orthonymic origin as one of the heteronyms.

24  Letter to Armando Cortes-Rodriques, January 1915 (cit. *The Poems of Fernando Pessoa* (trans. and ed. by Edwin Honig and Susan M. Brown), San Francisco, 1986, p. x).

25  Jean-Michel Rabaté, 'The Paradoxes of the Symptom in Psychoanalysis', *The Cambridge Companion to Lacan* (ed. Rabaté) Cambridge, 2003, p. 99. We can perhaps read this as a displacement to the realm of the unconscious of Pessoa's self-description as 'a nomadic wanderer through my consciousnesses' (*Always Astonished*, p. 117). On Pessoa and the Lacanian 'stade du miroir', see Jorge, *Être pluriel,* pp. 220–2. In Pessoa's writings, the mirror scene is as if acted out in a hall of mirrors, in a never-ending refraction of self.

26 Gilles Deleuze and Félix Guattari – committedly philosophers of the 'multiple' – are the most commonly cited. In *What is Philosophy*? Pessoa is on the list of modern writers described as 'hybrid geniuses' who inhabit 'difference like acrobats torn apart in a perpetual show of strength' and whose work unfolds as an endless proliferation of crossroads scenarios ('they branch out and never stop branching out'). There is also a Pessoan echo in the notion of 'conceptual characters' as 'the 'heteronyms of the philosopher', the latter's name as 'the simple pseudonym of his characters' (see Adam Morris, 'Fernando Pessoa's Heteronymic Machine', *Luso-Brazilian Review*, vol. 51, no. 2, 2014).

27 Appignanesi, *Other than Identity*, p. 43.

28 This finds an echo in the admonition of the English heteronym, Thomas Crosse, where ideas of shattering and breaking are linked to the idea of a 'scattering' into otherness and multiplicity: 'Learn not to associate ideas, but to break your soul into pieces instead. Learn how to experience sensations simultaneously, to scatter your spirit through your own scattered self' ('Preface to an Anthology of the Portuguese Sensationists', *Selected Prose*, p. 64).

29 Paz, 'Introduction', *A Centenary Pessoa*, p. 19.

30 Cit. Rui Gonçalves Miranda, 'Mostrengos', in Mariana Gray de Castro (ed.), *Fernando Pessoa's Modernity*, Woodbridge, 2013, p. 114.

31 The naming, of course, involves a pun, built from the Greek *outopia* signifying 'no place' and *eutopia* signifying 'better place'.

32 In some accounts (Foucault's for instance), utopia and heterotopia are less complementary than opposed, the utopian as the ideal blueprint for a future society and the heterotopian as actual and local spaces for 'a breaking of norms'.

33 On the 'counterfactual structure' of the heterotopian/utopian paradigm, see Kenneth Surin, *Freedom Not Yet, Liberation and the Next World Order*, Oxford, 2011, p. 271.

34 See Aino Rinhaug, 'Entirely against the Script: Reflections on the Utopian Figure', in *Bloch-Jahrbuch Träume gegen Mauern – Dreams against Walls*, 2009. Rinhaug highlights the narrative fragment in Bloch's *Traces* called 'Incognito to Oneself', which tells of the clown who, in responding to the ringmaster's routine question 'Who are you?', disappears into an experience of radical self-loss: he 'lost not only the thread but consciousness, at least of himself. He began to sway, flailed his arms about, mumbled the same thing over and over in a strange voice: "Don't know, don't know, don't know"' (*Traces*, Stanford, 2006, pp. 91–2).

35 Gilbert Ryle, *Collected Papers*, London, 1971, vol. 2, pp. 133–4.

36 The artificial island idea was, of course, Peter Thiel's, a fantasized extension of his very real land grab in New Zealand.

37 In a couple of interviews – one with *Get Wired Magazine* (21 May 2007), the other with the magazine, *Wargamer* (5 May 2010) – Ferguson tells of how he

was approached by Muzzy Lane, the computer game company that produced 'Making History'. At a stroke, Fergusonian history as the arena of the Great Game and its cognates literally became a game, the moves modelled in turn on war-gaming, and experienced by its player as 'really exciting, because normally counterfactuals happen in my head. Now they can happen on the screen'. The excitement is not without consequence. Ferguson's previous models for analysing World War 2 fall apart, and require a rethink. The yield of the rethink? Child's play: the game teaches him that his original counterfactual (if Britain had, with the support of France, gone to war with Germany in 1938, all would have been well sooner) had overlooked that in 1938 France was most unlikely to have played ball. Why it required a computer game to figure that out isn't explained. But it seems the input of his 13-year-old son proved decisive. It was thus perhaps no surprise that, when invited by the British government to advise, his pedagogical contribution to revamping the history syllabus in the English school system was the scarcely credible suggestion that the best way to introduce our children to the study of history is by teaching them war-gaming techniques (*Guardian*, 9 July 2010). This bright eventuality might, one presumes, include Ferguson's happily dystopian thoughts on acceptable collateral damage in 'strategically unimportant' countries (see Chapter 1). One very real danger in computer-gaming the past is that historian-players already notable for being amply endowed with self-confidence end up as delegates for the 'mind of God'.

**38** Manuel Portela and Antonio Rito Silva, 'Encoding, Visualizing, and Generating Variation in Fernando Pessoa's *Livro do Desassossego*', *Variants. The Journal for the European Society of Textual Scholarship*, 2016, pp. 12–13.

**39** Jerome McGann, *Radiant Textuality. Literary Studies after the World Wide Web*, London, 2001.

**40** One of the more interesting editing categories here is the class of textual items neither definitively adopted nor definitively discarded by the author, those that hover in a semi-limbo, on a literary shelf from which, under certain conditions, they could be or could have been taken down for use. Along with suggestions along these lines by McGann (for example, in connection with editions of Yeats), there is also the remarkable work of Johanna Drucker on Mallarmé's 'Un Coup de dés', the greatest throw of the dice in literary history, mirrored in the saga of its composition ('Diagrammatic and Stochastic Writing and Poetics', Eindhoven: Onomatopee, 2013).

**41** Syma Tariq, 'Fernando Pessoa and the multiple faces we show on the net', *Guardian*, 4 December 2010.

**42** The 'selfie' has become both an art object and a museum piece. See, for example, R. Kozinets, U. Gretzel and A. Dinhopl, 'Self in Art/Self as Art: Museum Selfies as Identity Work', *Frontiers in Psychology*, May 2017. There is also a now substantial literature in the field of social psychology on 'selfie-related behaviour', while the blogosphere is packed with entries in respect of aliases, fake names and pseudonyms represented as 'counterfactual identities'.

43  See Jiayang Fan, 'Beauty is Justice', *The New Yorker*, 18/25 December 2017. Everything that follows in my account is taken from Fan's article.

44  In 2014, HTC announced the launch of 'Desire Eye', the handset billed as the 'ultimate selfie' phone.

45  Gillian Terzis, 'Non-Friction', *The Times Literary Supplement*, 17 November 2017.

# INDEX

Aeschylus 96, 99, 172, 215 n.22, 216 n.33
Agrippa, Cornelius 208 n.3
Allen, Woody 149, 150, 185
alternative facts 6, 49, 50, 205 n.7
Althusser, Louis 63, 64
Angels 6, 67–78, 208 n.2, 208 n.3, 208 n.4, 209 n.6
Anjum, Rani Lill 17, 198 n.40
Anon, C.R 181
Anouilh, Jean 215 n.15
Anscombe, Elizabeth 209 n.5
antecedent 11, 12, 18, 28, 35, 38, 39, 40, 41, 42, 43, 44, 46, 96, 148, 197 n.38, 202 n.20
Anthony, Saint 106, 107
*apodosis* 11, 16, 18, 20, 25, 34, 41, 42, 43, 44, 46
Appiah, Kwame Anthony 227 n.41
Appignanesi, Richard 230 n.13, 231 n.19, 232 n.27
Apter, Emily 205 n.4
Aquinas, Thomas 69, 208 n.4
archive 24, 55–61, 64, 65, 81, 189, 196 n.26, 205 nn.9,10
Arendt, Hannah 144, 210 n.9
Aristotle 9, 13, 54, 125, 126, 158, 163, 204 n.1, 206 n.14, 216 n.30
art history 3, 6, 81
as if 9
Ascherson, Neal 197 n.35
Augustine, Saint 67, 102, 104, 105, 106, 107, 127, 136, 227 n.42
Ausonius, Decimus 127

Badiou, Alain 230 n.8
Bahun, Sanja 211 n.23

Balaam 113
Baldwin, Thomas 193 n.2
Balso, Nicole 230 n.8, 231 n.16
Banks, Arron 204 n.3
baroque 48, 77, 78
Barroso, José Manuel 36
Barthes, Roland 114
Beauchamp, Sally 179, 183, 186, 188, 230 n.7
Beauval, Bassagne de 140
Beckett, Samuel 53, 87, 146, 161, 164, 184, 188, 226 n.33
Becket, Thomas à 141, 206 n.18
behavioural psychology 3, 22, 145, 22 n.31, 223 n.33
Belfort, Jordan 36
Belkin, Aaron 203 n.23
Benatar, David 165, 227 n.38
Benjamin, Walter 6, 7, 47, 48, 71–5, 76, 77–8, 79, 82, 83, 187, 209 n.7, 210 n.9, 210 nn.9,10,12, 212 n.32
Biemann, Asher D 212 n.30
biology 3, 30–31, 62
birth 92, 97, 162–4, 166, 167, 169, 171, 175, 180, 182, 184, 226 n.34, 230 n.12, 231 n.21
*bivium* 92, 103
Blair, Tony 35
Bloch, Ernst 188, 203 n.22, 232 n.34
Bloom, Alfred 193 n.7
Bloom, Harold 179
Blumenberg, Hans 217 n.44
Boccaccio, Giovanni 99, 103
Bolaño, Roberto 23
Bonaparte, Napoléon 8, 196 n.26
Bonaventure des Périers 196 n.31

Bonnefoy, Yves 90-1
Borges, Jorge Luis 185
Boulogne, Valentin de 81
Bourdieu, Pierre 64, 208 n.27
Bourreau, Alain 219 n.56
Bouveresse, Jacques 178-9
Boyarin, Daniel 224 n.1
Braider, Christopher 218 n.48
Braudel, Fernand 13, 14, 194 n.10, 196 nn.28,29, 213 n.2
*Brief Encounter* 2
Brown, Susan M 230 n.10
Bruno, Giordano 79-81, 84
Burckhardt, Jacob 100, 217 n.38
Burdach, Konrad 83, 212 n.30
Bury, John Bagnell 203 n.27
buyer's regret 7, 146-7

Caeiro, Alberto 181, 182, 184
Calderòn, Pedro 164
Calvin, John 130
Campos, Àlvaro de 181, 182, 183, 184, 185, 186, 188
Capra, Frank 165, 208 n.1
Caroline, Princess of Wales 29
Carr, E.H. 35, 56, 60
Carracci, Annibale 106, 218 n.48
Carroll, Lewis 53
Cassin, Barbara 205 n.4
Castro, Fidel 36
categorical desire 175-6
causation 12, 17, 18, 28, 31, 32, 39, 42, 46, 60, 62, 76, 152, 160, 188, 198 n.39, 200 n.3, 203 n.27, 210 n.11
Cervantes, Miguel 113
*ceteris paribus* 38, 39, 41-2, 43, 202 n.20
Champaigne, Philippe de 212 n.31
chaos theory 28, 31, 44, 200 nn.2,3, 203 n.25
Chapeaurouge, Donat de 211 n.23
Charlemagne 141
Chaucer, Geoffrey 101
Chevalier de Pas 181
Chrysostom, John 127

Clubb, Dare 96
Cicero 103, 120, 127, 163, 196 n.24
Cimabue 82
Cioran, Emil 165, 175, 227 n.37, 229 n.12
Clark, Maudemarie 226 n.12
Clark, T.J. 82, 212 n.28
Clarke, Samuel 29
Clemens, Samuel 183
Cleopatra's Nose 8, 42, 44, 46, 137, 203 n.27
closeness 39, 41, 42, 43
Coelho, Eduardo 184
cognitive psychology 3, 5, 145
Cohen, Michael 223 n.30
Coleridge, Samuel Taylor 64
confucianism 32, 88
consequent 11, 16, 18, 28, 35, 36, 41, 42, 43, 44, 45, 46, 148
contingency 28, 42, 45, 77, 110, 113
Conway, Kellyanne 6, 52, 205 n.7
Corbyn, Jeremy 35
cosmology 3, 29, 33, 50
Courteau, Johanna 231 n.22
Critchley, Simon 230 n.8
Croesus 144
Crosse, Thomas 181
crossroads 7, 13, 26, 30, 76, 77, 78, 82, 84, 85, 88-91, 92-3, 95, 98, 99, 100, 101, 102, 103, 104, 106, 107, 108, 110-13, 114, 115, 116, 121, 122, 152, 154, 157, 174, 186, 190, 212 n.32, 213 n.6, 214 nn.11,15, 215 n.15, 216 nn.24,30,33, 217 n.37, 219, n.56, 220 n.4, 232 n.26
Cyranno de Bergerac 14
Cyrus 124

Dan-Cohen, Meir 154, 156
Dante, Alighieri 84, 87, 103-4, 125, 137, 218 nn.45,46,47
Davies, William 205 n.5
*dea virtus* 102, 116
Debray, Régis 5
decisions, decision-making 7, 18, 23, 34, 70, 85, 90, 98, 106, 110, 112, 113,

114, 116, 120, 121, 124, 125, 144, 145, 152, 153–6, 157, 158, 168, 172, 173, 174, 197 n.32, 214 n.11, 216 n.24, 218 n.48, 219 n.56, 220 n.4, 228 n.47, 229 n.6
Deleuze, Gilles 5
Deluermoz, Quentin 60, 196 n.30
Deng, Boer 199 n.51
DeRose, Keith 19
Derrida, Jacques 205 n.10
Dick, Philip K. 195 n.19
Dickinson, Emily 15
Dinhopl, A 234 n.42
Dinshaw, Minoo 59
Dionigi da Borgo San Sepulcro 99, 101, 105
Drucker, Johanna 233 n.40
Du Bellay, Joachim 131
Duccio 82
Duchamp, Marcel 186
Dufrenne, Mikkel 212 n.25
Dürer, Albrecht 73, 76, 78, 84
Durkheim, Émile 61, 62, 207 n.23
Duverny, Jacques 222 n.18
Dworkin, Ronald 201 n.4

economics 3, 39, 147, 223 n.33
Edgington, Dorothy 21, 198 n.43
Einstein, Albert 201 n.4
El Greco 68
Ender 65, 68
Erasmus, Desiderius 79, 116, 129, 130, 131, 153, 219 n.38, 225 n.5
eternal recurrence 157–9, 161, 225 n.19
*ethos* 173, 174, 185
Euripides 122, 216 n.30, 221 n.7
Evans-Pritchard, Edward, 76
Evans, Richard 9, 20, 193 n.4, 195 nn.16,17,21, 198 n.45, 202 n.20
experimental history 21, 61–62

Fabian, Johannes 6
fact of the matter 49, 53, 55
factual expression 63
*factum* 50, 63

*fait accompli* 52, 64, 207 n.26
*Faktum* 56, 63
Faulkner, William 1, 3, 8, 22, 52, 67, 74, 87, 92, 187
Febvre, Lucien 14
Ferguson, Niall 16, 33, 34, 189, 198 nn.39, 42, 200 n.3, 201 n.10, 202 n.13, 233 n.37
Ferry, Luc 226 n.25
fiction 7–10, 14, 17, 19, 32, 37, 50, 54, 58, 94, 101, 195 nn.20,21, 206 n.14, 214,15
Fielding, Henry 91
Fillon, François 142–4
Fingarette, Herbert 89
Flaubert, Gustave 24
Flood, Alison 206 n.18
Fogel, Robert 18
Fomo 144, 145, 146, 147
Foucault, Michel 94, 174, 215 n.18, 217 nn.35,40, 222 n.17, 227 n.58, 225 n.24
Fournier, Jacques 222 n.18
Franklin, Benjamin 9
Freud, Sigmund 45, 147
Friday, Joe 50, 51
Fulkerson, Laura 221 nn.8,9
Furetière, Antoine 139–40

Gallagher, Catherine 8, 194 n.15, 196 n.27, 199 n.46, 201 n.5, 204 n.31, 210 n.11, 219 n.59, 220 n.2, 227 n.41
gambler, gambling 95, 107, 108, 113, 114, 115, 116, 117, 128, 149, 153, 154, 216 n.24
game theory 18, 21, 223 n.33
Gell, Alfred 194 n.9
Gellner, Ernest 145
Genesis 22, 31
Geoffroy-Château, Louis-Napoléon 8
Geyer-Ryan, Helga 210 n.10
Gibbon, Edward 100
Giotto 68, 82
Glaesemer, Jürgen 209 n.8
Gloubermann, Mark 216 n.35

INDEX   237

Gonzalez, Louis  218 n.54
Goodman, Nelson  10, 11, 197 n.38
Gopnik, Adam  154
Gould, Stephen  30-1, 201 n.7
Gray, John  230 n.8
Grayling, A.C
Green, Peter  217, n.43
Greenblatt, Stephen  199 n.50
Gretzel, U  234 n.42
Griffith, R.Drew  93
Guattari, Félix  232 n.26

Hacking, Ian  20
Hadeln, Detlev Freiherr von  78
Hainsworth, Peter  217 n.39, 218 n.45
Halliwell, Stephen  99
Hamel, Christopher de  206 n.18
Hardouin, Jean  205 n.11
Hastings, Max  206 n.16
Hawthorn, Geoffrey  10, 14, 17, 82, 195 n.22, 197 nn.32, 37, 198 n.45, 212 n.27
Hecate  7, 88, 89, 99
Hegel, Georg Wilhelm Friedrich  8, 61, 106
Heidegger, Martin  2
Hénaff, Marcel  76
Herbert, George  27
Hercules  7, 84, 89, 102, 103, 104, 106, 112, 115, 116, 217 n.43, 218 n.48
Herodotus  34, 124, 216 n.32, 221 nn.10,11
Hesketh, Ian  201 n.7
heteronym, heteronymy  181-8, 189, 191, 230 n.8, 231 nn.15,21, 232 nn.26,28
heterotopia  187, 191, 232 nn.32,33
Heyd, David  171, 191, 232 nn.32,33
Hill, Rosemary  207 n.19
hindcast  16, 197 n.33
Hobbes, Thomas  222 n.17
Hobsbawm, Eric  35
Hobson, Suzanne  211 n.21
Hollander, John  185
Homer  11, 123
Honig, Edwin  230 n.10, 231 nn.15,24

Hoover, J. Edgar  37-41, 202 n.18
Horapello  78
Horkheimer, Max  75
Hume, David  17, 50, 53, 54, 62
Humphrey, Caroline  122, 222 n.14
Hyland, Martin  213 n.8

identity  7, 39, 106, 132, 133, 150, 151, 152, 154, 156, 157, 158, 160, 166, 167, 169, 170, 171, 172, 174, 176, 179, 183, 184, 185, 188, 190, 195 n.20, 218 n.48, 224 n.1, 225 n.14, 227 n.41, 228 n.53, 231 n.21
if only  22, 75, 96, 100, 122, 128, 133, 146, 147, 149, 220 nn.2,4, 221 n.7
Ignatius of Loyola  7, 92, 108-17, 127, 161, 218 n.54, 219 nn.59,60,61
Ingram, Edward  206 n.17
Inwagen, Peter van  203 n.26
Isidore of Seville  89
Isocrates  196 n.24

Jeremiah  88, 209 n.5
Jerome, Saint  80, 114
Jewel, John  130
Job  164, 167, 226 n.6
Johnson, Christopher  211 n.19
Jorge, Manuel dos Santos  231 nn.16,25
Judas Iscariot  127, 222 n.15
Jung, Carl  161
Junius Bassus  68
jurisprudence  3, 148
Jiayang, Fan  190, 234 n.43

Kafka, Franz  24, 121, 220 n.2
*kairos*  124, 127, 147, 225
Kanai, Ryota  23
Kant, Immanuel  53, 76, 158, 179, 208 n.3
Kennedy, John F  69
Kermode, Frank  9
Keynes, John Maynard  151
Kishik, David  210 n.9
Kissinger, Henry  34

Klee, Paul 6, 71-4, 75, 77, 78, 79, 83, 209 n.6, 212 n.32
Koselleck, Rheinhart 5, 206 n.14
Kozinets, R 234 n.42
Kraus, Dagmara 230 n.12
Kripke, Saul 183, 195 n.20
Kruschev, Nikita 69

La Rochefoucauld, François de 132, 137-9, 143, 144
Lacan, Jacques 45, 231 n.25
Lactantius 89, 217 n.44
Lahtinen, Mikkel 207 n.25
Lamont, Norman 120, 121, 219 n.1
Lampert, Jay 197 n.32, 214 n.11
laws of nature 29, 30, 39, 42, 43, 76, 157
Le Guin, Ursula K 211 n.14
Lebow, Ned Richard 195 n.21, 202 n.19, 203 n.26, 228 n.53
Lehrich, Christopher 76
Leibniz, Gottfried 29, 49, 70, 76, 174, 200 n.4, 201 n.5, 211 n.19
Lenin, Vladimir 187 n.35
Leonardo da Vinci 68, 73
Lessing, Doris 25
Lessing, Gotthold Ephraim 212 n.25
Lévi-Strauss, Claude 175-7, 78, 211 nn.19,23
Lewis, David 19, 38, 40, 43, 52, 195 n.20, 203 n.22, 206 n.14
Lezra, Jacques 205 n.4
Lincoln, Abraham 183
Lindbergh, Charles 9, 10, 37, 195 n.20
Linville, Mark 201 n.8
Livy 103
Lloyd, Geoffrey 26, 193 n.7
Llull, Ramon 219 n.57
Loeb, Paul S 226 n.26
*longue durée* 13, 169 n.28 197 n.35
Lossin, Rebecca 206 n.12
Louis the Pious 141
Louis, Saint 219 n.58
Luther, Martin 111, 114, 129, 130-1, 154
Lyapunov, Aleksandr 28

McCarthy, Cormack 27, 87, 88
McCarthy, Eugene 36
McGann, Jerome 189, 233 n.40
McInerney, Jeremy 214 nn.14,15
McKinney, Lawrence 149
McTernan, John 35
Machiavelli, Niccolò 127
Mackie, John Leslie 17
Macron, Emmanuel 142, 143
Magritte, René 186
Mair, Victor H 213 n.4
Makowski, Claude 211 n.23
Mann, Nicholas 217 nn.37,44
Mao Zedong 4
Marincola, John 216 n.32
Marx, Groucho 21, 24, 25
Marx, Karl 76, 210 n.9
matters of fact 53, 63, 205 n.5
Matthew, Saint 127
Meghill, Allan 42
Merriman, John 200 n.2, 202 n.14
*metameleia* 123, 125, 126, 146
*metanoia* 7, 22, 23, 119, 123-31, 132, 133, 135, 144, 146, 147, 151, 153, 187, 198 n.45, 220 n.4, 221 n.13, 222 n.17
Metternich, Klemens von 64
Michelangelo 68
Miéville, China 210 n.12
might-have counterfactuals 2, 5, 13, 14, 19, 22, 30, 33, 50, 68, 69, 70, 74, 81, 85, 124, 163, 171, 183, 187, 189, 196 n.26, 197 n.35, 198 n.45, 222 n.22
Milo, Daniel 21, 61, 62
Miranda, Ruis Goncalves 232 n.30
modal bewilderment 96, 115, 228 n.50
modernism 82, 177, 195 n.19, 212 n.28
*Mögklichkeitmenschen* 174
Molina, Luis de 70
Mommsen, Theodor 213 n.7, 217 n.44
Montaigne, Michel de 132-4, 135, 136, 137, 138, 140, 149, 222 n.22
Monteiro, Adolfo Casais 181, 184, 231 n.15

moral luck  121, 153, 154, 156
More, Thomas  130, 187
Morgenbesser, Sidney  18
Moriarty, Michael  223 n.25
Morris, Adam  232 n.26
Morris, Ian  31, 32
Mulligan, Kevin  229 n.5
Mumford, Stephen  17
Murat, Laure  8
Musil, Robert  175, 177–9

Nabokov, Vladimir  119
Nadal, Jérôme  114
Nagel, Thomas  59
Names  56, 57, 151, 183, 184
Naudé, Pierre Poiret  70
Nehamas, Alexander  157, 159
Nerval, Gérard de  183
Newton, Isaac  29
Nicole, Pierre  47, 204 n.34
Nietzsche, Friedrich  29, 74, 122, 145, 156–64, 165, 166, 169, 173, 174, 175, 217 n.38, 226 nn.26,27,31, 227 n.36
Nozick, Robert  172

O'Malley, John W  219 n.61
Oakeshott, Michael  207 n.24
Obama, Barack  91
*occasio*  127, 144
Ockham, William of  69, 70
Oedipus  2, 4, 7, 8, 18, 89, 90, 91, 92–9, 100, 116, 123, 170, 214 n.15, 215 nn.17,21, 216 nn.24, 31, 35, 217 n.36, 219 n.63, 227 n.35, 228 nn.47,48, 229 n.60
Olson, James M  223 n.31
options  11, 13, 14, 15, 16, 18, 32, 35, 81, 82, 83, 84, 92, 93, 94, 95, 96, 97, 133, 146, 154, 163, 169, 173, 191, 196 nn.26,28, 197 n.32, 214 n.15, 222 n.22, 228 n.47
oracles  2, 58, 90, 92, 95, 96, 98, 107, 144, 170, 189, 215 n.21, 216 n.32, 228 nn.46,37
Ovid  106

Pacwa, Mitch  219 n.59
*paenitentia, poenitentia*  127, 129
Pais, Abraham  200 n.4
Panofsky, Erwin  55, 56, 64, 79, 80, 81, 82, 83, 217 n.44
Parmenides  87, 213 n.6
Pascal, Blaise  24, 42, 44–8, 132, 134–7, 138, 143, 203 nn.24,25,26, 204 nn.31,32
Pasolini, Pier Paolo  216 n.24
Paul, Saint  22, 105, 108, 127, 135, 152, 224 n.1
Paulsen, Ronald  203 n.22, 208 n.28
Pavel, Thomas  9
Paz, Octavio  179, 187, 230 nn.8,9
people of possibility  176, 177
Persius  89
Pessoa, Fernando  7, 8, 177, 179–90, 191, 230 nn.8,12,14, 231 nn.15,18,23,25, 232 n.26
Petrarch, Francesco  7, 92, 99–108, 116, 217 nn.37,38,39,40,44, 218 nn.45,46,48,51, 219 n.63
Piaf, Edith  120, 121, 123, 219 n.1
Pizarro, Jeronimò  230 n.14
Planissoles, Béatrice de  128
Plato  125, 146, 199 n.46
Plutarch  44, 125, 163, 203 n.28
Politsky, Matthew  218 n.50
Polybius  61
Portela, Manuel  223 n.38
Posner, Richard  148
Possibilitarian  165, 177, 178, 179, 200 n.4
possible worlds  2, 9, 10, 29, 37, 38, 39, 40, 41, 43, 52, 70, 76, 81, 145, 148, 149, 150, 183, 195 n.20, 200 n.4, 203 n.26, 206 n.14, 227 n.43
*pothos*  124, 144, 221 n.9
Priest, Graham  193 n.2
Prince Albert  32, 33
Prince, Morton  230 n.7
Probability  16, 19, 20, 43, 148, 198 n.39, 199 n.46
*protasis*  11, 16, 18, 20, 25, 34, 41, 43, 197 n.38

Proust, Marcel 1, 164
providence, providential 29, 70, 82, 107, 108, 110, 112, 114, 115, 219 n.63
Pseudo-Dionysius 67
Pythagoras 89

Queen Victoria 32, 33
Quine, Thomas 62

Rabaté, Jean-Michel 231 n.25
Rabelais, François 14, 196 n.31
Raphael 68
Rathenau, Walter 20
Reagan, Ronald 36
Rees, Martin 30, 33
Reformation, Reformers 111, 115, 129, 135
regret 7, 22, 23, 80, 96, 115, 120–150, 151–5, 157, 159, 166, 171, 172, 183, 185, 187, 199 n.50, 219 n.1, 220 nn.2,4, 221 n.7,9,10, 220 n.17, 223 nn.28,30,32, 224 n.4, 225 n.11
Reis, Ricardo 181, 182, 183, 187, 231 n.18
remorse 80, 83, 121–8, 146
Renaissance 68, 78, 79, 80, 81, 82, 83, 89, 100, 102, 103, 127, 128, 136, 153, 212 n.31, 218 n.48
Renouvier, Charles Bernard 19, 20
*renvoi mirrorique* 186
Repentance 80, 121, 124, 125, 126, 127–39, 140, 172, 198 n.45, 22 n.17
revolution 12, 36, 74, 76, 197 n.35, 202 n.13, 222 n.17
Richelieu, Armand Jean du Plessis 135
Ricoeur, Paul 203 n.22
rigid designator 183
Rimbaud, Arthur 183
Rinhaug, Aino 232 n.24
Roannez, Charlotte de 135–6
Robbe-Grillet, Alain 215 n.17
robots 23
Rodrigues-Cortes, Armando 231 n.24
Roese, Neal J. 145

Roth, Philip. 9–10, 19, 37, 121, 195 nn.20,21
Rousseau, Jean-Jacques. 76, 77, 101
Runciman, Steven. 59
Russell, Conrad. 200 n.2
Rusten, Jeffrey. 215 n.16
Ryle, Gilbert. 188

Sacramento, Mario de. 231 n.22
Salmon, Wesley C. 200 n.1
Santayana, George. 206 n.15
Sartre, Jean-Paul. 125
*saudosismo* 185, 186
scale. 6, 13, 28, 31, 33, 37, 41, 42, 44, 45, 46, 61, 156
Scheffler, Simon. 175, 179
Schlegel, Friedrich. 71
Scholar, Richard 203 n.29, 222 n.22
Schopenhauer, Arthur 164
Schubert, Franz 231 n.18
Scipio. 103
Search, Alexander. 181
Seddon, R.F.J. 230 n.8
Seignobos, Charles. 87
self 101, 102, 106, 114, 121, 122, 132, 133, 134, 137, 139, 144, 146, 152, 153, 156, 157, 158, 160, 166, 172, 173, 174, 175, 176, 177, 179–91, 217 n.40, 224 n.5, 225 n.19, 226 n.27, 227 n.41, 228 n.52, 231 nn.21,25, 232 nn.28,34
selfie 144, 190, 191, 234 nn.42,44
semiophany 114
shoulda, coulda, woulda 19, 121
Sidgwick, Henry 43
Silenus 161–4
Sinatra, Frank 219 n.1, 223 n.30
Singaravélou, Pierre 60, 196 n.30
Smallman, Rachel 223 n.31
Smith, Adam 43
Smith, Stephen 197 n.35
Soares, Bernardo 181, 183, 185, 231 n.15
social facts 62
Sophocles 8, 92–9, 172, 214 n.15, 216 n.30, 227 n.43

*sortes* 107, 114
Stalnaker, Robert 38
Stendhal 25, 177
Stravinsky, Igor 89
Surin, Kenneth 232 n.32
Swedenborg, Emmanuel 208 n.3
Swedin, Eric G. 68, 69

Tariq, Syma 233 n.41
Taylor, Elizabeth 202 n.15
Taylor, L.C 231 n.20
Terzis, Gillian 234 n.45
Tetlock, Philip 43
Thatcher, Margaret 49, 63
Theodosius 141
Thompson, E.P. 35, 202 n.13
Thucydides 11, 124, 216 n.30, 221 n.11
Titian 5, 6, 7, 78–85, 212 nn.25,31,32
Tordoff, Robert 221 n.11
Trevor-Roper, Hugh 16
*trivium* 89, 93, 99
Trump, Donald 34, 35, 36, 41, 201 n.11, 202 n.17, 204 n.3, 223 nn.28,35
Tucker Avieze. 195 n.17, 202 n.20
Turing machine 22
Twain, Mark 183
Tyndale, William 130

utopia, utopianism 7, 14, 75, 78, 187–8, 190, 191, 194 n.15, 208 n.28, 211 n.14, 232 nn.32,33,34

Vaihinger, Hans 9
Valeriano, Piero 79, 80
Valéry, Paul 61
Valla, Lorenzo 129, 130
Van Gogh, Vincent
Vasari, Giorgio 83, 127, 144
Vermigli, Peter Martyr 130
Vernant, Jean-Pierre 95, 216 nn.23,24,33

Vidal-Nacquet, Pierre 216 n.23
Villon, François 140
Virgil 89, 104, 107
virtuality 114
Voltaire 29, 217 n.38, 220 n.2

Wallace, R.Jay 224 n.4
Warburg, Aby 68
Weber, Max 18, 42
Wender, Wim 68
wheel of memory 80
Whitehead, Alfred 64
Whitman, Walt 90, 95
Williams, Bernard. 4, 36, 96, 97, 121, 141, 152, 153, 154, 166–9, 172–3, 174, 175, 179, 186, 193 n.6, 194 n.11, 205 n.8, 216 nn.23,30, 225 nn.10,12, 227 nn.41,43, 228 nn.45,50,52,53, 229 nn.54,60, 231 n.21
Williams, Rowan 215 n.15
Williams, Shirley 3, 36, 202 .15
Wood, Michael 2, 3, 93, 95, 98, 216 n.24, 228 n.46
Wordsworth, William 10
would-have counterfactuals 17–19
wrongful identity 167–71, 228 n.45
wrongful life 167–71, 228 n.45
Wu-Kuang-ming 193 n.7

Xenophon 103, 124

Yaroufakis, Yanis 219 n.1
Yates, Frances 78
Yoga Berri 90
Yolo 21, 144, 145, 148, 223 n.32
*ypsilon* 89, 103

Zak, Gur 217 n.40
Zenith, Richard 230 n.11
Zimmerman, Jens 222 n.19
Zohar, n. 228 n.44

www.ingramcontent.com/pod-product-compliance
Lightning Source LLC
Chambersburg PA
CBHW050350230426
43663CB00010B/2061